ANDY ROONEY

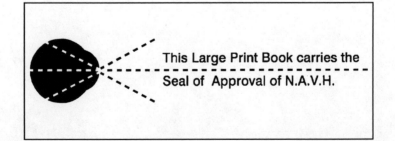

This Large Print Book carries the
Seal of Approval of N.A.V.H.

ANDY ROONEY

60 YEARS OF WISDOM AND WIT

*With an Introduction
by Brian Rooney*

ANDREW A. ROONEY

THORNDIKE PRESS
A part of Gale, Cengage Learning

Detroit • New York • San Francisco • New Haven, Conn • Waterville, Maine • London

GALE
CENGAGE Learning™

LIBRARY OF CONGRESS CATALOGING-IN-PUBLICATION DATA

Rooney, Andrew A.
  Andy Rooney : 60 years of wisdom and wit / by Andrew A. Rooney.
    p. cm. — (Thorndike Press large print nonfiction)
    ISBN-13: 978-1-4104-2284-2 (alk. paper)
    ISBN-10: 1-4104-2284-4 (alk. paper)
    1. American wit and humor. 2. Large type books. I. Title.
  PN6162.R629 2010
  814'.54—dc22   2009042970

Published in 2010 by arrangement with PublicAffairs™, a member of Perseus Books Group, LLC.

Printed in the United States of America
1 2 3 4 5 6 7 14 13 12 11 10

CONTENTS

5

TIMELINE

January 14, 1919

- Andrew Aitken Rooney is born in Albany, New York, to Walter Scott and Ellinor Rooney.

1932–1938

- attends The Albany Academy
- writes for student magazine *The Cue*

1938–1941

- attends Colgate University in Hamilton, New York, where he becomes editor of Colgate's magazine *The Banter*

1941

- drafted into the Army, heads to training in Fort Bragg, North Carolina, fol-

lowed by Camp Blanding, Florida
- arrested outside St. Augustine, Florida, for sitting in the back of the Army bus alongside African American soldiers

1942

- marries Marguerite Howard
- arrives in Perham Downs, England, with the 17th Field Artillery
- joins the Armed Forces newspaper *The Stars and Stripes* in their London office
- meets United Press reporter Walter Cronkite, *Stars and Stripes* correspondent Don Hewitt (who would become the executive of *60 Minutes*), and Edward R. Murrow

1943

- flies with the Eighth Air Force on the second American bombing raid on Germany

1944

- lands on Utah Beach in Normandy, three days after D-day
- encounters Ernest Hemingway at hotel

outside Paris and finds him ill-mannered
- enters Paris with the French Army the day the city is liberated from Germany
- *Air Gunner* (written with Bud Hutton) is published

1945

- discharged from the Army

1946

- *The Story of the Stars and Stripes* (written with Bud Hutton) is published
- MGM buys movie rights to *The Story of the Stars and Stripes* for $55,000 (Rooney and Hutton are hired by MGM to work on the script)
- assigned by *Cosmopolitan* to cover postwar Europe with Bud Hutton in ten pieces

1947

- returns to Albany, New York, and embarks on a freelance career
- *Conquerors' Peace: A Report to the American Stockholders* (written with Bud Hutton), which derives from the

Cosmopolitan assignment, is published
- daughter Ellen Rooney is born

1949

- joins CBS as a writer for megawatt radio and TV personality Arthur Godfrey; writes for *The Arthur Godfrey Talent Scouts* and *Arthur Godfrey Time* until 1955

1950

- daughters Emily and Martha Rooney are born

1951

- son Brian Rooney is born

1952

- begins his love affair with woodworking

1957

- adapts E. B. White's essay "Here is New York" for TV

1959–1965

- writes for *The Garry Moore Show,* for

Victor Borge, Herb Shriner, and Bob and Ray and contributes to CBS News' "The Twentieth Century," "Adventure," "Calendar," and *The Morning Show*

1962

- *The Fortunes of War: Four Great Battles of World War II* is published
- begins work with CBS *60 Minutes* correspondent Harry Reasoner on a series of TV specials that include pieces on bridges, hotels, and the English language

1964

- writes his first television essay, "An Essay on Doors"

1965

- writes television essay on Frank Sinatra narrated by Walter Cronkite and produced by Don Hewitt

1966

- receives Writers Guild of America

Award for best TV documentary for *The Great Love Affair*

1968

- writes *Black History: Lost, Stolen or Strayed,* narrated by Bill Cosby, and is awarded a Writers Guild Award and an Emmy Award for his script
- appears for the first time on television on the *60 Minutes* broadcast "Digressions" with Palmer Williams

1970

- quits CBS after their refusal to air his "An Essay on War"

1971

- "An Essay on War" is aired on PBS's *The Great American Dream Machine* and receives a Writers Guild Award; for the first time, narrates his own piece on air
- joins ABC, following Harry Reasoner

1972

- returns to CBS to continue to write,

produce, and narrate full-length pieces for *60 Minutes* and to write for various CBS broadcasts

1974

- writes and appears in his celebration of New York, "In Praise of New York City"

1975

- writes and stars in the CBS prime-time feature "Mr. Rooney Goes to Washington"
- is awarded a Peabody for the piece, as well as a Writers Guild Award for best TV documentary

1976

- writes and stars in the CBS prime-time feature "Mr. Rooney Goes to Dinner," for which he receives a Writers Guild Award

1977

- writes and stars in the CBS prime-time feature "Mr. Rooney Goes to Work"

1978

- Don Hewitt airs Rooney's humorous on-air segment "Three Minutes with Andy Rooney" as a summer fill-in for the "Point/Counterpoint" face-off between Shana Alexander and James Kilpatrick
- "A Few Minutes with Andy Rooney" replaces "Point/Counterpoint"
- receives an Emmy Award for "Who Owns What in America"

1979

- receives a Writers Guild Award for "Happiness: The Elusive Pursuit"

1979–present

- syndicated column is published and distributed through *Tribune Media*

1981

- *A Few Minutes with Andy Rooney* (the book) is published and quickly becomes a best seller
- is awarded a News and Documentary Emmy for "A Few Minutes with Andy Rooney"

1982

- *And More by Andy Rooney* is published
- receives a second Emmy award for "A Few Minutes with Andy Rooney"

1984

- *Pieces of My Mind* is published and becomes a best seller
- *Word for Word* is published

1989

- *Not That You Asked* . . . is published

1990

- suspended by CBS for three months for remarks that were perceived as racist and homophobic; re-hired four weeks later (*60 Minutes*' ratings fell 20 percent without "A Few Minutes with Andy Rooney")

1992

- *Sweet and Sour* is published

1995

- *My War* is published

1999

- *Sincerely, Andy Rooney* is published

2000

- *My War* is reissued and becomes a best seller

2002

- *Common Nonsense* is published

2003

- *Years of Minutes* is published
- awarded a Lifetime Achievement Emmy and the Ernie Pyle Lifetime Achievement Award

2004

- wife Marguerite (Marge) dies

2006

- *Out of My Mind* is published

INTRODUCTION
BY BRIAN ROONEY

It was not clear to me as a child what a writer does for a living. I thought my father just took the train to New York every morning before I was awake and came back in time for dinner. I was aware that he knew some famous people in radio and television, but he was not famous himself. I didn't have a clue what he did.

I went through most of grade school in the 1950s and 1960s with a pair of high black Keds and one pair of blue jeans that I wore every day until they ripped out and my mother bought another pair. I didn't know for many years that at the time it was about all my parents could afford.

My father made his living by the only thing he knew how to do, which was putting words on paper. He was blunt, outspoken, and opinionated. It turns out that he was paid money for being that way. But as a writer he lived by principles that often put his career and family at risk. Sometimes he was fired for what he said, and more than once he quit in disagreement with his bosses. He believes in thought, the written word, and that a person should stand for something more than his own good.

As a father he was the product of his time. He never said, "I love you," and never asked about my feelings. He encouraged me to play football, because that's what he had done, and tried to make it to as many games as he could.

He expected a certain amount of toughness in me. A broken finger was not an excuse to sit on the bench. When I was fourteen I ripped the cartilage in my left knee and came down with pneumonia the same week, but he woke me up one morning before catching the 6:02 to the city asking whether I would make it to play in the football game that day.

He gave me my first pocketknife and taught me how to use a hammer, a chisel, and a table saw. He'd tell me, "It doesn't seem right, but it's safer when your fingers are closest to the blade." We both still have all our fingers. He also taught me basic cooking. He showed me how to make a roux to thicken a sauce and to grill a steak medium rare.

He was reckless in ways that were fun. One Halloween he lined me up with my three sisters in the kitchen, handed us each a bar of soap, and told us to get out there and soap some neighbors' windows. He took us winter camping without a tent — we made our own igloo out of snow. It rained one night and as the igloo melted on my crew-cut head, I saw him standing over the fire trying to dry our clothes.

One year when there was a foot of snow on the ground, my father put my sisters and me on the toboggan, attached a rope to the bumper, and towed us around town with the Country Squire station wagon. He drove with his head hanging out the window, looking back to check on us. Going down steep hills when the toboggan started catching up with the rear wheels, he'd hit the gas and speed up.

He liked doing things with gasoline because during the war the army in Europe had done everything with gas: heating, cooking, even washing their jeeps to give them a low sheen. In the fall we piled up leaves for burning and my father would get out a jug of gasoline, sprinkle it on, step back, and throw in a match. It went *whump* and the leaves were instantly reduced to ashes. He'd say, "That's the best thing since the ETO." The ETO was the European Theater of Operations, bureaucratic jargon for the War, and he never ceased to be amused by the term.

For a man who's been in the army and hung around newsrooms all his life, he, surprisingly, does not use profanity. The only time I ever heard a dirty word from him was when I asked about the racist joke that got Earl Butz fired from his position as Secretary of Agriculture. When my father repeated it to me I was more shocked to hear the words from his mouth than I was by the joke itself. I was in my twenties and had never heard him use words like that.

He is a ruthless negotiator. One Saturday he said to me, "Come on, kid, we have to go buy a new station wagon." We drove over to the Ford dealer, where he identified the car he wanted, and made an offer a few hundred dollars below the sticker price, which at the time was a deep discount. The salesman said, "Sir, I can't sell it for that. It's the last car of its model in the whole New England sales district and I can get full price from someone else."

My father kicked his toe in the dirt and said, "I wasn't going to tell you this, but my wife and I wanted two of them exactly alike." We went home, made hamburgers, and started to watch a football game. When the phone rang and my father answered, all I heard him say was, "Now we're ready to talk." The salesman had found an identical station wagon only a few miles away.

It barely does justice to the sight of it to say that my father keeps a messy garage. The wooden shelves he built are loaded with cans of paint that have turned solid, several C-rations he brought home from World War II, dead tennis balls, a pair of hickory skis with bear trap bindings, and the rubber rain boots I wore in sixth grade. I'm sure there's a Brooks Brothers tie he tucked on the shelf after cleaning out his car in 1972. He has Ball jars filled with odd nuts and bolts, bottles of glue, and wooden tennis rackets. It's a mixture of useful junk, memories, and things he just can't stand to throw away.

He does not fuss about his looks. He buys good clothes but is permanently rumpled. You could put him in an Armani suit right off the rack and he would look as if he had slept in it. He is not inclined to ornamentation in his person, or in his writing. He is fond of quoting Thoreau that "if one has anything to say, it drops from him simply and directly, as a stone falls to the ground." He writes in simple declarative sentences that bear no excess. His clothes are wrinkled but his sentences are not.

As a writer, and as a man, he thinks he can create his own world. He doesn't care much for reading, except the *New York Times.* He likes to say, "I'm a writer, not a reader." He does not read fiction and I suspect he has read only a few books cover to cover since he was in college, and maybe not even then. His primary contribution to culture in the family was bringing home a 45 rpm copy of Del Shannon's "Hats Off to Larry." He says, "I am not interested in being diverted from my own thoughts." He doesn't like listening to music or going to the Broadway theater, although he has had season tickets to the New York Giants most of his adult life. His genius as a writer is not knowing much about what anyone else says or thinks. It's knowing exactly what *he* thinks.

Like good writing, he also knows good furniture and food and has worked to make his own, with varying success. He has a collection of expensive tools and piles of beautiful wood. He makes furniture, but if he makes a four-legged table, one leg is likely to be a tad short. He is impatient with details so when he makes a mistake he doesn't start over, he patches with glue, putty, and shims and keeps going. His pleasure is more in having the idea and doing the work than having the finished piece.

He is an excellent cook and rarely uses a recipe. His popovers may be the best anywhere in America: tall and hollow, crisp on the outside, buttery on the inside. He can grill a steak to the perfect pink, make Beef Stroganoff and curried shrimp. He believes there are few things that cannot be made better with salt, garlic, and butter. He makes his own ice cream because that's what you did growing up during the Depression, and it's always fun to lick the paddles when it's done. He makes peppermint ice cream for Christmas.

He is absentminded. One night, back when $100 was serious money and he didn't have much, he paid a taxi driver with a hundred dollar bill, thinking it was a single. Making chicken soup with the pressure cooker, he forgot about it until the top blew, spraying greasy broth all over the kitchen walls. He still refers to it as "The Great Chicken Soup Disaster." One year he made wine and corked it in soda bottles. That winter we would wake up in the middle of the night to muffled explosions in the basement.

My father resists authority. He doesn't like bosses or people in uniform. Sometimes in

New York, just for fun, he'd hail a police car and when it stopped he would say, "Oh, I'm sorry, I thought you were a taxi." Several times he has been arrested while standing up to cops who overstepped their authority, only to be kicked loose by the desk sergeant.

He has lived by a series of rules he set for himself and people around him. He says, "There are standards in this world." His rules are a mixture of low-brow philosophy and simple maxims for an orderly life that have both literal and figurative meaning. When we were kids he'd instruct us: "The last one in at night turn out the light over the garage." Anyone who didn't would hear about it in the morning. Another rule was, "You meet the train, you don't wait for it." As a teenager I would deliver him to the rail station, and he would climb the steps and reach the platform just as the doors opened. He thought less of the guys who had stood there waiting, wasting their time. He laid down the rule that, "The keys to the car belong in the ignition." He didn't want to fumble around looking for the keys to four cars casually dropped somewhere in the kitchen by one of six drivers. That ended one summer night in 1969 when the Thunderbird was stolen out of the driveway. When the cops who returned the car asked how the thieves had gotten hold of the keys, my father said, "They were in the ignition, where they belong."

My father likes to say "the same things keep happening to the same people." This is his idea of fate as determined by personality. He was always impressed by the B-17 pilots who brought the plane back to base all shot up when everyone else on board was ready to give up and die. His theory was that whatever thing in that guy that had gotten him into Yale and made him a pilot would also drive him to success in later life. "The same things keep happening to the same people." As a little boy I found this disturbing, particularly when I was cast as "third elf" in the Christmas play.

He can be a terror in a restaurant. If the food is not good, he says so to the waiter, the maitre'd, or anyone in the line of fire. The rule at work here: "If you want the attention of the chef, you have to start by being mean to the busboy." My favorite of all was his rule for civic involvement. We lived in a small town with a volunteer fire department. When the fire horn blew, no matter the hour, my father would leave the dinner table, or pull everyone out of bed in their pajamas, pack us all into the Ford Country Squire wagon, and peel out of the driveway to speed toward the glow on the horizon. He said, "When your neighbor's house is on fire, you have an obligation to go and watch it burn."

But the rule above all rules was this: "If all the truth were known about everything, the world would be a better place." He thinks governments should not have secrets and that there is no opinion or information too dangerous or hurtful that it cannot be told. Good ideas and good people would rise in a world in which all the truth were known. In his personal life, he believes in blunt honesty, which he will deliver anywhere from the breakfast table to the boss's office to the whole country. Just about every one of my parents' best friends went through a period when they were so mad they refused to speak to him.

His gruffness hides sentimentality. He clings to life and the people he loves like that old stuff in the garage. He would not likely weep at a wedding, but I know that over the years he has woken up in the middle of the night thinking about Obie Slingerland, his smiling high school quarterback, the best athlete anyone ever saw, who was killed flying a fighter in the Pacific. He still wakes up thinking about Obie. And when my mother died, he curled up on the bed like a child, crying her name. He loves life and wishes it would never end.

If your parents live long enough, you get to know them more as people than parents. I have come to know my father's failings, and boy, has he got some. Sometimes he carried his principles to the extreme, and he has not always lived by his own rules. But also I appreciate even more that he has stood for something all his life when so many people have not, and that while he became rich and famous, it could just as easily have gone the other way and he would not have done anything differently. I learned that a writer lives by his words.

■ ■ ■ ■

PART I
THE BEGINNINGS OF
A WRITING LIFE

■ ■ ■ ■

DRAFTED

People who have lived well and successfully are more apt to dismiss luck as a factor in their lives than those who have not. It's clearly true that over a lifetime the same things keep happening to the same people, good and bad, so it can't be luck. The process by which each of us acquires a reputation isn't independent of our character. It almost always depends more on the decisions we make than on chance occurrences.

The trouble with this smug thesis is that anyone crossing a street can be hit by a truck and the accident alters the person's life no matter how wise he or she was in making choices, so we can't claim luck never enters in. Maybe my life wouldn't have been much different if "Doc" Armstrong hadn't owned the pharmacy and been head of the draft board in the pleasant college town of Hamilton, New York.

It was sometime in May and there were still a few weeks of classes left of my junior year at Colgate University. My life was never the same again.

Most of my classmates had registered for the draft in their hometowns. Thinking the draft board in a college town would be sympathetic to the idea of letting students finish college before serving, I had chosen to register in Hamilton instead of in my hometown, Albany.

I had come to Colgate fresh out of The Albany Academy, a private school. My friends at public school thought The Academy was elitist, which I thought was wrong at the time. Now I think they were right but that there's a case to be made for the kind of elitism that existed there. In some part, at least, it was excellence. The Academy was an exceptionally fine secondary school that graduated a high percentage of people who succeeded in making good lives for themselves. Everyone in the senior class, known at The Academy as the Sixth Form, went on to college. The other boys and girls in Albany thought of us as rich kids because the tuition was $400 a year. Some few classmates were from rich families and no one let them forget it. We kidded Walter Stephens about being brought to school every day in a chauffeur-driven Pierce Arrow and our remarks to him were not very good-natured. In a world where everyone strives to make money, it's strange that a family with a breadwinner who achieves that goal is stigmatized and charged with the epithet "Rich!"

My father's $8,000 a year was considered good money during the Great Depression. When I was eight or nine, we moved out of a respectable middle-class house in the residential heart of Albany to a much nicer one with chestnut woodwork, a fireplace, and downstairs playroom, still in the city but further out. In addition to that home in Albany, we owned a cottage on Lake George, seventy miles north. There we had a Fay-Bowen, a classic old wooden boat, and I had my own outboard attached to a sturdy rowboat. My sister, Nancy, had a canoe. She wanted a fur cape for Christmas when she was seventeen but she didn't get that.

Dad traveled through the South for the Albany Felt Company as a salesman and he was worldly wise but my mother ran things. Part of her expertise was making Dad think he was boss. She was a great mother to have and I've often wondered how she was able to get so much satisfaction from doing for us what so many mothers today do without satisfaction. She liked to play bridge but I don't think she ever read a book. Being a mother was her full-time occupation.

Life at The Academy was very good. We used the school almost like a country club, often meeting there on Saturday morning to use the facilities or plan our day if we didn't have a team game scheduled. The Academy was not a military school, but it was founded in 1812 and during the Civil War it had formed a student battalion. The tradition was continued and once a week for about an hour and a half we put on funny old Civil War–style formal uniforms and marched in practice for Albany parades and our own competitive Guidon Drill. It was my first brush with military life. Although it was years before the thought occurred to me that I'd ever serve in the U.S. Army, I learned to detest everything about anything military at an early age. One day when we were to parade on the football field, I refused to march because I claimed it would damage the carefully kept field.

In the student battalion, everyone's aim was to become an officer in his Sixth Form year. The choices were made by two military aides who came to the school just once a week and a committee from the regular faculty. Shortly before the choices were to be made as to who the officers would be, Colonel Dormer, the school's military adviser who was with the New York State National Guard, lined up the Fifth Formers in the battalion and said that anyone who did not want to be considered for a position as one of the officers in his senior year should step forward.

It put me in a terrible spot. Everyone wanted to be an officer. I wanted to be one but my negative attitude toward the battalion was so well known to everyone that the colonel was, in a way, challenging me to put up or shut up. I had no choice but to step forward as the only person in the school announcing that he did not want to be considered for the honor of being an officer in the battalion.

The colonel thanked me for being honest and dismissed us.

It was lucky for me that several teachers on the faculty disliked the battalion as much as I did. When the announcement of their choice for officers was made three days later, my name was on the list. Because I was captain of the football team, president of the Beck Literary Society, and "one of the guys," it would have been difficult for them to leave me off the list because it would have called for an explanation to the younger kids in the school. And then some of the faculty members like Herbert Hahn were my friends. They knew, even though I had stepped forward in that bravado gesture, that I desperately wanted to be chosen. (Mr. Hahn otherwise distinguished himself in my eyes by stating in class one day in about 1936, "Hitler will get nowhere in Germany.")

The only problem for me at The Academy was that my marks were poor. That was a constant problem. My mother always signed my report cards and hid them from my father when he returned from a trip because she knew Dad would be angry about them. He had successfully made his way from the tiny Ballston Spa High School to Williams College and he couldn't understand my bad grades. Although I was puzzled over them, I never gave in to the idea that I was stupid even though there was some evidence of that. There were things I did well and it was easy for me to think about those and ignore failing marks in Latin, geometry, and French. It was further depressing evidence of how much we're like ourselves all day long, all our years. I still see traces of the way I performed in The Academy at age sixteen in things I do today. We're trapped with what we have and with what we have not. No amount of resolve changes our character. I do a lot of woodworking as a hobby and, considering how different the craft is from writing, it's interesting — and sometimes discouraging — for me to note, in introspective moments, how close my strengths and weaknesses in making a chest of drawers are to the strengths and weaknesses in my writing. I feel the same helplessness with my shortcomings on paper and in my shop as I do when it occurs to me that I'm overweight, not primarily because I eat too much but that I eat too much primarily because of some genetic shortcoming I got from my father and share with my sister.

Football was one of the things I liked best at The Academy. We had a good bunch of fellows on the team and a coach known as "Country" Morris who was just right. He knew the game and he was a decent man who expected decency from all of us. He had been a football star at the University of Maryland and he looked just the way a coach should look on the football field with his leather-elbowed jacket and his baseball cap pulled down over his eyebrows and cocked at a jaunty angle.

I was five feet nine inches, weighed 175

pounds, and played guard on offense and tackle on defense. Because of the attitude other kids in town had toward us at The Academy, it was particularly satisfying to beat one of the public high schools or a parochial school, and we did that quite often during the four years I played. My friend Bob Baker was a good football player but his family fell on hard times and he had to leave The Academy in the Fourth Form and go to Albany High and then play against us.

I was in or near tears for three days after the high-school game my senior year. We were undefeated during the season and heavy favorites to beat the high school. The high-school game ended in a scoreless tie and it was as if we had lost fifty to nothing. It seemed so important. Bob Baker was exultant and I suppose it took away some of the pain of his having had to leave The Academy.

In college, I soon realized I had conflicting interests. I was interested in writing, football, and philosophy. I thought I wanted to be a writer but didn't know where to start. What is called "English" in college is generally disappointing to anyone interested in learning how to write because, while I enjoyed having to read Byron, the English courses I was taking didn't have anything to do with learning how to put words down on paper in an interesting way. The courses I was getting were in English reading, not English writing. I didn't know at the time that you can't teach someone how to write. And I was discouraged to find grammar and English usage so much more complex than I'd previously thought it then to be.

Looking back at some of the things I wrote for Porter Perrin's "creative writing" classes, it's difficult to know why he thought I was worth encouraging. A good teacher hands out more encouragement than pupils deserve as a matter of teaching technique. You hear it from the teacher on the tennis court next to you. "Nice shot!" he says to the pupil who finally gets one over the net. Mr. Perrin did that with me and at least it gave me enough confidence, false though it may have been, to keep going.

Philosophy was all new to me. I had not known there were ideas like the ones we argued over in class. The great philosophers seemed to be maddeningly fair and indecisive, always too willing to consider another explanation. I had not known there was such a thing as pure thought for thought's sake only, independent of any practical result of having had it. I was fascinated by the application of philosophy to religion and became more convinced than ever that the mysteries of life, death, and the universe were insoluble and that God was as much a question as an answer.

Football was the thing I knew most about although some of the courses were easy. I took a biology course that was almost identical to, but simpler than, one I'd passed in The Academy. This was a freshman's dream come true.

At The Academy the linemen had already begun to trap block, which was considered a fairly sophisticated maneuver at the time, but my career as a football player at Colgate was checkered. I'd been heavy enough to be good in high school, but now at 185 pounds going up against linemen weighing 220 and 230 was a different experience. The first time I tried to move Hans Guenther out of the hole I was supposed to make for the fullback, Hans grabbed me by the shoulder pads, threw me aside, and tackled the fullback behind the line of scrimmage. Colgate had had an all-American guard a few years before my class who weighed even less than I did. The press had picked up the Colgate publicist's phrase "watch-charm guard" to describe him and it caught on. He was small but very fast and quick — not the

same thing on the football field. The freshman coach, Razor Watkins, thought he had
another watch-charm guard in me because
I was small. He was not prepared for a
player who was small and neither fast nor
quick.

No matter how I did on the field, I was
determined not to be a jock and let football
dominate my life. A lot of the young men
on the team were scholarship players who
had been recruited to play football. They
seemed crude to me and I became more
aware than I had been at The Academy that
I'd led a sheltered high-school life. None of
my friends there had smoked, we didn't say
"shit" or "fuck," and we didn't sleep with
our girlfriends. Sex was only a rumor to us.
I felt a sense of superiority that I recall now
with a mixture of pride and embarrassment.
I was right but it was self-righteous of me
to think so.

It was nonetheless true though that college often brings out the worst in perfectly
good young men and women. First-rate colleges like Colgate that get three times as
many applicants as they can accept choose
what they think are the best prospects. Go
to one of those colleges on a party weekend
and you wonder what the college applicants
who weren't selected must be like if these

young people attending the college are the cream of the crop.

I don't know what happens, but too often kids who have been bright and decent in high school turn into something else in college. I remember hearing of "Pig Night" at Yale where club residents were expected to bring a woman to the party who'd lay anybody. Colgate had fraternities, and there's some collective evil spirit that prevails in many fraternities and clubs. They offer sanctuary for boors and boorishness.

Colgate didn't bring out the best in me. I liked several of the teachers and their courses but I felt superior to a lot of what I saw there because I was looking at superficial things about the college and the students. It had a lot to do with my getting involved with a pacifist movement there.

Toward the end of my freshman year, I joined the Sigma Chi fraternity even though I felt the fraternity idea was foolish. Our house had been one of the fine old homes in town, and the fraternity had divided it up into a clutch of rabbit warrens that housed fifty of us in near-slum conditions. It was a good group of young men though, and it was an economically and socially practical way to live. The whole hocus-pocus of the fraternity mystique was foolish but dividing a campus up into groups of forty or fifty students and letting them work out their own food and housing is not a bad system.

For many years now I've returned all the Sigma Chi material that comes my way from the national headquarters with a note DECEASED on the envelope but nothing discourages the national organization from trying to honor anyone like me who they think might give them money.

When I got to college my marks improved dramatically, not through any genetic transformation but because I chose courses suited to a deformed intellect. This was one of the changes college life brought me. Another way I hoped to prove I wasn't a jock was by deciding to take piano lessons between classes and football practice. The wife of one of the professors undertook, at $2 for each one-hour lesson, to teach me. During my first lesson, I recall thinking that I clearly had more potential as a football player than I had as a musician. Piano playing didn't come easily to me. The teacher was quite a pretty woman and I was disappointed at myself, considering my motive for taking the lessons, for being thrilled when she put her hand over mine to move it over the keys. I found myself thinking more of the professor's wife than of the piano.

My third day of piano lessons turned out to be my last. I went directly from that lesson to football practice. It was a game-style scrimmage between the second team and the first team. During the second half of the scrimmage that day, I was playing opposite Bill Chernokowski, one of those gorilla-like athletes whose weight was mostly at or above the waist. He had short, relatively small legs and a huge torso with stomach to match. There are potbellied men who are surprisingly strong and athletic and "Cherno" was one of those. At 260 pounds he was the heaviest man on the squad.

As things turned out, it didn't matter where he carried most of his weight. When he stepped on the back of my right hand in the middle of the third quarter, that ended, for all time, any thought I might have had of being another Vladimir Horowitz.

At our fiftieth class reunion I had to revise my long-held opinion of Bill Chernokowski when I learned that his daughter was an outstanding cellist and Bill had season tickets to the New York Philharmonic. I couldn't have been more surprised, as my friend Charlie Slocum used to say, if I'd seen Albert Payson Terhune kick a collie.

Football became less important to me as I realized I was never going to be an all-American player. My career as a pianist now over, I began to think more about writing. There were two professors who interested me.

One was Porter Perrin, who was writing a book called *Writer's Guide and Index to English*. He became the closest thing I had to a friend on the faculty. The other was a Quaker iconoclast, Kenneth Boulding, who taught economics for the university and pacifism for his own satisfaction at night in meetings with students at his home. I don't know firsthand that he was brilliant; but it is an adjective that almost everyone used in referring to him.

When the college opened after preseason football, I had classes with both men. Boulding stammered badly and even though you knew it shouldn't have, it influenced the way you thought about him. During a class lecture, you were driven to pay careful attention because of the difficulty of following his broken speech. He was always surprising us, too. He'd be expounding some theory of economics that we barely understood when suddenly he'd drop in some mildly witty or unexpected remark. The class would erupt in raucous laughter, more from the sense of relief the class felt when Boulding got it out than by the humorous content of it.

When Boulding posted a notice on the bulletin board about a meeting of all those opposed to our entry into the war, I took that second opportunity to separate myself from the other football players and started going to his meetings. For some reason opposing the war seemed like an intellectual stand to take. It still seemed that way to Vietnam protesters. It was almost like not watching television now. There's a whole subculture in America of people who are proud of themselves for not watching television. They take every opportunity to tell anyone they can get to listen. I suffered something like that syndrome in opposing the war.

Boulding was a good teacher. The best teachers are not the ones who know most about the subject. The best teachers are the ones who are most interested in *something* — anything, and not necessarily the subject they teach. Boulding was consumed with the idea of pacifism and I've often thought of him as a good example of how little it matters that a college teacher is professing theories that are counter to popular and acceptable ideas of economics, religion, race, or government. His students were constantly propagandized by him but they ended up sorting things out for themselves. Being exposed to a communist professor in the 1930s didn't make communists of many students. Being exposed to the pacifist ideas of Kenneth Boulding didn't do his students any harm although if the parents of many of my classmates had sat in on some of those evening sessions in Boulding's home, they might have been reluctant to pay the next tuition bill to Colgate.

Quakers, like Christian Scientists, are frequently such decent, gentle, and seemingly reasonable people that they are not often considered to be religious fanatics. But they are generally more zealous than other Christians — most of whom, God knows, are zealous enough. The further a religion is from mainstream, the more devoted its followers are likely to be to it, and Quakers are down a long little rivulet.

Boulding may have been an economics genius, but he was definitely a religious nut. I was caught up with some of his ideas before I knew that and became convinced of the truth of one of his statements I've since seen attributed to both Plato and Benjamin Franklin: "Any peace is better than any war." I liked that a lot.

It was Boulding's contention that the conflict in Europe was none of the United States' business and even if it had been, war was an immoral way to pursue interests. The argument made sense to me, which gives you some idea how sensible I was when I was twenty.

On September 1, 1939, the day Hitler invaded Poland to begin World War II, I was in Hamilton where I'd arrived three weeks before classes began for football practice under the legendary head coach, Andy Kerr. I was so consumed with the game that one of the most momentous events in all history, Hitler's blitzkrieg, barely got my attention. I'd buy the *New York Times* several days a week but I didn't read much of it.

NAZIS TAKE BREST-LITOVSK

TURKS MASS ON SYRIAN BORDER

I couldn't have told you what country Brest-Litovsk was in nor did I have any idea what disagreement the Turks had with the Syrians.

It still was ten years before Senator Joseph McCarthy aroused the moderate and liberal population to protest his demagogic effort to expose and make jobless any American who ever had a conciliatory thought about socialism or communism. Before the war the isolationist Congressman Martin Dies

54

Jr. of Texas had already formed an Un-American Activities Committee that was McCarthy's forerunner. Isolationism was a popular movement, and outside the House it was organized as a group with the populist name "America First."

I participated in a debating society contest and the issue of the argument was "Resolved, that the American Press should be under the control of a Federal Press Commission." I'm pleased to be able to report that I was on the right side of that argument although I think the sides were chosen by a flip of a coin. We won the debate, but the fact that it could have been proposed as a subject for debate says something about the times — and we didn't have any easy time winning. The proposition would not be seriously considered today.

I didn't want to go to Europe to fight and die for what seemed to me to be someone else's cause. I hear the faint, far-away-and-long-ago echo of my own voice every time a congressman proclaims that "we shouldn't sacrifice the life of a single American boy" when the question comes up about our moving in to save a few hundred thousand poor souls being slaughtered in some foreign land. I decided I must be a Conscientious Objector. It was always capitalized because it was a formally recognized category of draft resisters.

This was when "Doc" Armstrong ended up forcing my hand, although he couldn't have known it since I'd never spoken with him. I had no idea that "Doc," the friendly, homespun tradesman with the gold-rimmed spectacles, was the head of the draft board. If "Doc" was around today, he could step into a role as the druggist in any pharmaceutical company's television commercial. His was the first drugstore I'd ever seen that didn't have a soda fountain, and that should have made me realize that "Doc" was a no-nonsense guy. There was something else I didn't know about "Doc" that I learned later. He was commander of the Madison County chapter of the American Legion and thought that every red-blooded American boy should serve his country — as he had in World War I — and right now.

He was not impressed by my attempt to delay enlisting by registering in Hamilton instead of Albany. It seemed to me as though I'd been hit by a truck the day I got the draft notice, sometime in May, a few weeks before the end of my junior year, stating I was to report for duty in the United States Army.

I had long, sophomoric, philosophical

discussions with my friends about resisting the draft. A young man I'd been in school with at The Albany Academy, Allen Winslow, had already refused to serve and was the first person to go to prison for that offense during World War II. I admired him.

Unwilling as I was, over the few months I had between the time I was drafted and the day I had to report, I wisely concluded that I probably wasn't smart enough to be a Conscientious Objector even though I agreed with those who were. All the Conscientious Objectors I knew, like Boulding, seemed bright, deep, introspective, and a little strange. I liked those traits in a person even though I didn't have them myself.

One of my dominating characteristics has always been that I'm not strange. I'm average in so many ways that it eliminates any chance I ever had of being considered a brooding, introspective intellectual.

When Boulding died in 1993, several people wrote me saying I'd been unfair in some of the things I'd said about him. Our opinions of people tend to alter slowly over the years and, if we don't update our relationship by talking to them, become untrue. I have opinions of a great many people that must be unfair and untrue, but I've repeated them so often they're set in my mind and

As a young Stars and Stripes *reporter in England*

serve my purpose when I'm casting characters for stories that illustrate a point. My opinion of Kenneth Boulding settled and changed moderately over the years without my having come on any new facts to justify the change. It may not be accurate. On the other hand, of course, it may *be* accurate.

After months of anguishing over it I realized that, while I was an objector, I could not honestly claim to be a conscientious one. On July 7, 1941, I reported for duty.

Meeting Marge

I'd been writing to Marge Howard, a girl I'd first met in Mrs. Munson's dancing class when we were thirteen. We had gone together, off and on, all through high school and college. I'd frequently made the drive from Colgate to Bryn Mawr, outside Philadelphia, where she was in college. She still points out that she was a year ahead of me in college although a year behind in age. It was a seven-hour drive each way and that took a lot of time out of the weekend.

One Friday afternoon I'd left after my one o'clock class and was driving a little too fast somewhere between New York and Philadelphia. In order to get to Bryn Mawr by 6 P.M. I was saving time by changing my clothes as I drove. This was before highways were "super" and at a time when all state policemen rode Indian motorcycles. A lot of the young men who showed up at Bryn Mawr on weekends were from nearby Princeton and, in order to fit in and conceal my Colgate affiliation, I had brought gray flannel slacks and a sports jacket and I wore Spaulding dirty white bucks (from buckskin) with red rubber soles. They were part of the Ivy League uniform of the era. It was said of a well-dressed Princeton student, "He's really 'shoe.' "

With my knees raised, I was holding the steering wheel on a straight course while I pulled my old corduroy pants down around my ankles with my two hands in anticipation of changing them for the gray flannels. I knew when I saw the flashing red light on the trooper's motorcycle behind me that I was in big trouble. The corduroys were in a never-never land, half on and half off, and when the cop came up to the side of my car and looked in the window he must have decided I was not only a speeder but a sex pervert. He ordered me to follow him to the house of a justice of the peace, with whom I assumed he had a business arrangement, and I paid a cash fine of $12, which was all but a few dollars of the money I had.

Margie graduated in the spring of 1941, a short time before I got my draft notice, and she was using her Bryn Mawr degree in art history to teach French, a language about which she knew very little, in a girls' school in Albany. In February or March we decided, long distance and me on a pay phone, to get married. I forget why we thought it was a good idea. Most of our friends were delaying marriage until after the war.

There was a major family argument over who would perform the ceremony. I was already set in disbelief and Margie, although brought up Catholic, had stopped going to church when she was sixteen. Margie's mother had always served fish on Fridays and was a serious mass-going Catholic. She was adamant that her daughter be married "in the church."

My mother's strongest religious belief was that she was not Catholic. She had always gone to great pains to point out that, even with the name Rooney, we were Presbyterians. My father and mother both grew up in the small town of Ballston Spa, New York, and there had been a moderate influx of Irish immigrants to the area in the late 1800s. My mother's parents were English and my father's had come from Scotland although their Irishness was not far behind them. When my father and mother were growing up, most of the Irish in Ballston were doing what first-generation immigrants have traditionally done in America — working at menial jobs and doing the housework for the establishment. It was a desire to distance herself from them that produced this Irish denial in my mother. It made me understand how benign prejudice can be at its inception.

After a lot of letter writing and telephoning during which we tried to come to some

Marge Rooney, on board the Staten Island Ferry

amicable agreement, Margie's father, an eminently sensible orthopedist who was in no way religious, wrote me a letter that was not unfriendly but was brief and to the point. He was obviously tired of the dinner-table conversation he was getting on the subject from Margie's mother.

"I don't give a damn who performs the ceremony," he wrote, "but if you're going to do it, I wish you'd do it and get it over with." I wish I had the letter. I don't know what happens to life-altering pieces of paper like that. I suppose I threw it away.

After reading Dr. Howard's letter, I realized that I didn't really care who married us either. It was a ceremonial formality, the religious overtones of which meant nothing to me.

Travel was difficult and the prenuptial negotiations had been so contentious that neither my parents nor Dr. Howard came to the event conducted in a bare-bones Army chapel used for Catholic, Protestant, and Jewish services. The priest, a lieutenant named Joseph Farrell, who was chaplain for the regiment, assumed that Margie was Catholic through the circumstance of birth, and inasmuch as I had told him I was not Catholic or anything else, decided it was what he called a "mixed marriage."

He was very friendly and casual about it, but he thought he ought to get permission from some higher authority in the church so he called the living quarters of his bishop. The bishop was on the golf course at the time but someone on the other end of the phone said he was commissioned to act in his name.

"Mixtae religionis," our priest said. "Okay?"

Evidently it was okay with this anonymous and somewhat suspect stand-in and we were married on the authority of a cleric well down the hierarchical ladder from the pope. I suppose I was predetermined to dislike this likable priest, and it seemed to me that Chaplain Farrell had a condescending air about himself during the ceremony which suggested that he felt marriage was for lesser mortals than himself.

We had dinner that night with a group of friends of Margie's father and mother who were staying at The Pinehurst Inn, near Southern Pines, North Carolina, which was for a time one of the great resort hotels in the country. Most of them were doctors and their wives, and I was uncomfortable with what I considered the off-color stories they were telling. "Off-color" is what we used to call a dirty joke. After dinner I returned directly to the barracks at Fort Bragg and, on the very next day, before we'd had a chance to live any married life, the Seventeenth Field Artillery was ordered south from North Carolina to Camp Blanding, Florida, and we were all restricted to the base until the move, which took place ten days later.

A MISSIVE TO MARGE FROM ENGLAND

Nov 30, 1942

Dearest Marg,

I have never put so many words on paper in one day in my life but I can't go another day without writing you.

Eight days ago I was transferred from the 17th to The Stars & Stripes. And except for frequent trips out of town I will be living permanently in London. The first week has been hell. I am not a good newspaper man, nor do I write particularly well at this point. But what I need is work and I'm getting it.

In the week with the paper I have seen more of England than Desk of Cook's Tours and have seen things Cook will never see. I have been out for four days covering the major air fields in the British Isles with a photographer. We got some good shots, and several stories — the best of which are not for publication.

Thursday I am going up with some sort of a formation of Flying Fortresses on what they are calling a "sortie." There are twenty other newsmen going so I hardly think we will hit the continent.

The S&S is put out by two boys who really

know what newspaper work is all about. Bob Moora and Bud Hutton. Hutton is the typical tabloid desk man — has worked on most NY papers. Moora is the stabilizer — five years with the Herald, two as night editor. (Moora says of Yank "If I ever get back there I'm going in swinging, what a bunch of glamour boys.") And I could think of a few examples of what he meant.

The editorial offices are in the Times building. The Times itself has shriveled into the bowels of its building and we work in three offices previously used by pages three, four and five of the Sunday Supplement.

You should see the Times function. About twenty seventyish English gentlemen come in each day about noon, retire to their rugged offices with a roaring fire place and a boiling samovar and ponder the days news. When a decision is made about using an item they call a secretary, have fresh crumpets sent in, pour the tea and chat. Then they dictate what they have to the secretary and while I'm not sure I think it then goes before the Board of Directors for approval previous to release.

It will be a sad Christmas for me and nothing merry for you I'm sure. I spent most of what money I had on twelve Wedgewood service plates and a Wedgewood bowl for Mother. I paid quite a bit for them, about $50 so I hope they get there intact. They are in three huge boxes and will probably be in several thousand less huge pieces when they get there.

I sent you something not nearly as nice but then Mrs. Rooney had no choice about being my mother and I thought it was time I did something decent for her. Next month and all months thereafter I will draw an extra $150. so when your birthday roll around etc. (By the by Lovie, that means that all in all I will kill about $250 a month. It will cost something to live here but not $250.)

If you volunteer for Red Cross work here, you will find me usually in the vicinity of Blackfriars near the Embankment but in the event that you don't get over I will see you sometime in 1943.

All my love forever,
Andy

At the end of World War II Andy Rooney collaborated with fellow *Stars and Stripes* reporter Bud Hutton to write an informative firsthand account of the Army's daily newspaper titled simply *The Story of the Stars and Stripes.* Written by and for soldiers, *The Stars and Stripes* was, as

Nov 30,1942

Dearest Marg,

I have never put so many words on paper in one day in my life
but I cant go another day without writing you.

Eight days ago I was transferred from the 17th to The Stars & Stripes.
And except for frequent trips out of town I will be living permanently
in London. The first week has been hell. I am not a good newspaper man,
nor do I write particularly well at this point. But what I need is work
and Im getting it.

In the week with the paper I have seen more of England than Cook of
Cook's Tours and have seen things Cook will never see. I have been out
for four days covering the major air fields in the British Isles with
a photographer. We got some good shots and several stories - the best
of which are not for publication.

Thursday I am going up with some sort of a formation of Flying
Fortresses on what they are calling a "sortie". There are twenty other
newsmen going so I hardly think we will hit the continent.

The S&S is put out by two boys who really know what newspaper work
is all about. Bob Moora and Bud Hutton. Hutton is the typical tabloid
desk man - has worked on most NY papers. Moora is the stabilizer - five
years with the Herald,two as night editor. (Moora says of Yank "If I ever,
get back there Im going in swinging,what a bunch of glamour boys.") And
I could think of a few examples of what he meant.

The editorial offices are in the Times building. The Times itself
has shriveled into the bowels of its building and we work in three offices
previously used by pages three,four and five of the Sunday Supplement.

gentlemen come in each day about noon,retire to their rugged offices with a roaring fire place and a boiling samovar and ponder the days news. When a decision is made about using an item they call a secretary, have fresh crumpets sent in,pour the tea and chat. Then they dictate what they have to the secretary and while Im not sure I think it then goes before the Board of Directors for approval previous to release.

It will be a sad Christmas for me and nothing merry for you Im sure. I spent most of what money I had on twelve Wedgewood service plates and a Wedgewood bowl for Mother. I paid quite a bit for them,about $50 so I hope they get there intact. They are in three huge boxes and will proba— bly be in several thousand less huge pieces when they get there.

I sent you something not nearly as nice but then Mrs Rooney had no choice about being my mother and I thought it was time I did something decent for her. Next month and all months thereafter I will draw an extra 150. so xxxxxx when your birthday roll around etc. (By the by Iovie,that means that all in all I will kill about $250 a month. It will cost something to live here but not $250.)

I f you volunteer for Red Cross work here,you will find me usually in the vicinity of Blackfriars near the xxxxxxxxxxxxxxxabout in the event that you dont get over I will see you sometime in 1943.

editor Bob Moora put it, a paper "for Joe." A morale booster and source for hard news about the American forces and the enemy's movements, the paper was also, in Rooney's words, a "refuge for eccentrics." Established by a corporal, a sergeant and a private, *The Stars and Stripes* was produced in the height of war and published in Rome, Paris, Frankfurt, Casablanca, and Liege. In their book, Hutton and Rooney offered readers vivid accounts of the perilous, sometimes tragic, sometimes hilarious life of newsmen covering the frontlines of battle.

As a twenty-four-year-old reporter for *The Stars and Stripes,* Andy Rooney boarded a B-17 bomber with the Eighth Air Force to fly on America's second bombing mission over Germany. In 1944 he landed on Utah beach, three days after the brutal invasion of Normandy. The day that Paris was liberated from Germany, Rooney entered the city with French forces. Rooney's front-row seat to the war afforded him a unique purview into the soldier's life and a crash course in delivering news under the most unforgivable conditions imaginable. The following selection from *The Story of the Stars and Stripes* offers a glimpse of that world.

PLACES OF BUSINESS

The *Times* of London is an institution. From the drab and motley cluster of brick and wooden buildings in the dingy shadows of Queen Victoria Street, on the edge of London's old city and just off the Thames, the *Times* does grammatically as it considers right, and in so doing molds an important (THE important, the *Times* is apt to feel and not without a lot of justification) portion of British public opinion. The *Times* does not hurry. Through its intricate, winding hallways linking the buildings that have been expanded with empire and time, *Times* editors walk with thoughtful mien, and they do it in fresh linen, with neckties, and coats. Sometimes, they do it with morning trousers, even in rationed wartime. The editors and subeditors are served tea in their offices at four on silver and china tea sets.

Maybe the *Times* is best summed up: its readers open their paper first to the editorials.

When *The Stars and Stripes* became a daily on November 2, 1942, it was at the *Times,* the first in a long line of journalistic step-parents to the daily paper of the army.

When *The Stars and Stripes* staff first clattered through their building, the sober edi-

With Bud Hutton, in a Hollywood publicity shot
Philippe Halsman, © Halsman Archive

tors of the *Times* looked up disapprovingly from under their green eyeshades. *Times* reporters, busy writing out their reports in longhand, lay down their pencils and pens as the unconscious Americans hit the floor, where only toes previously had tread, with heavy GI heels, making more noise than the building or any of its occupants had heard since the last nail (or wooden peg) was hammered in place hundreds of years before. There was a lot of walking to do to get where you were going at the *Times.*

The course from the street, near Blackfriars Bridge, to the *S&S* office in the *Times* led through hundreds of feet of narrow, winding corridors, up and down flights of wooden steps and around little corners.

Strangers groping their way to the office often felt like dropping small bits of paper, Boy Scouts of America–like, so they would be able to find their way out. The second night of the occupation of the *Times,* Bob Moora and Russ Jones started out to find a shortcut from the editorial offices to the pressroom, some four floors below, and eventually wound up in a black maze, literally unable to retrace their steps. They stood there and hollered for help until a small, gray *Times* employee came along and, completely unperturbed, led them back to the city room.

The labyrinth, which would have driven any intelligent American laboratory guinea pig insane, was some protection, though, from the thousands of screwballs who tried to get up to the office. Some of the Belgian bicyclists who wanted to insert ads in the paper, the refugee Poles who wanted to find their cousins from Scranton and the soldier with the self-heating bedroll for tired and cold soldiers got to know their ways to the editorial rooms, but thousands more must have given up, discouraged. We never found any parched skeletons, though, on the way out.

The *Times* got *The Stars and Stripes* daily printing job by underbidding all the other London papers for the job. It was on a reverse Lend-Lease basis, but they were doing it cheaply. It was almost a gesture of goodwill to their American allies. "Sure we'll print your little journal for American soldiers," they said in effect. What they definitely did not understand was that within a year and a half *The Stars and Stripes* would dwarf the *Times'* own circulation and would be published by a high-powered staff from whom "The Thunderer's" own editors frequently borrowed stories.

It probably was a merciful thing that the *Times* didn't realize what was happening until it was too late to stop it. From its venerable presses was coming an American tabloid newspaper, comic strips, pin-up photos of semidressed femininity, black headlines on page one; six days a week, four pages a day except Monday when there were eight and every one of them blatant by *Times* standards.

That first month of November, 1942, full of bold news for bold American headlines, such as the invasion of North Africa, gave the *Times* an idea of what it was going to be like. Before December, every newspaper in Fleet Street was sending a messenger boy to wait at the *Times'* pressroom, not for a copy of the Thunderer, but for *The Stars and Stripes.* So, too, the American news agencies. The British press picked up leads on stories, and frequently stories intact, albeit injecting into them the unique style of London journalism.

The Stars and Stripes was particularly proud of its roundup on the day's bombing activities during that period of the war when there was no fighting in Europe except that in the air; the paper literally was an Air Force trade journal. As such it had to know its business. The air story often ran for 1,500 words and included a meticulous report of heavy and medium bomber missions, their targets, and the background down to the number of tons that target already had absorbed, fighter-bomber sorties, strafings, aerial minelaying and just about everything else. The roundup was so capably handled that most London papers and American news bureaus there waited for it before writing their final stories of the night, sometime along about 11:30 P.M.

The *Times,* from the first day of war, had

begun its air story with a simple introductory sentence and then had printed verbatim the RAF communique, later adding whatever the Americans might have done. Its air editor finally got around not only to the *S&S* treatment of the story, but one evening broke down enough over a glass of mild-and-bitter to confess that he was "finding actually more enjoyment these days in treating the subject in your ah American manner. With some reservations, of course, some reservations."

The air war, then, accounted for the reproductions of diving fighters, burning bombers and formations that covered part of the walls of the *Stars and Stripes* office. The rest of the walls were covered with a miscellany of items stuck up haphazardly with paste. The pictures were predominantly "cheesecake," the trade term of Sergeant Ben Price, the Des Moines picture editor, for choice items from his stack of Hollywood girls more or less out of bathing suits.

From the walls the *Times* could have — and probably did — draw its own image of things to come after that first month. The *Times* people were very obliging, but they first began to realize they were in for real trouble the day the switchboard operator heard a voice from *S&S* make a request.

In the London office of The Stars and Stripes; *Rooney, standing in back, is looking over Bud Hutton's shoulder*

"Would you please tell the department in charge of knocking down walls that we would like to have the wall knocked down between our two offices?" the voice asked.

The operator, not realizing how surprised she was for a minute, said she would. Fifteen minutes or so later, two grayed men in overalls came into the city room, crowbars, sledges, hammers and saws over their shoulders. The Desk was a little taken aback, but pointed, and they dutifully knocked down the wall that time, the blitz and generations of *Times* men had left standing. That made the *S&S* offices in the building into one large room.

It was about thirty feet wide and twice as long. As you came in at one of two doors — the other was bolted shut and carried a nostalgically huge poster of a dish of American ice cream — there was a small rectangular niche about five feet deep and six feet wide at your left. There, for some reason, the light switch had been placed conveniently behind a desk and a heavy wooden cabinet. On the far side of the room was the Desk.

The city editor, through whom came all stories other than those from the newswires, sat on one side of the double desk. With the aid of the five telephones in front of him he sent reporters out to cover this largest local news beat in the world — the whole British Isles, the seas around them and the flak-filled sky all the way to Berlin.

The news editor, who handled all the wire copy, the news from home and the stories from other war fronts, sat across from him. Six other desks of varying sizes and states of disrepair were scattered around the room.

On a small shelf, nailed to the wall between the two windows, was the complete office library. There were eight books: a Jane's *Fighting Ships;* a Webster's dictionary; a Tacoma, Washington, telephone book; a 1939 *World Almanac;* Jane's *Aircraft of the World;* a French-English-German dictionary; an *Official Officers' Guide Book;* and a volume entitled *The Fox of Peapack.* Over the library, for handy reference, someone had scribbled in foot-high black crayon letters "IT'S ADOLF — NOT ADOLPH."

Running up the middle of the city room was a pipelike affair about six inches in diameter. It served as the office bulletin board although structurally its function was to hold the wooden ceiling off the wooden floor. Toward the top of the pipe, near the ceiling, there was a wicker wastebasket, wired fast. Ben Price tied it to the top of the pole one day when an order came down for all *Stars and Stripes* men to get an hour's exercise every day.

Price and a couple of staffers used to drag out a new case of pastepots every few days and get their exercise by tossing a few of the glass "balls" through the (waste) basket.

The boys got the greater part of their exercise in climbing up to retrieve the glass pastepot-balls until one day Charlie White staggered into the shop and through the thick lenses of his glasses turned red eyes on the basket. Charles was no athlete, but somehow the pastepot he grabbed from Ham Whitman's desk sailed truly through the air and into the basket. Charles was pleased, but irritated.

"Hell of a basket," he grumbled. "It's got a bottom." He climbed on a chair, jerked the basket down and kicked vigorously at its bottom. The kick carried too far. As a matter of fact, it carried Charlie's foot, ankle and knee on up into the basket, and carried Charlie completely off his feet so that he wound up threshing on the floor, the basket jammed up around his waist. In the confusion he lost his glasses, and his myopic eyes spun wildly as he kicked and wrestled with the basket.

At the height of Charles's battle with the wicker wastebasket, Lieutenant Colonel Llewellyn walked into the office, and where never in a sober moment would he have thought of saluting, Charles suddenly was seized with a self-martyring urge to stand up and salute. He did, and as he stood there, the basket still around his leg, glasses lost, thin hair mussed, coat up around the back of his neck, eyes glaring wildly and his balance a precarious thing, the character of

Hubert, Dick Wingert's cartoon hero, was born.

The thing had an aftermath. Because Charles had destroyed the bottom of the basket, when it was replaced on the pipe, the pastepots went right through, and, non-bouncing, splattered glue and glass across the room each time the mob exercised.

This, presumably, was the army.

On the walls, finally, in addition to the cheesecake, there were dozens of clippings, memos, pictures, and odds and ends of printed material. There were weekly notices of inspections and various formations, which eventually, as they were disregarded, came to have, you felt, a sort of pleading note in them. Sort of please, fellows, come on up to inspection this week.

One of the staffers' favorite headlines pasted to the wall was:

YANKS GET ABBEY FOR GI CHAPEL

It came from the first Thanksgiving in England. For the traditional American services, the friendly Britons gave up their most precious religious symbol, Westminster Abbey. It was a good story; it was worth a top head on page one. That meant thirty-point type, a size that simply doesn't permit the word "Westminster" to be squeezed into one line. The resourceful Desk solved it with their headline describing the venerable abbey as about to become a GI chapel. It shocked a few chaplains, but most of them understood there was no disrespect involved, and there had been a neat job of head writing.

Just behind the Desk was the favorite clipping of the city editor's. It served as text when anyone turned in a paragraph or more of meaningless copy, and it had been clipped from the November 25, 1941, issue of the very *Times* itself. It read (and there were a couple of staffers who came to be able to recite it by heart):

With a British Armoured Unit
LIBYA, Nov. 23
The battle of the tanks in Libya is still going on furiously. At the time of writing the issue is still in the balance. The Germans are fighting furiously to destroy the British tank forces and to break through the ring. The British are fighting with equal fury to prevent them. Both sides have given and taken some very hard knocks. The tank battles are an affair of sudden onslaughts in unexpected places. The battle is joined, broken and rejoined. Sometimes small groups only are involved; other times,

large groups . . .

It went on like that.

When the staff first moved into the offices there was just one electric light in the middle of the room. The Desk wanted a low, green-shaded light over each desk. The meticulous *Times* maintenance men obliged with a network of wires and lights.

Suspended from all sections of the ceiling and hanging at ruled heights above the desks, the wires presented a maze too intriguing to anyone who'd spent half an hour in the Lamb and Lark, the pub across the street, before coming back to the office late at night for extra work. You'd start one hanging light swinging in great circles, then another and another and when enough of them were wound around each other, the whole complex structure would come down. Next day the maintenance men would be upstairs, surveying the tangled mess, the chunks of ceiling plaster, and the blown fuses. They would say sadly, "The blast of those bombs is enough to shake down almost anything."

Which was all right and logical on nights when there was an air raid. But sometimes the lights came down after a raid-free night, and they said the same thing, and the staff finally decided they were simply nice, understanding guys who maybe had wanted to do the same thing in the staid *Times* all their lives but hadn't dared.

At frequent intervals, we received a formal announcement that "General Somebody" was coming down to the office to look around. There could have been no more absurd place for a military inspection; but one time the staff was told "for sure" that Lieutenant General John C. H. Lee, one of the army's most inspecting generals, was to visit us. We were ordered to take down the ridiculous display on the walls and clean up the office. Some of the memos and pictures pasted on the walls were part of the office, though, and taking them down was out of the question, even for General Lee.

Ben Price walked over to Fleet Street. He visited half a dozen little bookstores, buying road maps, maps of the canal system in Afghanistan, terrain maps of the territory adjacent to Shanghai, and weather maps showing general pressure areas between Iceland and England. He came back and the staff went to work hanging the maps from hooks or with thumbtacks on the walls.

With straight faces the staff explained to the officer in charge that no one could kick about legitimate maps in any newspaper office. General Lee, of course, like the others, never arrived. Most of the maps came down, and the urgent memos, the cheesecake, and the outdated headlines were visible again in all their dusty yellow uselessness. The weather map of the North Atlantic stayed. Ben said we might need to know someday how the weather was there.

The *Times* people never really got used to *The Stars and Stripes*. They tried, and some of the compositors eventually became as one with the staff. But mostly the *Times* just wondered.

In the first few days strange things happened in the composing rooms with compositors who never had worked for any paper except the *Times*. There was, for example, the mysterious disappearance of a particularly choice bit of cheesecake that had been sent up to the engravers one night. Somehow the picture and engraving disappeared completely, and there always has been an argument as to whether some venerable *Times* worker secretly slipped the picture of the seminude Hollywoodite into his pocket to contemplate in some lonely place or whether the *Times* man was a reforming purist who thought that in the best interests of the soldiers of England's ally the photo should be destroyed. If he simply wanted the picture for his own he was easily satisfied, because after that first week none ever disappeared again, and if he was a reformer he quickly gave us up for lost.

That first week at the *Times* was something English type compositors are going to talk about for a long time. On the sixth night, one linotype operator was carried off screaming mad, and he's in the booby hatch yet shouting about "the language of Shakespeare." Another compositor, setting heads, saw unfilled orders piling up and piling up and suddenly and stiffly fainted dead away; but in general they became familiar with what the editors wanted, and Jimmy Frost, the composing room foreman, and Bill Jolley, a stone man, got to be so expert in the American way of newspapering that they were worried about their postwar return to the *Times.*

Just as the *Times* became a little proud of the army paper it housed, so the army paper was proud of the *Times.* The staff learned the *Times* folklore complete through constant contact with the Thunderer's staff in the building — this was after *Times* editors decided we'd been there long enough for them to stop bowing stiffly from the waist when we passed in the corridors — and in the Printing House Square pub, Alf Storey's Lamb and Lark. There was a great store of *Times* stories, and probably the one the *S&S* liked best was that of the man with the little black bag.

When a new managing director was appointed by the *Times* board of directors, he started a thorough check through the books and offices of every branch of the organization. The new manager noticed an obscure little man in an oversized overcoat and carrying a little black satchel entering the building one Friday and made a mental note to find out who he was. The following Friday he saw the little man again and this time started asking who he was. The old-timers admitted they had seen the little man for years, but no one knew exactly who he was or what he did. He came Friday nights, carrying his black satchel, and left Monday mornings.

Over the weekend, the manager was checking some ledgers and came upon a small but inexplicable item. He asked one of the bookkeepers about it and was told the money went for meals brought in Saturday and Sunday from a small restaurant around the corner; the meals went to the little man who appeared each Friday night at the office.

On the third weekend, the manager searched through the dozens of little offices off the rabbit warren of corridors. Beyond one door he found the little man, with a little lunch spread out before him, his little black satchel at his side.

The little man was from the Bank of England. In the little black satchel he had five thousand pounds in cash.

Back at the turn of the century, along about the time of the Boer War, the *Times* wanted to send a man off to cover a big story on the Continent in a rush assignment. He had to leave on a Saturday afternoon, but there were no boats to the Continent that day because of a storm. Charter a boat, ordered the editor. The business office ruefully replied that there wasn't enough money in the place, it had been sent to the bank in the morning.

To prevent that ever happening again, the *Times* had asked that a representative of the Bank of England be on hand Friday evenings and stay until Monday mornings with five thousand pounds in cash.

Long afterward, when the *Times* had its own boats and had fully-manned bureaus on the Continent, no one had bothered to countermand the order, and the little man was still coming every Friday evening.

Stately *Times,* whose subscribers will doubt the world's end until they read it in your pages, institution of British dignity with morals like the collars of your directors, you were very kind; and if you were an old gaffer, the people who came to your house to work were brats, and you were very indulgent. You nodded and smiled when the people in Fleet Street got to calling your musty, cobblestoned old courtyard "Stars and Stripes Square," instead of the Printing House name it had borne so long. You even asked one of the brashest of the Americans to write book reviews for that book review section which is the double-distilled synthesis of *Times* conservatism and backed him up when he lampooned stuffed shirts. You gathered up the pieces when they were broken and you set the precedent for all the rest to come. As it was in the beginning, so always was *The Stars and Stripes,* and so the *Times* was home.

In 1944 Andy Rooney and Bud Hutton's *Air Gunner* — a vivid portrait of the American gunners engaged in the perilous air war against Germany — was published. An engaging account of what was arguably one of the most exciting and dangerous wartime posts, *Air Gunner* shed light on the at turns dramatic, mundane, and heart-wrenching experience of the twenty-somethings who flew into the eye of the storm, manned the guns, and scattered bombs as they screamed towards their targets. Offering a window into Air Force men (men who fail to be good "parade soldiers because they don't like to march in a line") *Air Gunner* was widely praised for its candid, intimate rendering of what a gunner's life entailed. In *The New Yorker,* then-editor Edmund Wilson praised it as, "The first piece of writing . . . which has really given me any idea of what it is like to operate a bomber . . . full of intimate observation of how people speak, feel, and behave." The following essay from *Air Gunner* gets to the heart of the matter.

COMBAT

A lot of air gunners were growing up during the years between 1925 and 1935 — a lot of gunners in America and in Germany. All over the world, public opinion was penduluming to the opposite extreme of World War I's emotional pitch. There were exposés, from time to time, of last-war propaganda. One of public opinion's favorite stories in the years 1925 to 1935 was of a truce which was declared one Christmas Eve during that first World War. Allies and Germans dropped their guns, the story went, and sang carols to each other across no man's land. A lot of gunners who were growing up liked that story; a lot of gunners in America and in Germany.

Those Americans who liked that story as youngsters grew up into air gunners who liked the story of Tyre C. Weaver, a top turret gunner from Riverview, Alabama. It maybe wasn't good for the war that they liked it, but they did. . . .

The copilot on the B-17 *Ruthie II,* on July 28, 1943, was redheaded Jack Morgan and he won the Congressional Medal of Honor for what he did that day. The navigator was Keith Koske, and "Red" Morgan always was embarrassed that Keith didn't get a higher award for what he did for the top turret gunner whose arm was blown off. It took a tougher kind of guts, a rarer kind, for what Koske did than what won the Medal of Honor, Red was always saying.

The top turret gunner was Tyre Weaver.

Ten boys started out in *Ruthie II* that day, and nine of them came back. One, the pilot, was dead in the arms of his copilot. The tenth man, the one that was missing, was somewhere in Germany. The crew didn't know whether he was dead or alive. He was somewhere in Germany without a left arm. The left arm was in the bomber, and Tyre Weaver was somewhere, dead or alive.

Ruthie II was within twenty minutes of the target when the pilot, Bob Campbell, of Liberty, Mississippi, took the controls from Morgan. Within three minutes a flight of German airmen slashed into the formation.

On their first pass, one German plane poured a stick of 20-millimeter shells into *Ruthie*'s midriff, puncturing the oxygen tanks above the ball turret gunner that supply the two waist gunners, the tail gunner and the radio man. A second later another flight of four F-W 190s screamed nose-on toward *Ruthie.* A cannon shell and one machine-gun bullet shattered the windshield, striking Bob Campbell in the head just above the temple.

The stricken pilot fell forward over the control column, wrapping his arms around it with a frenzied power. He was not killed instantly; and, partially conscious, he struggled instinctively with the controls.

The Fortress plunged forward out of the formation and Red Morgan wrenched at the controls to set the plane back on its course. By sheer strength, working against the force of the struggling pilot, Morgan pulled the ship level. Over the intercom he called for help but no one heard him. The plane's communication system had been shot out with the rear oxygen tanks.

In the top turret, Tyre Weaver twisted himself ahead of his mechanical turret, trying to make shots that were impossible from his position. They had all felt the impact of the blow that hit their pilot but none knew what had happened. It had looked as though they were going down; then somehow, someone had pulled them out. That was all they knew or had time to think of.

German planes circled on the fringe of the formation and barreled in for the attack once more. Tyre Weaver was hit. A flow of 20-millimeter shells ripped into his turret, and tore through his arm just below the shoulder, shearing it off close to the armpit.

Weaver dropped from the open half of his boiler-shaped turret into the runway leading to the nose compartment. Koske, the navigator, saw Weaver and quickly went to find out what had happened. Leaning over the gunner, who was not sure himself, for a few seconds, what had happened, Koske tore the white scarf from his neck and tried to wrap it tightly around the stump of arm. Red blood flowed fast into the white neckpiece, quickly spotting it and then, as the spot crept to the edges, soaking it in blood. The tourniquet was no good. The arm was gone so close to the shoulder that there was no pressure point left at which the blood could be choked off.

"I tried to inject morphine," Koske said, "but the needle was bent. I couldn't get it in and as things turned out it was best I didn't give him any.

"He had to have the right kind of medical attention, and right away, I knew that," Koske said. "We had almost four hours of flying time ahead of us and there was no alternative. There was only one place that he had any chance of getting medical attention quickly. I opened the hatch and adjusted Weaver's 'chute for him.

"He knew what I was doing all right and he was really good about it. He seemed to know somehow that it was his only chance. After I adjusted his 'chute I put the ripcord in his right hand. He must again have lost his sense of exactly what was happening because he pulled the ripcord immediately and the little pilot 'chute opened in the strong updraft coming from the open hatch below us. I gathered it all together again and tucked it under his good arm, making sure he was holding all the folds together. I got him into a crouched position right over the hatch and just toppled him out into space.

"The bombardier, Asa Irwin, had been busy with the nose guns because they were still coming at us from head-on. When I got back up there he had dropped his gun and was getting ready to toggle (release) the bombs. The target, the chemical works there at Hanover, was covered with smoke and we just dropped our bombs into it and picked up the guns and went to work again.

"Most of the attacks began to come from directly behind us so we couldn't do much about them up front. I tried to use my interphone several times but I couldn't get any answer. The last time I remember hearing anything over it was just after the first attack when I heard someone say they weren't getting any oxygen.

"Except for what seemed to be some pretty violent evasive action we seemed to be flying okay."

It was two hours and fifteen minutes later when Koske decided that he should go back and check with the pilot to see that everything was all right.

Slumped on the seat and covered with blood, he found his pilot, Bob Campbell. The back of his head had been blown off by a 20-millimeter shell which had entered the cockpit from the right, crossed in front of Red Morgan and hit Campbell.

"Red was flying the plane with one hand and holding Bob Campbell off the controls with the other," Koske said, "and there was no way he could call for help. The pilot was still alive and struggling drunkenly with the controls.

"Red told me we'd have to get Campbell out of the pilot's seat because the windshield was so badly smashed in front of him that he couldn't see out to fly, let alone land. He had to guide the plane by looking out the side window next to him."

Morgan and Koske struggled for thirty minutes to get the fatally injured pilot out of his seat and down into the catwalk at the rear of the navigator-bombardier nose compartment. The door of the escape hatch had been jettisoned when Weaver was dropped out and the bombardier had to hold the pilot to keep him from slipping out the opening.

Koske went back through the bomb bay of the plane to get help from the gunners in the rear of the plane. Opening the door to the radio room he found the radioman slumped on the floor. Stepping over the unconscious gunner Koske opened the door leading back to the waist gun positions and he saw the same seemingly lifeless heaps on the floor. Both gunners were unconscious. Realizing that the tail gunner and the ball turret gunner must also have been unconscious, Koske hurried back to tell Morgan that the oxygen system was shot out back there.

No one but Red Morgan really knows what he went through taking that ship in over Hanover with a crazed pilot. Alone for two hours he battled with a dying friend to save the lives of the others on the plane.

And no one but Keith Koske really knows what went through his mind as he decided to push Tyre C. Weaver through the hatch onto Germany.

It was five months later before anyone knew what had happened to Weaver that July day.

He'd gone out into the sky, and the parachute had opened. He'd come down about twenty-five miles from Hanover, and had been picked up almost as soon as he hit the ground. Some Germans took him to a hospital and a German surgeon treated him. His left arm was gone and he was in a bad way from shock and loss of blood. He got well, which was kind of a miracle, or else he had awfully good care, and when he was able to write he sent a postcard from Stalag

IV. That was in December, and some of the men Tyre Weaver flew with that day were still flying. They sat around the hut for a long time and talked to new gunners and told them the story they liked just about as well as that one about the truce on Christmas Eve, the one back in the other war.

That ship of Red Morgan's had returned that day with more drama and pathos aboard it than any that had ever returned before and any that has ever returned since. Combat, the real details of what happens when a man is without oxygen or without warmth at twenty thousand feet, the real details of what men feel when one of the other crewmen is seriously wounded over Germany hours from home, is hard to catch in words. Something happens to gunners in combat. They are greater men, finer men, and heroism and the ability to endure pain is on a grander scale. Back in their Nissen huts they can still complain about the fifty-degree cold and the absence of hot and cold running water; they still howl in pain if they stumble over a bed in the blackout coming in at night.

What happened in Red Morgan's plane wasn't a typical combat story and what happened to the crew of Francis Lauro's Fort in a raid on Bremen in January 1944, wasn't typical either, because too much happened. Mostly nothing happens to anyone on a bomber trip. Mostly the men just sit and wait to be attacked or to be hit by flak. There is always one raid — maybe two — in a gunner's tour of operations that stands out in his mind as the roughest he ever made. For Lauro's crew it was that January haul to Bremen.

They got into the target and bombed, all right. On the way out the trouble began when Murray Schrier began having trouble getting a breath. Murray was the ball turret man and after he'd told the pilot over the intercom that his oxygen mask was frozen he climbed up out of the ball turret and started for the radio room before he fainted.

The right waist gunner, Bill Heathman, grabbed Schrier and dragged him into the radio room. There was only one outlet for the oxygen masks to be plugged into in the radio room, and the radio operator, Nelson King, cut his own oxygen off and plugged Schrier's extension line in there. The waist gunner and the radio operator started to work on Schrier, trying to bring him around.

King fumbled through his heavy gloves with the hose attachment and finally started to hook the mask to the ball turret gunner's face. The oxygen mask hooks onto two small fittings on the gunner's helmet in the old-type oxygen system that crews first used and it was an old-type mask they were trying to fit to Schrier's face. King pulled off three layers of gloves he had on, exposing his hands to the fifty-below-zero temperature in the radio room, in order to tie the mask to the unconscious ball turret gunner's face.

Feeling the lack of oxygen after he took his line off the main system to give it to Schrier, King plugged into one of the small emergency oxygen bottles. As he finished the job of tying the mask to his ball turret gunner's helmet King toppled over on top of Schrier. The bottle he had plugged into was frozen and he had been getting no oxygen.

Heathman, the third man, was almost exhausted himself by that time. The other waist gunner, Gerald Will, left his gun and came into the radio room to help after calling Lauro on the intercom to tell the pilot that they were having trouble there. Will hooked his oxygen tube into the walk-around bottle he had beside him and walked forward.

With the green oxygen bottle under his arm Will got as far as the ball turret just outside the radio room before he realized that, like King's bottle, his outlet valve was frozen stiff. He turned and started back for his waist position where he could plug back into the main line which was still flowing all right, but he never made it. Halfway back to the waist window he collapsed on the floor of the bomber. Three men were lying unconscious and without oxygen.

Heathman, the only one still conscious, called forward over the interphone for help. Walt Green and Emanuel Greasamar, the bombardier and copilot, took walk-around bottles from the nose compartment and started back to the radio compartment.

"With six men tied up in the radio room our luck changed," Francis Lauro, the pilot, said. "It got worse. Our number two engine started acting up and then several F-W 190s showed up on the fringe of the formation.

"The bombardier called up to me and suggested that we go down a few thousand feet where it was warmer and where the boys would be able to get a little oxygen, but he hadn't seen the fighters. They would have piled into us if we'd left the formation for a minute and there was an undercast with probably several squadrons of German fighters under it just waiting for some sucker to drop below it. All I could do was hold the ship in formation and sweat it out.

"The Jerry fighters made a pass at us and

it was nice timing if they'd only known it. In the nose the navigator, Emery Horvath, did a good job with the nose guns, while Dewey Thompson up in the top turret sprayed them from there."

In the radio compartment the copilot and the bombardier had revived Will and Schrier with the emergency oxygen bottles they had brought back. King, the second to go out, was in the worst condition and he came around more slowly than the others. When Schrier saw King's hands, which were left bare when King took his gloves off to fix Schrier's mask, he opened his flying jacket and put King's hands under his armpits. Finally the others fixed King's mask and he started to revive. He had been out a long while though and he came back fighting. The men in the radio room had to call for more help when King, a big, strong Nebraska farmer, started lashing out with his hands and feet. Heathman and Greasamar alone couldn't hold King down as he thrashed around the radio room.

The top turret gunner, Dewey Thompson, answered the final SOS from the radio room. He hurried back through the bomb bay and helped hold the struggling King.

When Thompson opened the door to the radio room he saw King thrashing around, lashing out with his fists. When his great swollen white hands struck the floor of the ship or the sharp edge of some piece of radio equipment bits of frozen flesh would chip off like shavings gouged out of a hunk of ice. The battered hands didn't bleed. They were frozen through.

It was too late for them to think of gloves. No gloves would have fit those hands, swollen to more than twice their normal size. Finally King settled down, regaining full consciousness, and Green sat on the floor next to him and again put the horribly battered and frozen hands inside his bombardier's warm jacket.

King's hands didn't start to bleed until the Fort was within sight of England. Down below five thousand feet the blood started moving through his chilled veins and out into the frozen hands.

"I didn't see King's hands until we got down on the ground," Lauro said. "Frostbite was no word for what had happened to his hands. One of the flight surgeons looked at them and I looked at the doc and what he was thinking wasn't pretty. King had saved Schrier's life with those hands."

And that is about where the story of one crew's memory of their roughest trip ends. Bill Heathman, Nelson King, Murray

Air Gunner, *the first Rooney-Hutton collaboration*

Schrier and the rest will yell again when they crack their shins and stub their toes, and they'll complain the next time there is no hot water or heat in the room at home. But that day they were greater men.

Forrest Vosler, too, was great one day.

Forrest was the radio operator–gunner on a Fortress called *Jersey Bounce Junior.* He was twenty-two years old.

It was a long daylight haul into Germany when the Air Force was beginning to step up its pounding of the Nazis' aircraft production plants. *Jersey Bounce* was plugging along in formation when a double burst of flak smashed two engines and sent the Fort reeling from formation. It leveled off, but the Luftwaffe fighters had seen it and closed in for the inevitable kill. Somehow the gunners beat them off. Tracer poured from the waists and tail, the nose guns yammered steadily and from both turrets came an almost drumfire pounding. The radio gun was firing, too.

Finally, a 20-millimeter shell crippled the tail gun. From the radio hatch, a covering fire swept back past the fin and rudder and at length the fighters went away.

When the fighters had gone, the crew began to check up on each other. You all right? Roger. Waist? Roger. Radio? RADIO? Vosler, are you . . . One of you guys go up there from the waist and see if Vosler's all right.

Vosler wasn't all right. The first attack, the one that had knocked out the tail guns, had left him with half a dozen 20-millimeter splinters in his legs and thighs. The tail guns had gone out and he'd fired his gun despite the pain, and the fighters had pressed in once more. A 20-millimeter shell had burst next to the radio hatch and jagged hunks of steel ripped into his head and face. Where his eyes should be there was a great gash of red and dead white bits of flesh. The gunners tried to patch Vosler up, but they couldn't give him morphine because a man with a head wound suffers from morphine and may die. They were still trying to fix his wounds when the intercom clicked:

"Pilot to crew. Gas getting low. We'll have to get rid of everything we can."

They threw out everything within reach, but the gas was running out and so was time. So Vosler sat down to his radio. He couldn't see it, but he knew where everything should be. His cold fingers told him what the others could see with their eyes — the radio had been smashed by cannon fire. Vosler was the kind of kid who a few minutes before had fought on with his single gun even after the cannon shell had hit him. Working now by touch alone, hearing the steady, even drip of blood that soaked through the bandages and fell on the folding counter of his radio desk, he fixed an emergency set. He switched on the power and told one of the others where to set the dials so they would be on the emergency channel.

The noise of the key as it called for help was louder than the drip of the blood on his extended arm.

When he had sent out an SOS, telling base they probably would have to crash land in the sea, he fainted. The others revived him, and he called base again. He fainted again. They revived him.

The gas was lower now in the tanks. Still too much weight. The crew searched the ship for more spare weight. They had cleaned her out before. In the radio room, unable to see, still feeling his radio and keeping base advised of what was happening, Vosler made a decision. He asked the other gunners to fix his 'chute and throw him out. That would be 175 pounds less. That might make the gas reach. He was pretty badly off, anyway. Would they? Please.

They said no.

The little lights on the instrument panel had been on a long time. No gas, they winked. No gas, no gas, no gas. *Jersey Bounce Junior* settled to the Channel, mushed toward the wave tops as the last of the engine's power died away. They hit. The dinghies went out the hatches. Someone hoisted Vosler. Take care of Vosler, you guys. Right, got him. Take care. Take care.

Out on the wing of the sinking plane, the tail gunner, who had been wounded, started to slip down into the sea. Vosler was nearest. He couldn't see, but he could hear the kid call for help, and finally his groping hand found the wounded man and held him for a long time until the rescue launch arrived and took them back to being warm and dry.

The doctors think that Forrest Vosler may be able to see enough but of one eye, the right eye, to distinguish the Congressional Medal of Honor they've recommended should be his for the day's work in *Jersey Bounce.*

The gunners don't like to think about what goes on in Dick Blackburn's mind sometimes when he thinks about the targets that filled his ring sights the day of the Regensburg haul. Probably everything was all right. Probably . . .

It was on August 17, 1943, and the sun was hot and a big blob of flame up there with the formations of Fortresses heading for Regensburg and then on to Africa. In the tail of one B-17 was Staff Sergeant Richard A. Blackburn, from Port Republic, Virginia.

There were fighters that day, more fighters than anyone in the Eighth Air Force ever had seen at one time. There were all kinds of fighters, though for the most part they weren't the cream of the Luftwaffe, by any means. They were fighters from the inner ring of defenses, second-line fighters and third-line fighters. Somewhere along the route, as the Forts droned deeper and deeper into the Reich, the district luftfuehrer must have got worried. He must have figured this was an all-out affair. So he called out everything that could fly. There were Junkers 87 Stukas up there, and big four-engined Focke-Wulf 200s and half a dozen kinds of medium bombers.

It was rough, because there were such a lot of them, and it was a long way through the lanes of fighters, but the Fortress gunners were having a field day. And Dick Blackburn was having his share of the fun. For a solid hour and a half Dick tracked German fighters with his guns, opened up with short bursts as they came in, shot at single-engined jobs and two-engined Ju 88s and four-engined bombers pressed into emergency service. He sat there and shot at them and the squint in his eyes grew tighter and tighter because always there was that bright sun to stare up into and worry if it held more fighters.

Blackburn's Fort got to Africa finally, and the crew had a hell of a time bartering with the Arabs, whom they learned to call "Ayrabs," and getting their tired plane ready for the trip back. But Dick Blackburn didn't have much of a time. He didn't say much, just spent most of the days they were there stretched out on his back in the shade of the B-17's wing, closing his eyes against even the reflection of the hot African sun.

When the ship took off for England, Blackburn was back in his tail position same as ever, but still not saying much. He didn't have much work to do on the way to the target, an easy one, Bordeaux, and there wasn't any enemy plane in the sky for hours.

Finally Blackburn saw what he thought was a German fighter bearing in on them. He started to press his microphone switch and then he wasn't sure. It looked like one.

"Tail gunner to ball turret. Tail gunner to ball turret. Is that a Ju 88 coming in at five o'clock?"

"Are you kidding, Blackburn?"

"No. Is it? Is it?"

"Blackburn, that's another Fortress just a little out of formation."

When they were over the English Channel, and the danger was gone, Blackburn went up to the radio room. He picked up a package of K rations and the other gunners, who had come to the radio room too, saw him squinting at the large lettering on the package.

"Funny," Blackburn began slowly, "but I can't tell whether that's breakfast . . . dinner . . . supper . . . or —

"For Christ's sake! My eyes!"

When they got back to base, the other gunners led Blackburn to the flight surgeon, who peered into the angry red eyeballs that had searched for German fighters in the August 17 sun and sent Blackburn to bed. For a good many days the gunner couldn't even see the food they had to spoon into his mouth. After a while, though, the doctors looked at his eyes and said that if he was careful his eyes would be pretty good again, someday. He was through firing and sighting, though. They said that the long hours of staring up into the flaming sky, searching for German planes, had injured the delicate tissues of his eyeballs, had injured the nerves. They said it had begun to happen while he was still peering and firing that day on the way to Africa. They said it had been a wonder he could see anything at all that day.

Blackburn agreed with them. It had been hell, staring up into the sky, trying to catch those single-engined fighters, and the twin-engined ones, and the four-engined ones. The Germans had used an awful lot of four-engined planes that day, an awful lot. . . .

It's on those rainy nights, when conversation in the hut dies away and a gunner flops onto his sack, too weary to talk, too weary to write letters, and sinks into a sort of mental void, that the inevitable quality of his job comes home to him. It comes in phrases that roll on and on through his brain, and his face will be without expression as it happens to him, except maybe the lines at the corners of his eyes will begin to form and the hard part of the corners of his mouth will draw down a little tighter.

The gunners in a Liberator hut talked for a long time about Dick Castillo, and they waited a long time for word to come back through the International Red Cross. This man and that man in Castillo's crew was reported a prisoner. This man and that man . . .

Dick, who came from Springfield, Ohio, and was a staff sergeant, was tail gunner in the Liberator *Rugged Buggy*. The other crews saw what happened to him, and told about it.

Rugged Buggy was on her way in to a German target in the summer of 1943, before the Libs went down to Africa for the Ploesti oilfields mission, when flak smashed the number three engine. German fighters saw the feathered prop and came in, as they always do, firing as the Lib slipped from formation. Other crews could see *Rugged Buggy* almost heave herself up as the pilot tried to nurse her back to the shelter of the other planes' guns, but little by little *Rugged Buggy* dropped away.

Two of the attacking pack of twenty Focke-Wulfs went down as the crippled plane's guns poured out thousands of rounds, but the other Nazis pressed the attack. Cannon fire silenced the Lib's waist guns, and great rents and wounds began to show in her wings and tail and fuselage. *Rugged Buggy*'s defensive fire slowed. Finally, only Dick Castillo's tail guns were firing, traversing back and forth, framing one attacker just long enough to beat him off, then swinging to another quarter. The tail guns seemed almost to be shooting around corners, to be firing everywhere at once. Over their radio, the leader of the German fighter element ordered his pilots to spread out and smash this *verdammte* Yankee gunner.

That was the beginning of the end. While one trio of fighters attacked from dead astern, engaging Castillo's fire, the others cut in from the sides. Maybe they planned it the way it happened, maybe they didn't, but other crews in the formation of B-24s up above saw enemy fire crisscross just forward of Castillo's tail position, saw the fabric tear loose in great sheets, saw the bare skeleton of *Rugged Buggy*'s vertebrae exposed.

The Lib slipped off on one wing, and still Dick Castillo was firing. Two enemy aircraft definitely were destroyed by the hosepipe of death that splurted from *Rugged Buggy*'s tail guns.

Another burst of cannon shells ripped into the fuselage of the B-24 as that second F-W went down, and the other crews, from their places higher in the sky, saw *Rugged Buggy*'s entire tail section, in which Dick Castillo still fought, break slowly away from the rest of the plane, pause a moment to tear loose the last shreds of well-molded aluminum bracing, and then flutter off by itself, twisting over and over as the forward part of the ship plummeted straight to earth.

Black dots and then white parachutes appeared in the wake of the falling forward section of the plane. From the slowly twisting tail section, where Dick Castillo fought, there came nothing except, just as it dropped into the undercast and was lost to the others' view, one last spurt of whitish tracer fire that arced up into the sky, and then there was no more.

It was always that last burst of fire that streaked across the minds of the Liberator gunners in their huts those dull evenings.

Every now and then word came from the Red Cross that another of the *Rugged Buggy* crew had turned up as a prisoner of war in Germany. The gunners kept waiting for word from Dick Castillo.

Combat is hard to catch in words. You say, maybe, twenty-millimeter shells smashed the turret, ripped through the fuselage. But no phrase will tell the empty five seconds in the guts of every man aboard as they waited and even felt to know whether that had been THE attack. Or you say, Fire began to glow within the engine nacelle and eat slowly back into the wing, and no words you own can measure the limitless courage it takes for men in that plane to watch flame consume the very thing that bears them aloft, yet struggle not just to live but to strike back.

You write down what they did and tell how things were. But that isn't all of combat. Combat is shells and fire and no oxygen, and it is also, maybe mostly, what happens in an airman's guts and his mind. The split-second things you can tell. They happen and are dealt with by reflex, and there is no element of mind in them. But sometimes, after the split-second things have happened, there follow long minutes and hours that airmen call the time "the men get separated from the boys." Those are the minutes and hours of eternity in which fires smother under extinguisher foam or roar on to explode fuel tanks and bombs, in which shattered tail surfaces stick by shreds to get you home or flutter off and start the crazy, spinning plunge to earth. Such times are of the mind and the viscera, and speak an infinite horror; you can tell little of them.

■ ■ ■ ■

PART II
MR. ROONEY GOES
TO WORK

■ ■ ■ ■

After the Second World War, Andy Rooney returned to Albany, New York, to embark on a freelance writing career. In 1949, after finishing *Conquerors' Peace,* a book on postwar Europe, Rooney joined CBS to write for the radio and TV personality Arthur Godfrey on his shows *Arthur Godfrey's Talent Scouts* and *Arthur Godfrey Time.* In 1956 he left Arthur Godfrey, and by 1959, he had started to write for *The Garry Moore Show* — a popular CBS

Early days in the CBS television studios

comedy program. In 1962 Rooney began collaborating with CBS newsman Harry Reasoner to write and produce a series of popular hour-long specials narrated by Reasoner on everything from bridges and chairs to women and the English language. By the 1970s Rooney was writing and producing a series of trenchant prime-time *60 Minutes* segments on war, New York City, Washington, dining, and working in America. In his signature forthright style, Rooney reported the pieces from the ground up, crisscrossing America to take its collective pulse, all the while opining,

conjecturing, cracking wry jokes, and sharing his refreshingly honest wisdom.

CHAIRS

There is so much that is unpleasant and dull about living that we ought to take every opportunity presented to us to enjoy the enjoyable things of life. None of us can afford to become immune to the sensation of small pleasures or uninterested in small interests. A chair, for instance, can be a small and constant joy, and taking pleasure from one a sensation available to almost all of us all the time.

It is relatively easy to say who invented the light bulb but impossible to say who built the first chair. They took one out of King Tut's tomb when they opened it in 1922 and King Tut died fourteen hundred years before Christ was born and that certainly wasn't the first chair, either. So they've been around a long time. If there was a first man, he probably sat in the first chair.

Chairs have always been something more

than a place for us to bend in the middle and put our posteriors on other legs in order to take the weight off our own. They have been a symbol of power and authority, probably because before the sixteenth century only the very rich *owned* real chairs. The others sat on the floor at their feet in most countries.

A throne is the ultimate place to sit down and there are still something like twenty-five countries in the world that have thrones, and leaders who actually sit on them.

The Peacock Throne of Persia is one of the most elaborate, but I don't know what happened to that. It belonged to the King of Persia, but Persia is called Iran now and, of course, they don't have a king. The leaders they have now usually sit on the floor. I suppose this is their way of reacting against the idiocy of a throne but I hope they haven't discarded theirs. It was crusted with rubies and diamonds and was supposed to be worth $100 million twenty years ago. In today's market I should think it would bring $500 million, although I don't know who it would bring it from.

I've seen pictures of it but, personally, I wouldn't give them $50 million for it, and if the average American housewife got hold of it, she'd probably put a slipcover over it.

I didn't mean to get off on thrones but some kings and queens have more than one. Queen Elizabeth has one in every Commonwealth country, presumably in the event she wants to sit down if she visits one of them. She has five in London alone and several more at palaces around England. I'd hate to have to reglue a throne.

If the United States had a king, I suppose there'd be a throne in the White House. Too bad there isn't, in a way. It could be more of a tourist attraction than the Washington Monument.

Theoretically the royal chair is never sat in by anyone but a nation's ruler, but it's hard to believe that a few of the cleaning ladies and some of the kids around the castle don't test it out once in a while. I can imagine the guards in a state prison fooling around in the electric chair, too. "Hey, Joe. Look at me. Throw the switch!"

The closest thing we ever had to a throne was that big rocking chair John Kennedy intimidated people with. A visiting dignitary could be disarmed by its folksy charm and overwhelmed by its size and mobility.

There's nothing else like chairs that we have in such great numbers. We know how many cars there are in this country and how many television sets, but we don't have the vaguest idea how many chairs there are. I'll bet if everyone sat down in one, there'd still be fifty empty chairs left over for each one of us.

Over the past fifty years the most-used piece of furniture in the house has been the kitchen chair. Like anything that gains wide acceptance, it turns out to be useful for a lot of things it wasn't built to do. The kitchen chair is for sitting on, for throwing clothes over, for hanging jackets on, for putting a foot on when you're lacing a shoe and as an all-purpose stepladder for changing light bulbs or for getting down infrequently used dishes from high and remote parts of kitchen cabinets. It has usually been painted many times, hurriedly.

If the kitchen chair isn't the most sat on, the one the American working man comes home to every evening must be. (The American working woman doesn't have a chair of her own.) It's the one in which he slumps for endless hours watching football games on television. It's the one in which he is portrayed in cartoons about himself and it's usually the most comfortable chair in the house. It's a chair you sit in, not on.

It isn't so much that the American male takes this throne as his prerogative. It's that women don't usually like a chair that mushy.

It's a comfortable chair, though, and for all its gross, overfed appearance, I'm not knocking it. It serves as a bed when it's too early to go to bed. It's a place where you can take a nap before turning in for a night's sleep.

In big cities you see a lot of overstuffed chairs being thrown away outside apartment houses. I always think of the old Eskimo women they put out on an ice floe to die.

The kitchen chair and the overstuffed living-room chair are the *most* sat on, and there are always a few chairs in every home that no one ever sits on. Everyone in the household understands about it. There are no rules. It is just not a chair you sit on. It may be in the hall by the front door, used mostly for piling books on after school. Or it may be silk brocade with a gold fringe, in the back bedroom. It may be antique and uncomfortable or imperfectly glued together and therefore too fragile for the wear-and-tear that goes with being sat on regularly.

Sometimes there is no reason that anyone can give why a chair isn't sat on. It's like the suit or dress in the closet that is perfectly good but never worn. The unsat-upon chair in a home really isn't much good for anything except handing down from one generation to the next.

In hotels they often put two chairs not to be sat in on either side of the mirror across from the elevator on every floor.

There aren't as many dining-room chairs as there used to be because there aren't as many dining rooms. Now people eat in the kitchen or they have picnics in front of the television set in the living room. It's too bad, because there's something civilized and charming about having a special place for eating. It's a disappearing luxury, though. These days everything in a house has to be multi-purpose, folding, retractable or convertible.

Dining-room chairs on thick rugs were always a problem. They made it difficult or impossible for a polite man to slide a chair under a woman. As soon as any of her weight fell on the chair, the legs sank into the pile and stopped sliding. If she was still eight inches from where she wanted to be, she had to put her hands under the seat and hump it toward the table while the man made some futile gestures toward helping from behind her. It took a lot of the grace out of the gesture.

The other trouble with a good set of dining-room chairs was that at Christmas or any other special occasion when you wanted them most, there weren't enough of them. This meant bringing a chair or two in from the kitchen or the living room and ruining the effect of a matched set.

If dining-room chairs are the most gracious, folding chairs are the least. I suppose someone will collect those basic folding, wood chairs they kept in church basements and sell them as antiques someday soon, but they're ugly and uncomfortable. Maybe they were designed to keep people awake at town meetings.

The Morris chair was invented by an English poet named William Morris. He's better known for his chair than his poetry. A man takes immortality from anywhere he can get it, but it seems a sad fate for a poet to be remembered for a chair. I make furniture myself and I hate to think of any table I've made outlasting my writing, but I suppose it could happen.

Very few chairs survive the age in which they were designed. The Windsor chair is one of a handful of classics that have. The Hitchcock is another. If the time comes when we want to place a time capsule to show people on another planet in another eon what we sat on, we should put a Windsor chair in to represent us. You have to choose something better than average as typical.

The rocking chair probably comes closer than any other article of furniture to delineating past generations from present ones. People sat in them and contemplated their lives and the lives of people they could see passing by from where they sat. People don't contemplate each other much from chairs anymore. When anyone passes by now, he's in a car going too fast for anyone to identify him. No one is sitting on the front porch watching from a rocker anyway.

Rockers were good furniture. They were comfortable and gave the user an air of ease and contentment. They give the person sitting in one the impression he's getting somewhere without adding any of the headaches that come with progress.

From time to time furniture makers say there's a revived interest in rocking chairs, but I doubt this. For one thing, the front porch has probably been closed in to make the living room bigger and anyway people don't want anything as mobile or folksy as a rocker in a living room filled with electronic gear.

Comfort in a chair is often in direct ratio to the relationship between the height of the feet and the height of the head. People are always trying to get their feet up. Very likely there is an instinct for self-preservation here because the closer anyone's feet are to being on a level with the head, the less work the heart has to do to get the blood pumped around.

During the years between World War I and World War II, everyone's dream of a vacation was a boat trip somewhere on the *Mauretania,* the *Leviathan* or one of the *Queens* to Europe. In their dreams, the man and the woman were stretched out in the bright sunshine on deck chairs in mid-Atlantic. Not many people go by boat anywhere anymore, though, and the deck or steamer chairs were redesigned and moved to the backyard. The wood in those deck chairs has been replaced by tubular aluminum and the canvas by plastic straps. They wouldn't have lasted five minutes on the deck of the *Mauretania* in a stiff breeze.

At some time in the last hundred years, we reached the point where more people were working sitting down than on their feet. This could be a milestone unturned by social historians. We have more and more white-collar people and executives sitting in chairs telling people what to do and fewer and fewer people on their feet actually doing anything.

The sitting executives found that they weren't satisfied not moving at all, so they invented a chair for executives that swivels, rolls forward, backward or sideways and tilts back when the executive, who used to have his feet on the ground, wants to lean back and put them on his mahogany desk.

In many offices the chairs provided for men and for women are symbols that irritate progressive women. The chairs often represent clear distinctions in the relative power of the sexes there. The executive male has his bottom on a cushion, his elbows on armrests. At the desk outside his office, the secretary, invariably a woman, sits erect in a typing chair about as comfortable as an English saddle.

It's a strange thing and probably says a lot about our rush through life that the word "modern" has an old-fashioned connotation to it when you're talking about design. I think of Art Deco as modern. It must be because what we call "modern" is just a brand-new design about to become obsolete. Someone is always coming up with what is known as a modern chair. It looks old and silly in a few years but is still referred to as modern.

There are modern chairs that have not become obsolete because they're so good. Some of them are forty years old but they're still called modern. Charles Eames designed that plastic bucket seat on tubular legs that will not go out of style. Mies van der Rohe designed the Barcelona chair that you have in the outer lobby of your office if you're a rich company. That's going to last like the Windsor and the Boston rockers because it's comfortable and simply attractive.

Considering how much time we spend sitting, it's strange our chairs don't fit us better. No size 6 woman would think of wearing a size 14 dress but a size 48 man who weighs 250 pounds is expected to sit in the same size chair a 98-pound woman sits in. To some extent a chair in a room is considered community property, but in most homes a family arranges itself in the same way day after day when it settles down, and more attention ought to be given chair sizes.

Certain purposeful chairs have been well done but with no regard to the size or shape of the occupant. The electric chair, the dentist's chair, the theater seat or the airplane seat are mostly well designed, but again every chair is the same size. We're not. I suppose it would be difficult to sell theater tickets by seat size or for a dentist to have more than one chair depending on whose tooth ached. But the fact remains: people don't take the same size chair any more than they take the same size shoe.

Even though most public seating furniture must have seemed comfortable to the people who designed it, it seems to have been designed and sat on for the test under laboratory conditions. These conditions don't exist in a movie theater or on a crowded airplane.

In the theater chair, the shared armrest has always been a problem. The dominant personality usually ends up using the one on both sides of the seat in which he or she is sitting and the occupants of the adjacent seats get either none or one, depending on who flanks them on the *other* side. The shared armrest may be part of what's known as the magic of the theater, but it's a constant source of irritation to anyone watching a bad movie.

The average airplane chair is a marvel of comfort and we could all do worse than to have several installed in our own homes. The problem on board, of course, is the person in the seat next to you. The seats are usually lined up three across, and if the plane is full the middle seat can make a trip to Europe a nightmare. It is no longer a comfortable place of repose; it's a trap and you're in it.

At a time when all of us are looking for clues to our character, it's unusual that no one has started analyzing us from the way we sit in chairs. It must be at least as revealing of character as a person's handwriting and an even more reliable indicator of both personality and attitude than, say, palmreading.

The first few minutes after you sit down are satisfying ones, but no matter how good it feels to get off your feet, you can't stay in one position very long. Sooner or later that wonderful feeling you got when you first took the weight off your feet goes away. You begin to twitch. You are somehow dissatisfied with the way your body is arranged in the chair but uncertain as to what to do about it.

Everyone finds his own solution for what to do with feet. No two people do exactly the same thing. The first major alteration in the sitting position usually comes when the legs are crossed. The crossing of legs seems to satisfy some inner discontent, the scratching of a psychosomatic itch deep inside.

It's amusing to see how often we use a chair designed to be used one way in a manner so totally different that even the originator could not have imagined it. We straddle a chair, sitting on it backwards with our arms where our backs are supposed to be and our chin on our arms; we sit sideways in a lounge chair with our legs draped over one arm and our backs leaning against the other arm. We rock back in chairs that are not rockers, ungluing their joints. We do things to chairs we wouldn't do to our worst enemy, and chairs are among our best friends.

You'd have to say that of all the things we have built for ourselves to make life on earth more tolerable, the chair has been one of the most successful.

MR. ROONEY GOES TO DINNER

You see so many things that all of us have done badly that life can be depressing unless you look for some of the things we've done well. And there are some.

Take something as basic as eating, for example.

It's absolutely necessary that we eat to survive, but we could do that by stuffing food in our mouths with our hands, so we can congratulate ourselves for having turned eating into a civilized and often very pleasant little ceremony called either breakfast, lunch or dinner.

All of us enjoy the ceremony and one of the special treats we give ourselves once in a while is eating out in a restaurant.

There are 400,000 restaurants in the United States and if you ate three meals a day in restaurants for seventy years, you could only eat in 76,000 of them.

Obviously I haven't gone to all 400,000 restaurants in the United States to make this report. Chances are I didn't go to the one you like best or least. I didn't even go to the one *I* like best.

My job may seem good to some of you . . . but I've got a tough boss. Several months ago he gave me an order. "Travel anywhere you want in the United States," he told me. "Eat in a lot of good restaurants on the company . . . and report back to me."

I took money, credit cards and a lot of bad advice from friends and set out across the country.

People argue about where the best restaurants are in the United States.

Boston, San Francisco and New Orleans have always had good places. Florida has had some for a long time. New York has a hundred that would be the best in town anywhere else. But there have been some changes for the better in places that didn't used to have *any* good restaurants.

The South is getting over Southern cooking, for instance. Places like Cincinnati,

135

Mr. Rooney goes to dinner

Kansas City, Pittsburgh, even South Bend, Indiana, have excellent restaurants. You can get a gourmet meal in Houston, Texas, or Phoenix, Arizona.

There are a few places that puzzle me, though. For instance, I don't suppose there's a place in the whole world that grows as much good food as Iowa does. They brag about it. And yet a gourmet tour of Iowa would be a nonstop trip.

The biggest trend is a leveling out that has taken place. It's harder to find that great little undiscovered place in a small town, but more often than before you can find a restaurant that serves at least acceptable food. The Rotary Club usually meets there.

There's more dependable mediocrity than there used to be. It isn't going to be very good, but it isn't going to be very bad either. And because most of it's frozen, it's going to be the same in Maine as it is in Oklahoma.

What's happened to all the good and bad little independent restaurants, of course, is all the big chains and the fast-food places. Many independents have been driven out of business.

There are the big steak chains, for instance. They often serve beef treated with tenderizer and are called something like the Beef and Bourbon or the Steak and Stein. They and the fast-food places bring in billions of dollars a year. Most are owned by big corporations with other interests: Pillsbury owns Burger King, for example.

Hamburgers are the big seller, a lot more American than Mom's apple pie now because Mom isn't baking pies much these days. The chicken places have come up fast in the last ten years and there are pizza parlors everywhere. You don't have to go to Mexico to get a taco.

The biggest and most successful fast-food operation is, obviously, McDonald's. There are 3,232 of them — and counting. They've driven thousands of individually owned diners and cafés out of business. The drive-ins have been victims in a lot of areas.

A typical meal in McDonald's costs about $1.75. The hamburger is good ground meat, the French fries are excellent and the shake is an imitation milkshake made with thickeners to give the impression it's made with ice cream — which it isn't.

McDonald's restaurants are probably a reflection of our national character. They're fast . . . they're efficient . . . they make money and they're clean. If they're loud and crowded and if the food is wastefully wrapped, packaged, boxed and bagged . . . let's face it, Americans, that's us.

There's nothing really distinctive about American cooking. "American cooking" isn't even a phrase like "French cooking." That accounts for why our best restaurants serve someone else's native dishes.

Italian restaurants are most popular. Thirty-six percent of all Americans who eat out eat in Italian restaurants at one time or another. Thirty-five percent, according to the National Restaurant Association, eat in Chinese restaurants. French restaurants are most popular with people who make more than $25,000 a year.

But we have everything. In the last ten years there's been a population explosion of Japanese restaurants. They serve steak, shrimp or chicken along with bean sprouts and onions — and it's all cooked right there in front of you. The man doing the cooking is part chef . . . part show biz . . . and part Kamikaze pilot.

One of the good things about these places is they never serve you a piece of anything you can't eat . . . no bones, no fat. I've never been to Japan. For all I know, they don't eat like this over there. Someone told me there's a Benihana of New York in Tokyo.

Part of the fun of eating out is doing something different. Japanese is different. How many times in the last few weeks have you come home from work to find your husband fixing sukiyaki for you?

The other kind of Japanese restaurant is the sushi bar. Five years ago you couldn't have told me I'd ever eat a piece of raw fish. Now I'm addicted to sushi. Sushi is carefully boned and carefully sliced raw fish . . . tuna . . . squid . . . mackerel . . . eel . . . octopus . . . served with cold rice wrapped in seaweed. Sounds good, doesn't it? It's always attractively served on a board. It looks like a Japanese painting.

Scandinavian smorgasbord places are

popular, too: Americans like the idea of helping themselves to all they want. It's as if they were getting something free.

I ate in one called the Copenhagen one day — with a friend. He's a smorgasbord expert.

WALTER CRONKITE: This is a Danish something.

ROONEY: Lingonberries.

CRONKITE: That's right. That's what it is. That's the word I was groping . . .

ROONEY: You were grasping for.

CRONKITE: And they're marvelous.

ROONEY: What is this pink stuff?

CRONKITE: That pink stuff is some very interesting . . . pink stuff there. I think it's beets. I believe. I don't know. I'm not sure what that is. I've never taken it. It looks repulsive, to tell you the truth. How about shrimp? Beautiful shrimp?

ROONEY: Yeah, I'll have a shrimp. I notice they leave the shells on them, though. I figure that's to make it hard so you don't take too many.

CRONKITE: Any restaurant you go to where the dessert tray is brought in like this, every table the reaction is the same. People recoil. They're obviously making the statement to their friends. "I . . . I

140

shouldn't. Oh, no, I shouldn't. Take that away. I don't want to even look at that."

ROONEY: "But maybe I'll just have a little bit."

CRONKITE: But then they come back.

WAITRESS: And these are special ones over here. They're made of almond paste.

ROONEY: I really shouldn't.

CRONKITE: No, I shouldn't either . . . so have one.

ROONEY: Oh, thank you.

Like everything else, there are trends in the restaurant business — fashions in what a restaurant looks like. Years ago, many good restaurants had those white tile floors with lots of mirrors around and waiters who worked there for a hundred years wearing white aprons that came to their ankles.

In the past twenty years restaurants have gotten very conscious. Too conscious, probably. In the sixties, most new restaurants with any pretensions at all looked like this. As you came in, there was usually a coat of arms in the lobby. The dominant color was red, the lights were low and there was often a candle on the table held in one of those small bowls covered with white netting.

The menu was predictable . . . steak, shrimp, chicken, filet of sole and South

African lobster tail . . . meaning they didn't really have a chef.

They were pleasant enough and there are still a lot of them around — but there's a new trend. In the trade it's called "the theme restaurant." Eating in one, according to the ads, is an adventure.

If you want to start a theme restaurant, you can go to J.B.I. Industries in Compton, California. They can make the inside of your place look like anything from a submarine to a men's locker room.

Carolyn Steinbach is production manager.

ROONEY: How many of these do you do a year? How many restaurants do you design, roughly? Would you guess?

STEINBACH: Well, we did something like three hundred and fifty last year.

ROONEY: Could you show some of them to us?

STEINBACH: Certainly.

ROONEY: A pirate ship.

STEINBACH: A pirate ship.

ROONEY: Hey, what would it cost somebody to come up with a pirate ship in a restaurant like that?

STEINBACH: Our pirate ship runs somewhere around six thousand dollars.

ROONEY: Gosh, I'll be darned.

STEINBACH: This is our tin goose . . . seating on both wings, seating behind the engine and then down the center of the —
ROONEY: The kids get a kick out of this?
STEINBACH: Right. They really relate well to something like this.

Out back, it looked like Santa Claus's workshop. We talked to president Jay Buchbinder.

ROONEY: Well, now, wouldn't something like that make kids stay longer in a restaurant so the restaurant would have a smaller turnover? I mean, is that a factor?
BUCHBINDER: Well, it might even speed up the process of eating, because if you go in with little children, the children will want to play on the trains, so they might eat faster and then the parents will want to leave more quickly. We've even tried to get design involved in the restroom areas where people might say, "Well, gee, they have nice clean restrooms. We'll stop there because the restrooms are nice and we'll also buy our food." So everything goes as a total package situation.
ROONEY: You don't make any little engines for the restrooms or anything?
BUCHBINDER: There can be little decors in

the restroom areas, little train plaques or little car plaques. So when you go into a fast-food operation, it's like going into a finer restaurant now. They're giving you every courtesy that you might have in a better restaurant.

Workmen were finishing a new plastic replica of an old airplane to ship to a McDonald's opening in Glen Ellyn, Illinois. We were curious about how a hamburger would taste eaten in a plastic airplane, so a few weeks later, after it had been installed, we went to Glen Ellyn.

ROONEY (to cashier): Same price whether I eat it here or in the airplane?
CASHIER: Yes.
ROONEY: I guess I'll eat it in the airplane.

It seems as though everywhere you go they're trying to take your mind off the food. It's got so it's almost as though they were embarrassed to look like a restaurant.

The most successful theme chain is Victoria Station. Just five years ago three young Cornell Hotel School graduates started buying up old boxcars for a few thousand dollars each. Now they own 250 of them and they're using them in 46 restaurants around the country. In five years, sales went from nothing to $47 million.

The difference between this and the all-American diner is that Victoria Station serves mostly roast beef and steak. And, of course, for cooking steak and roast beef you don't need a French chef; you need a smart American kid who can cook meat.

They also have a help-yourself salad bar. They've become very popular in American restaurants too. You come along and just help yourself to as much of everything as you want. I suspect that people might take a little more lettuce than they'd get if the waiter gave it to them. On the other hand, lettuce is a lot cheaper than help. And it sure saves on the help.

The food is pretty good at Victoria Station, but just as in most other gimmick restaurants, food takes second place.

As a person who likes to eat, I am just vaguely worried about the food business being taken over by entrepreneurs rather than by restaurateurs but even if it isn't the gourmet restaurants that are making the money, there are still a lot of impractical optimists who keep opening what they hope will be the perfect restaurant.

I'm seated at a table at the most expensive

restaurant in the United States, the Palace in New York City.

Two of us just dined here. You don't eat at the Palace; you dine. And I have the check . . . brought on a silver platter. For two people: dinner . . . $179.35.

A lot of expensive restaurants are sneaky with their checks but there's nothing sneaky about the Palace. They lay it right on the line. Two dinners, $100. Two cocktails at $5 each, $10. A bottle of wine, $25. That was the second cheapest bottle on the menu, by the way. Tax. That all comes to $145.80. Plus 23 percent for service. That's $33.55 for tips, for a total of $179.35.

ROONEY: I thought maybe you could tell me what it was I had if I went over the menu.

FRANK VALENZA, owner: The first appetizer you had was the salad de Palace, which is fresh lobster with truffles, walnut oil, artichoke bottoms and a vinaigrette dressing.

ROONEY: I thought it was pecan oil.

VALENZA: No.

ROONEY: Walnut oil, aha. Well, they fooled me there. And then I had — this is the gazpacho?

VALENZA: Gazpacho, very thin gazpacho,

made with fresh vegetables and a little garniture on the side.

ROONEY: Made of what?

VALENZA: Tomato, garlic, peppers, onions, all your fresh vegetables. But just the essence of the vegetables.

ROONEY: Garlic seasoned with a little tomato?

VALENZA: Yes.

ROONEY: And . . . fish.

VALENZA: You had the fresh filet of sole filled with a mousse of salmon with a crayfish sauce. And then we had a little sherbet to cleanse the palate. Then, the main course, I believe you had the . . .

ROONEY: The rack of lamb.

VALENZA: Rack of lamb that was roasted with fresh aromatic herbs and naturel au jus. And for dessert, a little chocolate truffle. It's ice cream mixed with pastry cream. It's dipped in a very rich chocolate with little nuts and then we put it in the freezer.

ROONEY: Do you get people in here ever who are surprised at the cost?

VALENZA: Once in a while. Saturday night a lady came by and asked the price and I told her and she said, "I'm coming back with a boyfriend. I'm going to get a rich boyfriend to take me in." They came down and made a reservation. They sat down. The gentleman opened the menu and there was the price and he jumped up.

He said, "Well, I just ate dinner and I thought this was just an after-theater snack." And we said, "Thank you, maybe another day." And the lady winked at me and she said, "Well, we'll try again."

ROONEY (to camera): The surprising thing about the Palace is how good it is. The food is excellent. As a matter of fact, I plan to come over here real often . . . and bring the kids.

Two of the best lunches I ever had, I ate standing up . . . and within an hour of each other. Both places serve the same thing, oysters. Felix's is on Iberville Street in New Orleans and the Acme Oyster House is right across from it.

Every restaurant has its own way of doing things and if you don't know what it is, it's easy to look dumb the first time you go in a place.

ROONEY: What is the difference between the ones that are three dollars a dozen and the ones that are two-seventy-five?

MAN (cutting oysters open): . . . table.

ROONEY: Oh, the table. If I eat them at the

table, they're more? Are some of them harder to open than others?

MAN: Some of them are hard, some of them's easy.

ROONEY: But they're alive until you open them, is that right?

MAN: Yes, sir.

ROONEY: You mean I just ate a dozen live oysters?

It's always hard to find a good place to eat when you're driving in an unfamiliar part of the country, particularly if there are three or four people in the car who don't agree where you're going to eat. You get to one place and it looks fair but you decide to pass it up. You drive ten miles and you wish you'd stopped there, usually.

The trouble with most country inns is the same thing that's wrong with so many restaurants. They're fake, an imitation of the real thing.

The food in most country inns now comes from the city . . . frozen.

Being good at picking a place to eat is a matter of experience . . . prejudice acquired over years of eating out. Deciding which restaurant *not* to go to is important. . . . There are little things you look for.

I have as many as fifty little reasons for

steering clear of certain places. Just for example:

- I am very suspicious of a restaurant that says it is Polynesian and has flaming torches outside.
- If a Chinese restaurant serves chop suey and chow mein, I assume that it isn't very good . . . or very Chinese.
- Cute names on restaurants, such as Dew Drop Inn, suggest that the owners aren't very serious about their food. Watch out for places named after a new movie.
- Places that advertise "Home Cooking" don't interest me. If I want home cooking, I'll eat at home.
- And I'm put off if there's a sign in the window saying "OPEN." Restaurants with OPEN signs usually leave them there even when they're closed.
- I'm not attracted to an establishment that puts more emphasis on liquor than on food.
- Usually I avoid a restaurant located in a shopping center.
- And if a restaurant is connected with a bowling alley, it isn't where I'm going to spend my money for food.
- I don't eat where there's music, either.

Sometimes two things that are great by themselves are ruined when mixed. Food and entertainment are best kept apart.

- It's hard enough to get waited on in a restaurant that thinks it has enough help without going to one with a sign in the window advertising for waiters.
- And when I stay in a hotel or a motel, I never eat in the restaurant attached to it unless it's snowing.

There are just as many things that attract me to a restaurant:

- I'm a sucker for a place bearing the first name of the owner. If it's called "Joe's," I go in.
- I'm attracted to a restaurant that has a menu written with chalk on a slate.
- And to me, a real sign of class is a restaurant that refuses to accept credit cards.

If you've always thought of a menu as just a list of the food a restaurant serves, you're wrong. Menus are a big business by themselves and a lot of restaurants spend a fortune making theirs look good.

We went down to a studio one day when they were filming a new cover for a Howard

Johnson menu. The food was fixed in a kitchen near the studio. They try to be honest about it . . . but nothing ever looks *smaller* in the picture on the menu. For instance, they weigh the meat all right, but then they barely cook it so it doesn't shrink.

In the course of doing this report, we've looked through and collected several hundred menus. You can tell a lot about a restaurant from a quick look at its menu . . . even from the outside of it. For instance, if there's a tassel on the menu, you can add a couple of dollars per person.

Here's the Captain's Seafood Platter. The trouble with a restaurant called the Captain's Seafood Platter in Kansas City is that all the fish comes frozen, and by the time it's cooked in hot fat, you can't tell the oysters from the French fries.

The Lion's Paw . . . "Homemade Cheesecake." You always wonder whose home they mean it was made in.

Don Neal's Mr. T-Bone. He's a musician, I guess. This is the kind of a menu that's so cute you can hardly tell what they have to eat. "Rhapsody of Beef" . . . Roast Top Sirloin. "Symphony of the Deep" . . . Baked Lake Superior Whitefish. "Taste Buds in Concert" . . . Breast of Chicken Almondine.

Here's a place called the Bali Hai, a Polynesian restaurant. The "Pu-Pu Platter," they have. "Shrimp Pago Pago." I never know about the drinks in a place like this. Here's one called "Scorpion Bowl." I hate drinking from a glass with a naked girl on it.

This is a Spanish restaurant, La Corrida. Picture of a bullfight. They've just killed the bull, I guess.

I'm not a vegetarian, but I hate being reminded of the animals I'm eating. I'll eat almost anything, too, but there are a few things I'm narrow-minded about. Rabbit I don't eat, tripe, calves' brains, snails. I know I'm wrong, but I just don't eat them.

Karson's Inn in Historic Canton. This is one of those menus that tell you more about a town than you want to know. "Welcome to Karson's Inn in Historic Canton. . . ." It goes on and tells you all about how interesting Canton is.

Here's one from Troggio's in New Castle, Pennsylvania. This one tells you about how interesting New Castle is.

This is the Lamplighter, a family restaurant. It's one of those where they tell you about the family. "For over 50 years the Ferri Family has enjoyed serving the finest food to nice people like you. . . ." They like me.

This is another one: the Presuttis'. Mama and Poppa Presutti are on the cover there. And, yep, they tell you about the Presuttis here. "In 1933, Mr. and Mrs. S. Presutti converted their home into a restaurant." It goes on. You know, fine, but what have they got to eat?

This is something called the Shalako. It's one of those menus with a lot of writing in it. I always figure if I wanted to read, I'd go to a library. It says, "The Shalako is the most important religious ceremony performed by the Zuñi Indians." And it goes on for three pages. You can imagine a waiter standing there while you read this history of the Zuñi Indians.

Here's a place called the Parlour. I wonder where this is? Oh, there is no doubt where this is: "It is dusk in St. Paul. Sunset's fading light reflects a red ribbon on the meandering Mississippi River. The skyline is silhouetted against the blue-gray haze."

A menu.

We had a not particularly reliable survey made of menus and we have the results for you. According to the count we made, the most used words on menus were these, in order of frequency:

1. "Freshly"
2. "Tender"
3. "Mouth-Watering"
4. "Succulent"
5. "On a Bed of"
6. "Tangy"
7. "Hearty"
8. "Luscious"
9. "To Your Liking"
10. "Topped with"
11. "Savory"
12. "Tempting" and "Delicious" (Tie)
13. "Surrounded by"
14. "Golden Brown"
15. "By Our Chef"
16. "Seasoned to Perfection"
17. "Choice Morsels of"
18. "Delicately" and "Thick" (Tie)
19. "Crisp"
20. "Not Responsible for Personal Property"

"Freshly" was far and away the first.

"Savory," Number 11, was interesting. Actually, on menus where the dinner was more than $7.50, it was usually spelled with a "U." S-A-V-O-U-R-Y.

"Surrounded by." "Surrounded by" and "On a Bed of" are a lot the same, but "On a Bed of" actually beat out "Surrounded by."

"Golden Brown." Almost everything is "Golden Brown." Sometimes the lettuce is golden brown.

"By Our Chef." Even places that don't have a chef say "By Our Chef."

"Seasoned to Perfection." "Choice Morsels of." "Delicately" and "Thick" were tied for 18. Number 19 was "Crisp." And Number 20 on our list of most used words was "Not Responsible for Personal Property."

Wine menus. Last year was a very good year for wine menus.

Anyone who orders wine in a restaurant always wonders how much the same bottle would cost him in a liquor store. We thought we'd find out.

ROONEY (in liquor store): What's the price of the Chauvenet Red Cap?

LIQUOR-STORE OWNER: Six-ninety-nine.

ROONEY (from menu): Chauvenet Red Cap . . . twenty dollars a bottle. This is at the restaurant called the Michaelangelo. Let's see. Liebfraumilch, Blue Nun . . . ten dollars. (To liquor-store owner) What do you get for Blue Nun?

OWNER: Three-eighty-nine.

ROONEY (from menu): Mouton Cadet

Rothschild, 1970 . . . twelve dollars. (To liquor-store owner) This Mouton Cadet. What do you get for that?

OWNER: Three-ninety-nine.

ROONEY: You don't lose any money on that, either.

OWNER: No.

ROONEY (from menu): Château Malijay . . . six-forty-five.

OWNER: That's a Côte du Rhône . . . one-ninety-nine.

ROONEY (from menu): Here's a bottle of Pouilly-Fumé de la Doucette, 1971 . . . eighteen dollars. (To store owner) What do you get for that?

OWNER: La Doucette, Pouilly-Fumé . . . We sell it for six-ninety-nine.

ROONEY (from menu): This is a restaurant in Las Vegas. Here the Lancers Rose is eleven dollars. (To store owner) Lancers Vin Rosé?

OWNER: Lancers sells for four-twenty-nine.

ROONEY: I always thought this was the kind of a wine where the bottle was worth more than the drink. I guess you wouldn't want to comment on that?

OWNER: No. I'd rather not.

Everyone complains about wine snobs. Snobs of every kind have a bad reputation

157

in America. No one understands that it's the snobs who set the standards of excellence in the world. There are art snobs, literary snobs, music snobs, and in every case it's the snobs who sneer at mediocrity. The gourmets are the food snobs. Without them we'd all be eating peanut-butter sandwiches.

Like the gourmets, wine snobs know what they're talking about. So if you're going to drink wine, get to know something about it. Be prepared to pay too much for a bottle of wine. Be your own wine snob . . . it's part of the fun.

A good rule of thumb is, if you can afford a wine, don't buy it.

I went to the National Restaurant Association Convention in Chicago and everywhere I wandered someone was pushing food or drink at me.

Everyone who sells anything to restaurants had an exhibit, so there were garbage cans . . . corn cookers . . . can openers . . . wall decorations . . . seating arrangements . . . and devices to keep bartenders from stealing.

Restaurants sell 20 percent of all the food eaten in the United States. They are first in the number of retail business places. In other words, there are more restaurants than any other kind of store. We did a lot of poking around at the convention and we got a frightening look at what some restaurants are going to be feeding us.

1ST EXHIBITOR: Well, this is a soy protein with about 60 percent protein and it goes into . . .

ROONEY: What does it do?

1ST EXHIBITOR: Well, it stretches out products like tuna salad by about 30 percent.

ROONEY: What do they use it in, in addition to tuna fish?

1ST EXHIBITOR: It goes into egg salads. It's used to extend all kinds of meats, either uncooked as meat patties or it might go into precooked entrees . . . sloppy Joes, chili con carne.

ROONEY: Is it any good?

1ST EXHIBITOR: What kind of a question is that?

ROONEY: Now, what is this here?

2ND EXHIBITOR: These are our Morning Star institutional link sausage–like flavor product.

ROONEY: Sausage . . . like?

2ND EXHIBITOR: Sausage-like flavor.

ROONEY: They're artificial sausage?

2ND EXHIBITOR: They're artificial sausage. They have no cholesterol, no animal fat.

ROONEY: What *do* they have?

2ND EXHIBITOR: Well, they're made out of various vegetable proteins . . . soy protein, wheat protein. We use egg albumen to hold it together.

ROONEY: Are you a chef?

2ND EXHIBITOR: No. I'm trained as a biochemist.

ROONEY: Now what is this machine?

3RD EXHIBITOR: This is a mechanical meat tenderizer.

ROONEY: You put the meat on there?

3RD EXHIBITOR: Put the meat on here. It'll pass through underneath the needle. The needle will come down and penetrate the meat and break down the tissue.

ROONEY: So a restaurant could buy this and really buy less expensive meat?

3RD EXHIBITOR: That's right.

ROONEY: Now, I would call that orange juice canned. Not fresh.

4TH EXHIBITOR: Fresh frozen.

ROONEY: Fresh frozen. Right.

ROONEY (looking at ingredients): Now, "standard chicken base." How, do you pronounce that ingredient?

5TH EXHIBITOR: It contains hydrolyzed vegetable protein.

ROONEY (reads ingredients): "Salt, chicken fat, monosodium glutamate, dehydrated

160

chicken, dextrose, dehydrated vegetable, spices and spice extract, bicalcium phosphate, citric acid."

5TH EXHIBITOR: Right.

ROONEY: That's chicken base?

5TH EXHIBITOR: That's right.

ROONEY: It tastes like chicken?

5TH EXHIBITOR: Exactly. Four ounces of it tastes like an extra gallon.

ROONEY: You put just four ounces of this hydro . . .

5TH EXHIBITOR: And that's the basis for . . . in other words, if you want chicken noodle, you throw noodles in.

ROONEY: How many restaurants *don't* use anything like this?

5TH EXHIBITOR: Almost 100 percent of the restaurants use it. If they don't, then you're way on the other side of the . . . You can't exist today.

ROONEY: You mean without the artificial stuff?

5TH EXHIBITOR: It's not artificial really. You've got monosodium glutamate. You've got extracts. You've got fats. The real thing mixed with the chemical. This can feed or this can substitute or feed a thousand people per chicken, where you might have to take a hundred chickens. . . .

ROONEY: The chickens must love it.

5TH EXHIBITOR: You're a nice fellow.

Restaurants are one of the few good examples left of really free enterprise in America. There isn't much government control of them and the good ones prosper. The bad ones usually, though not always, go out of business.

The best restaurants are operated by people who like food better than money. The worst ones are run by people who don't know anything about food *or* money.

So that's our report on eating out in America. The camera crew is glad it's over because they say they're tired of spending their dinner hour watching me eat.

During the time we've been working on it, many friends and others here at CBS have been stopping me in the hallway to ask one question. It's a question I haven't mentioned so far in the broadcast . . .

But the answer, as of this morning . . . fourteen pounds.

In Praise of New York City

It's been popular in recent years to suggest that Nature is the perfect condition, that people have done nothing to the earth since they got here but make a mess of it. Well, that's true about some places but untrue about others.

New York City is as amazing in its own way as the Grand Canyon. As a matter of fact, you can't help thinking that maybe Nature would have made New York City look the way it does if it had had the money and the know-how.

When people talk about New York City, they usually mean the part of the city called Manhattan. Manhattan is a narrow rock island twelve miles long. Being an island is an important thing about New York because even though no one thinks much about it from day to day, they have to go to quite a bit of trouble to get on it and off it. This makes being there something of an event and people don't take it so lightly. New York isn't like so many places that just sort of dwindle away until you're out of town. In New York, it's very definite. You're either there or you aren't there.

The twenty-eight bridges and tunnels don't connect Manhattan with New Jersey and the four other boroughs. They're for entering and leaving New York. Where from or where to is of secondary importance. It may be some indication of the significance of the event that it costs $1.50 to cross the George Washington Bridge entering New

York, nothing to cross leaving it.

The Brooklyn Bridge is a cathedral among bridges. Coming to Manhattan across it every morning is like passing through the Sistine Chapel on your way to work. You couldn't be going to an unimportant place.

Although two million people work on the little island, only half a million of those who work there live there. As a result, a million and a half people have to get on it every morning and off it every night. That's a lot of people to push through twenty-eight little tunnels and bridges in an hour or so, but it's this arterial ebb and flow that produces the rhythm to which this heartless city's heart beats. There must be something worth coming for when all those people go to that much trouble to get there.

Although it isn't the outstanding thing about it to the people who live or work there, New York is best known to strangers for what it looks like. And, of course, it looks tall.

The World Trade Center has two towers, each a quarter of a mile high. The New York office worker isn't overwhelmed by the engineering implications of flushing a toilet 106 floors above the street.

The buildings of the city are best seen from above, as though they were on an architect's easel. It's strange that they were built to look best from an angle at which hardly anyone ever sees them. From the street where the people are, you can't see the buildings for the city. The New Yorker doesn't worry about it because he never looks up.

You have to talk about tall buildings when you talk about New York, but to anyone who has lived for very long with both, the people of the city are of more continuing interest than the architecture. There is some evidence, of course, that the New Yorker isn't all that separate from his environment. If dogs and masters tend to look alike, so probably do cities and their citizens.

The New Yorker takes in New York air. For a short time it trades molecules with his bloodstream and he is part city. And then he exhales and the city is part him. They become inextricably mingled, and it would be strange if the people didn't come to look like the city they inhabit. And to some extent like each other.

While the rest of the nation feels fiercely about New York — they love it or they hate it — New Yorkers feel nothing. They use the city like a familiar tool. They don't defend it from love or hate. They shrug or nod in knowing agreement with almost anything

165

anyone wants to say about it. Maybe this is because it's so hard to say anything about New York that isn't true.

New Yorkers don't brood much, either. They go about their business with a purposefulness that excludes introspection. If the rest of the country says New Yorkers lack pride because they have so little to be proud of, the New Yorker shrugs again. He has no argument with the South or the Midwest or Texas or California. He feels neither superior nor inferior. He just doesn't compare the things in New York with those anywhere else. He doesn't compare the subway with Moscow's or with the Metro in Paris. Both may be better, but neither goes to Brooklyn or Forest Hills and for this reason doesn't interest the New Yorker one way or the other.

New York is essentially a place for working but not everyone works in a glass cube. The island is crowded with highly individual nests people have made for themselves. There are 100,000 Waldens hidden in the stone and steel caverns.

The places people work and live are as different as the people. If a Hollywood façade is deceptive because it has nothing behind it, a New York façade is deceptive because it has so much. You can't tell much

At the Stork Club in Manhattan with fellow Arthur Godfrey colleagues; left to right: Andy, Chuck Horner, Mug Richardson, Frank Dodge, Hank Miles

about what's inside from what you see outside. There are places within places. Houses behind houses. Very often in New York ugliness is only skin deep.

New York is the cultural center of mankind, too. Art flourishes in proximity to reality, and in New York the artist is never more than a stone's throw from the action. The pianist composes music three blocks from a fight in Madison Square Garden. A poet works against the sound of a jackhammer outside his window.

There are wonderfully good places to live in New York, if you have the money. A lot of New Yorkers *have* the money. Some of the grand old brownstones of an earlier era have been restored. There are no living spaces more comfortable anywhere. There are charming and unexpected little streets hidden in surprising places throughout the city. They attract the artist, the actor, the musician. The insurance salesman lives on Long Island.

The city is crowded with luxury apartments, so even if you don't own your own brownstone, there's no need to camp out.

The average living place is an apartment built wall to wall with other apartments, so that they share the efficiency of water and electricity that flows to them through the same conduits. They're neither slums nor palaces.

If you can afford $2,500 a month for a three-bedroom apartment, you can live in a living room with Central Park as your front yard.

Several hundred thousand people do have Central Park for a front yard and it's certainly the greatest park on earth. It's a world of its own. No large city ever had the foresight to set aside such a substantial portion of itself to be one complete unbuilt-on place. It occupies 25 percent of the total area of Manhattan and yet any proposition to take so much as ten square feet of it to honor a Polish general or an American President brings out its legion of defenders.

There are crimes committed in the Park, but to say the Park is unsafe is like saying banks are unsafe because there are holdups. Life is unsafe, for that matter.

Most American cities have rotted from the center and the merchants have all moved to a place under one roof out in the middle of a suburban parking lot. Downtown was yesterday. New York is still vital at its core. It's the ultimate downtown. And if the biggest businesses are centered in New York so are the smallest.

Macy's, Gimbel's, Bloomingdale's are all here and so are the big grocery chains. But the place you probably buy your food is around the corner at a butcher's where you can still see both sides of a piece of meat.

If you want a rare and exotic cheese from Belgium, it's available, or maybe you need a gear for a pump made in 1923. All there somewhere in the city. If you're seven feet tall, there's a store that'll take care of you or they can fit you with pants if you have a waist that measures sixty-four inches.

There's nothing you can't buy in New York if it's for sale anywhere in the world.

Money doesn't go as far in New York but it doesn't come as far, either. All the numbers for all the money in American are handled in Wall Street on lower Manhattan. The banks, the businesses and even the government do most of their money shuffling and dealing there.

If a civilization can be judged on its ability not only to survive but to thrive in the face of natural obstacles, New York's civilization would have to be called among the most successful. For example, for what's supposed to be a temperate climate, New York has some of the most intemperate weather in the world. It's too hot in the summer, too cold in winter. During all its seasons, the wind has a way of whipping the weather at you and the rain is always coming from an angle that umbrella makers never considered.

The funny thing about it is that Nature and New York City have a lot in common. Both are absolutely indifferent to the human condition. To the New Yorker, accustomed to inconvenience of every kind, the weather is simply one more inconvenience.

New Yorkers learn young to proceed

against all odds. If something's in the way, they move it or go under it or over it or around it, but they keep going. There's no sad resignation to defeat. New Yorkers assume they can win. They have this feeling that they're not going to be defeated.

People talk as though they don't like crowds, but the crowd in New York bestows on the people it comprises a blessed anonymity. New Yorkers are protected from the necessity of being individuals when being one serves no purpose. This blending together that takes place in a crowd is a great time-saver for them.

New York can be a very private place too. There's none of the neighborliness based solely on proximity that dominates the lives you share your life with in a small town. It's quite possible to be not merely private but lonely in a crowd in New York. Loneliness seldom lasts, though. For one thing, troubles produce a warmth and comradeship like nothing else, and New York has so many troubles shared by so many people that there's a kind of common knowingness, even in evil, that brings them together. There is no one with troubles so special in New York that there aren't others in the same kind of trouble.

There are five thousand blind people making their way around the city. They're so much a part of the mix, so typical as New Yorkers, that they're treated with much the same hostile disregard as everyone else. Many of the blind walk through the city with the same fierce independence that moves other New Yorkers. They feel the same obligation to be all right. "I'm okay. I'm all right."

It might appear to any casual visitor who may have taken a few rides about town in a taxicab that all New Yorkers are filled with a loudmouthed ill will toward each other. The fact of the matter is, though, that however cold and cruel things seem on the surface, there has never been a society of people in all history with so much compassion for its fellowman. It clothes, feeds, and houses 15 percent of its own because 1.26 million people in New York are unable to do it for themselves. You couldn't call that cold or cruel.

Everyone must have seen pictures at least of the great number of poor people who live in New York. And it seems strange, in view of this, that so many people still come here seeking their fortune or maybe someone else's. But if anything about the city's population is more impressive than the great number of poor people, it's the great number of rich people. There's no need to search for buried treasure in New York. The great American dream is out in the open for everyone to see and to reach for. No one seems to resent the very rich. It must be because even those people who can never realistically believe they'll get rich themselves can still dream about it. And they respond to the hope of getting what they see others having. Their hope alone seems to be enough to sustain them. The woman going into Tiffany's to buy another diamond pin can pass within ten feet of a man without money enough for lunch. They are oblivious to each other. He feels no envy; she no remorse.

There's a disregard for the past in New York that dismays even a lot of New Yorkers. It's true that no one pays much attention to antiquity. The immigrants who came here came for something new, and what New York used to be means nothing to them. Their heritage is somewhere else.

Old million-dollar buildings are constantly being torn down and replaced by new fifty-million-dollar ones. In London, Rome, Paris, much of the land has only been built on once in all their long history. In relatively new New York, some lots have already been built on four times.

Because strangers only see New Yorkers in transit, they leave with the impression that the city is one great mindless rush to nowhere. They complain that it's moving too fast, but they don't notice that it's getting there first. For better and for worse, New York has *been* where the rest of the country is going.

The rest of the country takes pride in the legend on the Statue of Liberty: "Give me your tired, your poor, / Your huddled masses . . . / The wretched refuse of your teeming shore. . . ." Well, for the most part it's been New York City, not the rest of the country, that took in those huddled masses.

Millions of immigrants who once arrived by ships stopped off in New York for a generation or two while the city's digestive system tried to assimilate them before putting them into the great American bloodstream. New York is still trying to swallow large numbers of immigrants. They don't come by boat much anymore and they may not even be from a foreign country. The influx of a million Puerto Ricans in the 1960s produced the same kind of digestive difficulties that the influx of the Irish did in the middle 1800s.

New York's detractors, seeing what happens to minority groups, have said there is just as much prejudice here as anywhere. New York could hardly deny that. The working whites hate the unemployed blacks. The blacks hate the whites. The Puerto Ricans live in a world of their own. The Germans, the Hungarians, the Poles live on their own blocks. Nothing in this pot has melted together. The Chinese and the Italians live side by side in lower Manhattan as though Canal Street was the Israeli border. There's no intermingling, and in a city with almost two million Jews even a lot of *Jews* are anti-Semitic.

In spite of it all, the city works. People do get along. There is love.

Whether New York is a pleasure or a pain depends on what it is you wish to fill your life with. Or whether you wish to fill it at all. There is an endless supply of satisfaction available to anyone who wishes to help himself to it. It's not an easy city, but the cups of its residents runneth over with life.

It's a city of extremes. There's more of everything. The range of notes is wider. The highs are higher. The lows lower. The goods, the bads are better and worse. And if you're unimpressed by statistics, consider the fact that in 1972 the cops alone in New York City were charged with stealing $73 million worth of heroin. There are 1,700 murders

175

in an average year.

Neither of those statistics is so much a comment on crime as it is a comment on the size and diversity of New York City.

No one keeps a statistic on Life. The probability is that, like everything else, there's more of it in New York.

An Essay on War

We are all inclined to believe that our generation is more civilized than the generations that preceded ours.

From time to time, there is even some substantial evidence that we hold in higher regard such civilized attributes as compassion, pity, remorse, intelligence and a respect for the customs of people different from ourselves.

Why war then?

Some pessimistic historians think the whole society of man runs in cycles and that one of the phases is war.

The optimists, on the other hand, think war is not like an eclipse or a flood or a spell of bad weather. They believe that it is more like a disease for which a cure could be found if the cause were known.

Because war is the ultimate drama of life and death, stories and pictures of it are more interesting than those about peace. This is so true that all of us, and perhaps those of us in television more than most, are often caught up in the action of war to the exclusion of the ideas of it.

If it is true, as we would like to think it is, that our age is more civilized than ages past, we must all agree that it's very strange that in the twentieth century, our century, we have killed more than 70 million of our fellowmen on purpose, at war.

It is very, very strange that since 1900 more men have killed more other men than in any other seventy years in history.

Probably the reason we are able to do both — that is, believe on one hand that we *are* more civilized and on the other hand wage war to kill — is that killing is not so personal an affair in war as it once was. The enemy is invisible. One man doesn't look another in the eye and run him through with a sword. The enemy, dead or alive, is largely unseen. He is killed by remote control: a loud noise, a distant puff of smoke and then . . . silence.

The pictures of the victim's wife and children, which he carries in his breast pocket, are destroyed with him. He is not heard to cry out. The question of compassion or pity or remorse does not enter into it. The enemy is not a man, he is a statistic.

It is true, too, that more people are being killed at war now than previously because we're better at doing it than we used to be. One man with one modern weapon can kill thousands.

The world's record for killing was set on August 6, 1945, at Hiroshima.

There have been times in history when one tribe attacked another for no good reason except to take its land or its goods, or simply to prove its superiority. But wars are no longer fought without some ethical pretension. People want to believe they're on God's side and he on theirs. One nation does not usually attack another anymore without first having propagandized itself into believing that its motives are honorable. The Japanese didn't attack Pearl Harbor with any sense in their own minds that they were scheming, deceitful or infamous.

Soldiers often look for help to their religion. It was in a frenzy of religious fervor that Japanese Kamikaze pilots died in World War II with eternal glory on their minds. Even a just God, though, listening to victory prayers from both sides, would be understandably confused.

It has always seemed wrong to the people who disapprove of war that we have spent much of our time and half of our money on anti-creation. The military budget of any major power consumes half of everything and leaves us half to live on.

It's interesting that the effective weapons of war aren't developed by warriors, but by engineers. In World War I they made a machine that would throw five hundred pounds of steel fifty miles. They compounded an ingeniously compressed package of liquid fire that would burn people like bugs. The engineers are not concerned with death, though.

The scientist who splits an atom and revolutionizes warfare isn't concerned with warfare; his mind is on that fleck of matter.

And so we have a machine gun a man can carry that will spit out two hundred bullets a minute, each capable of ripping a man in two, although the man who invented it, in all probability, loves his wife, children, dogs, and probably wouldn't kill a butterfly.

Plato said that there never was a good war or a bad peace, and there have always been people who believed this was true. The trouble with the theory is that the absence of war isn't necessarily peace. Maybe the worst thing Adolf Hitler did was to provide evidence for generations to come that any peace is *not* better than any war. Buchenwald wasn't war.

The generation that had found Adolf Hitler hard to believe was embarrassed at how reluctant it had been to go help the people of the world who needed help so desperately. That generation determined not to be slow with help again and as a result may have been too quick. A younger generation doesn't understand why the United States went into Vietnam. Having gotten into the war, all it wanted to consider itself a winner was to get out. Unable to make things the way it wanted them, but unwilling to accept defeat, it merely changed what it wanted.

DWIGHT EISENHOWER, 1962: "I think it's only defense, self-defense, that's all it is."
JOHN KENNEDY, 1963: "In the final analysis it's their war. They're the ones that have to win it or lose it."
LYNDON JOHNSON, 1969: "But America has not changed her essential position. And that purpose is peaceful settlement."
RICHARD NIXON, 1974: "But the time has come to end this war."

There are a lot of reasons for the confusion about a war. One of them is that the statesmen who make the decisions never have to fight one themselves. Even the generals don't fight the battles.

Professional soldiers often say they hate war, but they would be less than human if they did not, just once, want to play the game they spent a lifetime practicing. How could you go to West Point for four years and not be curious about whether you'd be any good in a war?

Even in peacetime, nations keep huge armies. The trouble with any peacetime all-volunteer army is that the enlisted men in one are often no smarter than the officers. During a war when the general population takes up arms, the character of an army changes and for the better.

In the twentieth century there is open rebellion between the people who decide about whether to fight or not and some of the young men being asked to do the fighting. It hasn't always been that way. Through the years, even the reluctant draftees have usually gone to battle with some enthusiasm for it. Partially the enthusiasm comes from the natural drama of war and the excitement of leaving home on a crusade. It's a trip to somewhere else, and with the excitement inherent in an uncertain return. It is a great adventure, with the possibility of being killed the one drawback to an otherwise exciting time in life.

There have been just and unjust wars throughout history but there is very little difference in the manner in which people have been propagandized to believe in them. Patriotism, sometimes no more knowing or sophisticated than pride in a high-school football team, is the strongest motivator. With flags enough and martial music enough, anyone's blood begins to boil.

Patriotic has always been considered one of the good things to be in any nation on earth, but it's a question whether patriotism has been a force for good or evil in the world.

Once the young men of a country get into a battle, most of them are neither heroes nor cowards. They're swept up in a movement that includes them and they go where they're told to go, do what they're told to do. It isn't long before they're tired and afraid and they want to go home.

True bravery is always highly regarded because we recognize that someone has done something that is good for all of us, certainly at the risk and possibly at the expense of his own life. But in war, the mantle of virtue is pressed on every soldier's head as though they were all heroes. This is partly because everyone else is grateful to him and wants to encourage him to keep at it. All soldiers who come home alive are heaped with the praise that belongs to very few of them . . . and often to the dead they left behind.

In part, at least, this accounts for why so many men like being ex-soldiers. Once the war and the fighting are done with and they are safe at home, it matters not that they may have served in the 110th emergency shoe-repair battalion. In their own eyes, they are heroes of the front lines.

Even in retrospect, though, a nation has always felt an obligation to honor its warriors. The face of the earth is covered with statuary designed for this purpose that is so bad in many cases that were it not in honor of the dead, it would evoke not tears but laughter.

During and since World War II, the United States alone has bestowed ten million medals and ribbons of honor on its soldiers, many of them for acts calling for as little courage as living a year in Paris.

Bravery is as rare in war as it is in peace. It isn't just a matter of facing danger from which you would prefer to run. If a man faces danger because the alternative to doing that is worse or because he doesn't understand the danger, this may make him a good soldier but it is something other than bravery. Stupidity faces danger easier than intelligence.

The average bright young man who is drafted hates the whole business because an army always tries to eliminate the individual differences in men. The theory is that a uniformity of action is necessary to achieve a common goal. That's good for an army but terrible for an individual who likes himself the way he is.

Some men, of course, like the order imposed on them. They like the freedom from making hard decisions that mindless submission to authority gives them.

There is always more precision on the drill field back home than there is on the battle-field. Uniformity of action becomes less precise as an army approaches the front. At the front it usually disappears altogether. It is not always, or even usually, the best marchers who make the best fighters.

Everyone talks as though there was noth-ing good about war, but there are some good things and it's easy to see why so many people are attracted by it. If there were no good things about war, the chances are we would find a way not to have another.

A nation at war feels a unity it senses at no other time. Even the people not fighting are bound together. There is a sense of common cause missing in peacetime. Accomplishments are greater, change is quicker ... and if progress is motion, there is more of it in war-time. A nation at peace is busy gratifying itself, overeating, over-dressing, lying in the sun until it's time to eat and drink again.

If war brings out the worst in people as it has been assumed it does, it also brings out the very best. It's the ultimate competition. Most of us live our lives at half-speed, using only as much of our ability as is absolutely necessary to make out. But at war if a man is actually fighting it, he uses all his brain and all his muscle. He explores depths of his emotions he didn't know were down there and might never have occasion to use again in his lifetime. He lives at full speed, finding strength he didn't know he had accomplishing things he didn't know he could do.

The best thing about war is hard to describe, is never talked about. Most of us get a warm sense of fellow feeling when we act in close and successful relationship with others, and maybe that happens more in war than any other time. There is a lonesomeness about life that no one who has experienced it likes to talk about, and acting together for a common cause, men often come closest to what they ought to be at their very best.

It is paradoxical but true that in war when man is closest to death, he is also closest to complete fulfillment and farthest from loneliness. He is dependent, dependable, loved and loving.

And there is another thing about war. If there is love in us, there is hate, too, and it's apparent that hate springs from the same well as love and just as quickly. No one is proud of it but hate is not an unpleasant emotion and there is no time other than wartime when we are encouraged to indulge ourselves in an orgy of hate.

The worst of war is hell but there isn't much of the worst of it and not many soldiers experience even that much.

A soldier at war doesn't feel the need to answer any questions about it. He is exhausted by the battle.

He is busy destroying and it does not occur to him that he will have to help rebuild the world he is pulling down.

He often mistakes the exultation of victory for a taste of what things will be like for the rest of his life.

And they are only like that for a very short time.

■ ■ ■ ■

PART III
A FEW DECADES
WITH ANDY ROONEY

■ ■ ■ ■

In 1978 "Three Minutes With Andy Rooney," a short segment that featured Rooney opining on all things praiseworthy, annoying, and worthy of inspection, was aired at the end of *60 Minutes.* Initially a summer stand-in for "Point/Counterpoint," a debate segment between liberal writer Shana Alexander and conservative columnist James Kilpatrick, by the end of the season "Three Minutes" had become "A Few Minutes with Andy Rooney" and had

The home of "A Few Minutes"

Photo by Irving Haberman

assumed the primetime spot. The people
had spoken. Andy Rooney's no-nonsense
approach to life hit a nerve. With "A Few
Minutes" Rooney firmly established himself
as a beloved contrarian, a man who liked
to poke holes in common wisdom, remind
his viewers of values worth upholding, moments worth relishing, and the rewards of
skepticism. In its past thirty-one seasons,
"A Few Minutes with Andy Rooney" has
won millions of fans. Broadcast from
Rooney's paper-strewn, lovingly cluttered
walnut desk at CBS (a desk that he built),
Rooney's on-air time is a refreshingly

clear-eyed look at the perils and joys of the world we live in.

THE MAN BEHIND THE DESK: INTRODUCING ANDY ROONEY

To begin with, here are some clues to my character. It seems only fair that if you're going to read what I write, I ought to tell you how I stand:

— I prefer sitting but when I stand, I stand in size 8 1/2 EEE shoes. There have been periods in my life when wide feet were my most distinguishing characteristic.

— When it comes to politics, I don't know whether I'm a Democrat or a Republican. When I was young I was under the mistaken impression that all Democrats were Catholic and all Republicans were Protestant. This turns out to be untrue, of course, and I've never decided which I am. Those of us who don't have a party affiliation ought to be able to register under the heading "Confused."

— I like cold better than hot, rice better than potatoes, football better than baseball, Coke better than Pepsi. I've been to Moscow three times and don't like that at all.

— This morning the scale balanced at 203 pounds. I'm 5'9". My mother always called me "sturdy" and said I have big bones. A little fat is what I am.

— I have an American Express card but often leave home without it and pay cash.

— The following are among the famous people I have met: Richard Nixon, George McGovern, Arthur Godfrey, Frank Gifford, Barry Goldwater, Art Buchwald, Jimmy Stewart and Carol Burnett. I have never met Teddy Kennedy although I've seen a lot of pictures of him.

— I have been arrested for speeding.

— I speak French, but Frenchmen always pretend they don't understand what I'm saying.

— It is my opinion that prejudice saves us all a great deal of time. I have a great many well-founded prejudices, and I have no intention of giving up any of them except for very good reasons. I don't like turnips and I don't like liver. Call it prejudice if you wish, but I have no intention of ever trying either again just to make sure I don't like them. I *am* sure.

— I don't like anything loud.

— Fiction doesn't interest me at all. I haven't read a novel since *Lorna Doone.* I meant to read Hemingway's *The Old Man and the Sea* when it came out, but I didn't. Fiction takes too long for the ideas contained in it. I'm not interested in being diverted from my own life.

— Good ideas are overrated. It makes more difference how a writer handles an idea than what the idea was in the first place. The world is filled with people with good ideas and very short of people who can even rake a leaf. I'm tired of good ideas.

— When I write, I use an Underwood #5 made in 1920. Someone gave me an electric typewriter, but there's no use pretending you can use machinery that thinks faster than you do. An electric typewriter is ready to go before I have anything to say.

— I know a lot about wood, ice cream, the English language and Harry Reasoner. In other areas I have some serious gaps.

— Writers don't often say anything that readers don't already know, unless it's a news story. A writer's greatest pleasure is revealing to people things they knew but did not know they knew. Or did not realize everyone else knew, too. This produces a warm sense of fellow feeling and is the best a writer can do.

— There's nothing mystical or magic about being a writer. A writer is just a person who writes something. There are almost no people who are not dentists who can fix teeth, but there are a lot of people who aren't professional writers who write very well. This is one of the reasons why being a writer is tougher than being a dentist.

— I admire people who don't care what anyone else thinks about what they do, but I'm not one of them. I care what people think and would not want you to know how much I hope you like what I write.

AN INTERVIEW WITH ANDY ROONEY

"Anyone attracted to the rugged features of his handsome countenance might at first glance fail to observe the piercing intelligence of Andy Rooney's steel-blue eyes."

That's the way I'd like to have an article about me begin. In the past year I've been interviewed twenty times by reporters and none of them has started a piece that way. The articles have been friendly and many of them well done but no one who reads anything about himself is ever totally satisfied. Do they have to point out I'm grumpy? Must the reporter mention that my clothes are unpressed? Is it necessary to say that I'm overweight and getting gray?

194

A proud trio of Emmy award winners; (left) camera-man Walter Dombrow and (center) producer Bud Benjamin

What follows are some guidelines for reporters who wish to interview me in the future. I'd like to have the report go more like this:

"Rooney, who wears his expensive but tasteful clothes with a casual grace that conceals his position as one of the style setters in the men's fashion world, talked to this reporter in his hotel suite where he draped his taut, muscular frame over an easy chair.

"Considered by critics to be the leading

essayist in print and broadcasting, Andy was disarmingly diffident when this reporter compared his work with that of Mark Twain, Hemingway, Robert Benchley, E. B. White, Walter Lippmann and Art Buchwald.

" 'Shucks,' he said modestly as he dug his toe into the deep pile rug of the carpet in his penthouse suite, 'I don't know about that.'

"Although it is not widely publicized," this article about me would continue if I had my way, "Andy Rooney might well be known as a modern-day Chippendale, were his mastery of the cabinetmaker's art not overshadowed by his genius with the English language.

"On the tennis court, Andy's serve has often been compared to that of John McEnroe. He moves with a catlike quickness that belies his age.

" 'Andy is wonderful to work with,' says his wife, Marguerite. 'He's always good-natured and a joy to have around the house. I can't recall an argument we've had in all the years of our marriage.'

"Rooney's four children, Ellen, Martha, Emily and Brian, are all perfect, too.

"On the average day, Andy rises at 4:30 A.M. By 6:00 A.M., because of his unusual ability to read six hundred words a minute, he has finished two newspapers and *Time* magazine. His photographic memory enables him to store anything he has read for long periods of time and it is partly this ability that makes it easy for him to turn out three interesting, accurate, informative and perceptive essays each week.

"Of his friend, Harry Reasoner says, 'I only wish I could write as well as Andy does.'

"During our interview, Rooney got several telephone calls. William Buckley called to ask his advice on a point of grammar. There was a call from someone identified only as 'Ron' asking for advice on the economy. A third call came from E. F. Hutton asking Andy how he thought the stock market would behave in the days ahead."

I'm going to clip this out of the newspaper now and carry it with me wherever I go. If a young reporter wishes to interview me, I'll show it to him, just to give him some idea how I think his report should read. There's no sense having reporters waste a lot of time getting the facts.

SARTORIAL SHORTCOMINGS

From time to time it is brought to my attention that I'm not the best-dressed man in the world. Someone wrote once that I looked as though I slept in Grand Central Station every night. I have four grown children who unfortunately aren't afraid of me and they've never hesitated to point out my sartorial shortcomings, either. The least they could do is lie a little if they really love me.

I'm relatively unaware of how I look in clothes. I usually look once in the mirror when I dress in the morning but that only shows me myself from the chest up.

I don't know where I go wrong. I buy pretty good clothes but one of us is usually the wrong shape.

Maintaining clothes in good condition is as hard as keeping a house painted and in working order. For example, it's inevitable that you're going to get a spot on a necktie or the lapel of a coat once in a while. I keep all kinds of spot remover at home and in the office and I've never had any success with any of them. That spray can, with the powder in it, just plain doesn't work for me. I've used it a dozen times on grease spots and the same thing always happens. The grease spot is gone and I'm left with a big, plainly visible splotch of white chalk imbedded in the fabric. Nothing takes that out, ever.

Most brands of spot cleaner use carbon tetrachloride. I've tried to remove a thousand spots from a thousand neckties with carbon tet. All I get is a ring bigger and more obvious than the original spot.

I've seen women remove spots successfully. They say you just have to keep rubbing in circles. I've rubbed spots in circles with carbon tet until I was blue in the face from the fumes and I still get nothing but a big ring and a smelly tie.

In the morning I often take a pair of pants, a shirt or a coat into the back room where we have an iron set up. My intentions are good. I don't want to burden my wife with my problems and I want to look neat. I don't want to embarrass my friends or my family.

I have yet to iron a pair of pants that end up with fewer than two creases down the front of each leg. I'd like to have one of those machines the dry cleaners have. They just lay a pair of pants on there any which way, they pull down that handle, there's a big whoosh of steam and presto! the pants are perfect.

Shirts? Who can iron a shirt? I've never ironed a shirt yet that didn't look worse when I finished with it than it did when I started.

Neckties are smaller but they're at least as hard to iron as a shirt. You'd think they'd be easy but if you press down on a tie, you get the imprint of the lumpy lining on the front of the tie. As a result, many of my ties look like my pants.

During the summer I often carry a tie in my pocket instead of wearing it. Many of them never recover during the winter.

It's a good thing socks don't show much because if my kids think my pants and jackets look bad, they should see my socks. I've given up trying to put them on right side out because at least half the time I don't even have a pair. I just look for two socks in the drawer that are somewhere near the same color. I haven't had pairs of socks in years.

The funny thing is that I have a clear idea in my mind what someone well dressed looks like. I know what I want to look like and sometimes I realize I'm unconsciously thinking that's what I *do* look like. Obviously I'm dreaming.

I had several friends in school who were always well dressed, and I can go around for days thinking I look more or less the way they looked. Marshall always looked just right. Then someone will casually tell me I look like an unmade bed and I'm

At home in the country, in Lake George

brought back down to earth.

The only thing for me to do is take the position that clothes don't make the man.

A WORLD-CLASS SAVER

There is a pair of crutches leaning against the wall opposite the oil burner in our basement. I'm not sure who ever used them. They've been there as long as I can remember. I suppose one of the kids broke something once or maybe we bought them for my mother the year she broke her hip.

No one ever used the crutches much, I know that. I was looking at the rubber tips last weekend and they're almost new. I suppose I've kept them because, in the back of my mind, I know someone's going to break something again someday . . . me, maybe. They're an unpleasant reminder of that possibility every time I see them, though, and I think I may throw them out. If anyone breaks a bone, we'll just start fresh with a new pair. Crutches cost about twenty dollars. It would be worth coming up with that when we need them rather than having these crutches staring me in the face every time I go downstairs. On the other hand, maybe I'd better keep them just in case.

It's this kind of thinking that makes me realize I lack the executive's decision-making ability. I hem and haw, never quite making up my mind whether to keep something or throw it out.

For example, I finally got at going through about five big cardboard boxes of scripts I wrote for a radio show with Garry Moore and Durward Kirby. The show was on five days a week for ten minutes each day. I wrote it for five years, so you can imagine the stacks of paper involved. The scripts I have even include the commercials.

For twenty years I've saved these scripts with the five boxes taking up valuable space.

What am I saving them for? I thought to

myself. In a hardheaded moment, I dragged a major plastic trash can down to the cellar from the garage and started dumping the scripts in it.

I needed help carrying the can upstairs, and when I finally got it out in the driveway for the trash pickup, I started idly looking through some of them.

Gee, I thought to myself, some of these are pretty good. Like most writers, I'm not my own harshest critic. Ten minutes later, I was taking the scripts out of the trash container and putting them back in the boxes.

This is no way to clean up.

Margie saves clay flowerpots. I hate clay flowerpots and, if I think I can get away with it, I throw them out.

She hates the coffee cans, old broken dishes, odd lengths of wood and the assorted junk I save, and she throws out any of them she thinks I won't notice. Sometimes there's been an undeclared war between us. If I find she's thrown out some of my treasured junk, I retaliate with her flowerpots.

The boxes of scripts are back down in the basement now, right where they were before. Saving them was part sentiment, part the practical thought that I might find a use for them someday, but it was neither of those that brought me to the point of putting them back in the boxes. What did that was something different altogether.

It occurred to me that for twenty years I'd kept them; for twenty years they'd taken up space; for twenty years they were part of my life. If I threw them out then, all the space they've taken and all the thoughts I'd had about them in those twenty years would have been for nothing. In that case, I might as well have thrown them out the day I wrote them. This is the kind of thinking that makes a saver. A good saver can always think of a reason not to throw something out.

Being, as I am, a world-class saver, don't look for those crutches in my trash can anytime soon, either.

BORN TO LOSE

I'm a world-class loser.

There are very few people better at losing things than I am.

Last night, as I was getting into bed, I thought to myself, "Maybe losing stuff would make an essay." So I scribbled some notes about it on a piece of paper, turned out the lights, and went to sleep.

I cannot find the piece of paper I wrote the notes on about losing things. I got down on my hands and knees and looked under the bed. Nothing. It's not mixed in with the sheets. It's not in my pajama pocket and it isn't on my dresser. I'll find it a week from now.

Over the years, I've lost thousands of things. One reason I lose so much is that I have so much. I am an acquirer of things, a possessor. Once I get something, I keep it . . . unless I lose it, of course. It's hard to find a place to put all of my possessions, so they're just left around. They tend to get lost or, perhaps, covered over by other possessions.

My shoehorn was gone this morning. I had to stand there trying to worm my feet into my shoes without breaking down the backs.

I lose fingernail clippers at a great rate . . . and sunglasses.

If I need a screwdriver, I can only find the one with the Phillips head when I'm dealing with a single-slot screw. And, naturally, vice versa.

Where do all the flashlights I buy go?

Someone gave me a beautiful fountain pen for Christmas. I can't find it. I don't use it; I just don't want to lose it.

At this very moment I cannot find my driver's license. I'm driving 150 miles upstate tomorrow and it's illegal to drive without a license, but I'm going to make the trip anyway.

"I really do have a license," I'll explain to the policeman if I'm arrested for speeding. "I just can't find it."

This goes over big with policemen. I know because I've tried it before.

I have regular places where I look for things I can't find. They're never in those places. We have dozens of little drawers in tables and chests around the house, and I always look in those for things I can't find. Nothing. I've looked in those drawers ten thousand times and have yet to find a single missing item in them. I don't know why I persist in looking there.

In the office, Jane is good at finding things but she often doesn't realize I've lost what she finds; so she doesn't tell me she has it. The items are just the same as lost as far as I'm concerned.

Several years ago, I got a small lump of money for one of my books, so I decided to invest in the stock market. Someone knowledgeable about money told me to buy Exxon. I bought Exxon. It did very well, but after the unpleasantness in Alaska, I was embarrassed to be an Exxon stockholder and decided to sell my shares. If I ever ran for office, some reporter would discover that I owned a small amount of Exxon stock and ruin my chances for election by revealing it.

I'd sell the stock in a minute if I could find the stock certificates. The man who sold the stock to me said there was a process I could go through to recover my stock without the certificates. It would cost me about 1 percent of the stock's value. This fellow sent me a letter describing how to go about recovering my investment but I can't find his letter.

The value of an item doesn't seem to have anything to do with my ability to lose it. For example, I lose a lot of things of very little value in the refrigerator. Last Saturday, I wanted lunch and remembered I'd put some leftover rice in the refrigerator. I could not find it and everyone else swears they didn't eat it.

Things are even easier to lose in the freezer than in the main part of the refrigerator. If our refrigerator could be preserved for scientists of the year 3000, they'd find a treasure trove of gustatory Americana in there that I've lost.

My idea of heaven would be to die and awaken in a place that has all my lost things.

My Name's Been Stolen

Two years ago, someone broke my car window, took some things from the glove compartment and a suitcase I had left on the back seat. Twenty years ago, I had a motorbike stolen from my garage. In the Army, at Fort Bragg, someone went through my footlocker and took $20 I had saved for the day I could get a twenty-four-hour pass. These were the only brushes with crime I'd had in my life until recently. Now, several thieves have taken something of great value from me — my name.

More than a year ago, people started sending me copies of an e-mail that was appearing on computers all over the country. It was a list of about twenty comments, each one or two sentences long, under my byline. The piece was titled, "In Praise of Older Women — By Andy Rooney." It was sappy and obviously nothing I might have written, but harmless. While I didn't like the idea of someone using my name as his own, I didn't try to do anything about it.

Several months after I first saw the e-mail, a man named Frank Kaiser wrote asking why I had put my name on something he had written in 2000 for his syndicated column called "Suddenly Senior." I called

Frank immediately and he accepted the fact that someone else had taken what he wrote and put my name on it.

There have been two other instances of someone distributing a list of opinions under my name. What would make someone write down a series of personal observations and distribute them using my name as the author? It mystifies me.

About a year ago, I became aware of a more serious theft of my name and it is so hurtful to my reputation that it calls for legal action against the thief. Hundreds of people have written asking if I really wrote the twenty detestable remarks made under my name that have had such wide circulation on the Internet.

The list of remarks begins: "I like big cars, big boats, big motorcycles, big houses and big campfires."

It continues:

"I believe the money I make belongs to me and my family, not some governmental stooge with a bad comb-over who wants to give it away to crack addicts for squirting babies."

"Guns do not make you a killer. I think killing makes you a killer."

"I have the right NOT to be tolerant of others because they are weird, different or tick me off."

Some of the remarks, which I will not repeat here, are viciously racist and the spirit of the whole thing is nasty, mean and totally inconsistent with my philosophy of life. It is apparent that the list of comments has been read by hundreds of thousands of Americans, many of whom must believe that it accurately represents opinions of mine that I don't dare express in my writings or on television. It is seriously damaging to my reputation.

The only good thing to come out of this incident is the dozens of letters I've received from people saying they know me well enough to know I didn't write the comments. There must be many more, however, who are ready to believe I did write them.

I have tracked the e-mail back to an address in Tucson and a Web site called CelebrityHypocrites.com, which is owned *by* a man named Dave Mason. Mr. Mason lists as his address, 405 East Wetmore Road, No. 117 PMB 520, Tucson, AZ 85705. I was in Tucson recently and foolishly went to that address thinking it might be Mason's home or business. I'd like to know more about Mason, but the address was a commercial mailbox business and I didn't wait around for him to show up so I could confront him. If it is Dave Mason who has stolen my name, I demand that he put out a retraction that reaches as many people as his fraudulent e-mail did.

On Writing:
There Is No Secret

Writers are repeatedly asked to explain where they get their ideas. People want their secret. The truth is there is no secret and writers don't have many new ideas. At least, they don't have many ideas that a comic strip artist would illustrate with a light bulb over their heads.

New ideas are one of the most overrated concepts of our time. Most of the important ideas that we live with aren't new at all. If we're grown up, we've had our personal, political, economic, religious, and philosophical ideas for a long time. They evolved out of some experience we had or they came from someone we were exposed to before we were twenty-five. How many of us have changed our opinion about anything important after we were twenty-five because of some new idea?

Like almost everything else that gets popular, new ideas and the concept of creativity have been trivialized. People are passing off novelty for invention. Not many products have been improved with a new idea compared to the number whose quality has been diminished by inferior workmanship and the use of inferior materials. The shortage we face in this country is not new ideas, it's quality work.

Much of the progress of the world has come through genuine creativity but we've cheapened the whole concept by treating creativity as if it were a commodity that could be bought and sold by the pound.

Colleges teach courses in "creative writing" as if a course in just plain writing weren't enough. Trying to teach someone to be creative is as silly as a mother trying to teach her child to be a genius.

I don't know where we all got the thought that ideas come in a blinding flash or that we can learn how to be struck with creative new ideas. Not many ideas come that way. The best ideas are the result of the same slow, selective, cognitive process that produces the sum of a column of figures. Anyone who waits to be struck with a good idea has a long wait coming. If I have a deadline for a column or a television script, I sit down at the typewriter and damn well decide to *have* an idea. There's nothing

At his desk, with his beloved Underwood typewriters behind him

magical about the process, no flashing lights.

Creativity is a by-product of hard work. If I never have another really new idea, it won't matter. Enough writers are already exploring the new, the far-out, and the obscure. We don't understand the old ideas yet. I'm satisfied trying to quantify the obvious.

We have our ideas. What we need now are more people who can do something good with them.

IT'S A WRITER WHO MAKES A FOOL OF HIMSELF

Writing is difficult. That's why there's so little of it that's any good. Writing isn't like mathematics where what you've put down is either right or wrong. No writer ever puts down anything on paper that he knows for certain is good or bad.

When I was in The Albany Academy, I won a writing prize and, because I was not otherwise a good student, it was the academic high point of my years there. Several years later, I came home from college and looked at the things I'd written to win the prize in high school and winced. They were so bad.

In college I was a prolific contributor to the school literary and humor magazine. When I got out of the Army, four years after college, I reread what I'd written in college and couldn't believe I'd ever been so young

215

or written so badly.

In the Army, I was assigned as a reporter to the newspaper, *The Stars and Stripes,* and spent three years covering World War II and learning from the great war correspondents like Hal Boyle, Bob Considine, Homer Bigart, Dick Tregaskis and Ernie Pyle. It seemed to me I was finally growing up as a writer.

In several boxes in my basement I have every issue of *The Stars and Stripes* printed during the time I was on the staff and they contain hundreds of stories I wrote. I like having them as mementos but I'd be embarrassed to have anyone else read them.

All this self-criticism of what I wrote in the past seems like a not-unnecessarily modest attitude on my part but lately it has worried me. When do I get good? How come what I wrote last year, last month, last week and even yesterday, doesn't seem quite right, either? How come every day I think that for the first time I'm beginning to get the hang of writing but when I reread it the following day I realize I still have a ways to go? When do I arrive as a writer?

I have finally come to the sad realization that I will never write anything today that looks as good as it should to me tomorrow. It's the writer's albatross.

The syndrome is common among writers and, to some extent, it protects them. If writing wasn't difficult and often even demeaning, more people would be doing it. The competition would be greater. In motion pictures, television, newspapers and book publishing, there are hundreds of producers, directors, publishers, editors and salesmen standing around waiting to get what the writer has put down on paper so they can change it, package it and sell it. Producers, directors and editors don't become writers. Writers, seeing where the good life and the money are, become producers, directors and editors. It's so much safer.

It's the writer who makes a fool of himself and reveals how shallow he is by putting every thought he has on paper, where everyone can see it, read it and put it away to read again tomorrow. Those who merely speak their thoughts are safe. The spoken word drifts away and evaporates in the air, never to be held against the speaker.

"You know what I mean?" the speaker asks, as a substitute for thinking it out and putting it down on paper.

The writer may not think much but he has to know what little he thinks to get it down on paper at all. If someone knows what he's doing, he ought to be able to tell you, and if someone knows what he thinks, he ought to be able to write it down. If he can't, the chances are he doesn't have a thought.

The computer people are trying to make writing easier but they won't succeed. They make computers with writing programs, just as if there was some kind of magic that could help. All a writer needs is something to say, a blank page and an instrument with which to mark words on it. No word processor with a "writing program" will ever help a writer have something to say. No program ever designed will help make writing any better. It may make typing easier, the page neater and the spelling perfect but it won't improve the writing. Writing can't be turned out by machine, doubled, divided, added to and subtracted from, the way numbers can. The English language is more complex than calculus because numbers don't have nuances.

Several years ago someone wrote me asking if I understood how lucky I was to have my opinions printed and read by other people. I said I did appreciate it. I find something ridiculous about it, too. I even try to forget it. If I thought about how many people were going to read what I wrote every time I sat down at my typewriter, I'd freeze. Who is this person so presumptuous as to think anyone gives a damn what he has to say?

If writing is difficult, it's also one of the most satisfactory jobs in the world. Before I won that prize in high school, I already knew what I wanted to be when I grew up. I wanted to be a writer. I wish I was a better one ("were a better one," if you prefer, I don't) but I enjoy being the one I am. If I was forced to choose between appearing on television and writing the words to appear on paper, I wouldn't hesitate for a second. I'd give up television.

Igor Stravinsky, the musician, said, "I experience a sort of terror if I sit down to work and find an infinity of possibilities open to me. No effort is conceivable. I stand on nothing. Endeavor is futile."

Stravinsky said that what he grabbed for on such occasions were the seven notes of the scale. With the limitations they imposed, he could go to work.

A writer needs boundaries too, or he can't get to work. This book isn't a play, a novel or a history. I've set out to write a series of short essays. Within the boundaries of that form, I can go to work.

I hope the essays look okay to me tomorrow.

The Journalist's Code of Ethics

To what standards do newsmen and women adhere and how should everyone be made to adhere to them?

It is unlikely that reporters and editors are any more or less honest and ethical than doctors but I envy doctors their Hippocratic Oath, the creed they swear to when they become physicians. It's a little out of date but it has a grandeur to it that is timeless.

"I swear by Apollo, the physician," it begins.

That's not much of a beginning, but it improves even though it needs rewriting.

The Hippocratic Oath asks the young doctor to take care of the physician who taught him as he would take care of his own parents. Most young reporters don't feel all that kindly toward the editors who taught them their profession.

The Hippocratic Oath also asks the young doctor to do only what is right for his patients and to do nothing that is wrong. He promises to give no patient deadly medicine and not to induce an abortion for any pregnant woman.

The young doctor promises not to seduce any males or females and not to reveal any secrets.

If journalists had an oath of their own, it would differ from the doctor's.

The journalist certainly wouldn't start by swearing to Apollo and probably not even to Walter Lippmann or Ed Murrow. The oath should be simple and direct. I was thinking of some things that ought to be in it.

Here are some suggestions for "The Journalist's Code of Ethics":

— The word "journalist" is a little pompous and I will only use it on special occasions.

— I am a journalist because I believe that if all the world had all the facts about everything, it would be a better world.

— I understand that the facts and the truth are not always the same. It is my job to report the facts so that others can decide on the truth.

— I will try to tell people what they ought to know and avoid telling them what they want to hear, except when the two coincide, which isn't often.

— I will not do deliberate harm to any persons, except to the extent that the facts

With the 60 Minutes *crew; circa 1983: left to right: Morley Safer, Mike Wallace, Ed Bradley, Harry Reasoner, Dan Rather, Andy Rooney, Don Hewitt (executive producer)*

harm them and then I will not avoid the facts.

— No gift, including kind words, will be accepted when it is offered for the purpose of influencing my report.

— What I wish were the facts will not influence what investigation leads me to believe them to be.

— I will be suspicious of every self-interested source of information.

— My professional character will be superior to my private character.

— I will not use my profession to help or espouse any cause, nor alter my report for the benefit of any cause, no matter how worthy that cause may appear to be.

— I will not reveal the source of information given to me in confidence.

— I will not drink at lunch.

It needs work but it's a start on an oath for reporters and editors.

A REPORT ON REPORTING

A few weeks after I first appeared on *60 Minutes,* I got a call from a drug company selling aspirin. They asked if I would do a commercial for them because, they said, my voice sounded just right for someone with a headache.

This was the first time I ever realized I had a nasal, vaguely unpleasant-sounding voice. The money they offered was interesting but I told them I was a journalist and that journalists didn't do commercials.

Although I'd never dream of doing any commercial, I often make a sales pitch for journalism. I like the news business and intend to say good things about American journalism and the reporters and editors

2007: front row, left to right: Lesley Stahl, Bob Simon, Morley Safer; back row, left to right: Andy Rooney, Scott Pelley, Katie Couric, Steve Kroft

who work in it whether for broadcast or print. My desire to tell you how highly I regard reporters and editors is prompted by several negative stories that have appeared in recent years about dishonest reporting. The stories are dismaying to all of us who work in news. We know they reinforce the negative opinion many Americans have of us. We want to be loved and respected.

USA Today announced that, after a thorough investigation by a committee under the leadership of distinguished journalist John Siegenthaler, it had determined that one of *USA Today*'s star reporters, Jack Kelley, had invented many of his stories from war zones. He'd also borrowed information from other newspaper reporters and often added quotations he'd invented to make his stories livelier.

USA Today did the wrong thing when it kept Kelley on the job long after some of its own staff members suspected he was a fraud, but did the right thing when it had the matter investigated. I don't recall offhand any other company selling a product that paid to have an investigation conducted of some aspect of its own business and then made public the details of what it did wrong. The report said Kelley's stories had often been dishonest and that the editorial staff had been lax in not finding this out sooner. Half a dozen newspapers recently have fired reporters for dishonest or unethical reporting.

While *USA Today* has never been a paragon of editorial excellence, it has capably filled the gap left by good local newspapers in towns and small cities across the country that don't pretend to cover national and international events. Many people who buy *USA Today* buy two newspapers.

Believe it or don't, but I can tell you that newspaper or television reporters, working at *USA Today* or elsewhere, are more concerned about the ethical standards of their profession than the people in any other business. I don't think car dealers, manufacturers or clothing store operators worry much about the impact of their life's work on fellow Americans. Journalists think of themselves as belonging to an exclusive club and are proud of their membership.

The fact that news has become a profitable venture for large corporations has not always been good for people in the business. The disappointing fact is that a large part of the American public reads a newspaper and watches television news more for entertainment than information. This has contributed to the profit-driven companies' tendencies to deal less seriously with the truth in favor of entertainment. The truth is often less interesting than rumor or gossip and our good newspapers are to be congratulated for their imperfect resistance to being entertainers.

I've met hundreds of news people during my sixty years in the business. In World War II, I lived in a press camp with twenty-five and met my first bad apple reporter. He wrote for a news magazine and was ostracized by the others because he regularly put quotes in the mouths of anonymous soldiers he had not interviewed and described events he had not seen.

There's one in every crowd, but what I want to say in this commercial for journalism is this: Reporters are more honest and ethical than the people in any other line of work. It's just very difficult to get the whole truth and tell it accurately.

BIG BUSINESS

There is no more interesting or important work in the world than being a reporter. That's my opinion, of course, and being at least in part a reporter myself, it's natural I'd think so.

The word "reporter" isn't quite right for the job, though, because it only describes half of it — the half where you tell the reader or the listener what you've learned. The other half of a reporter's work isn't described by that word. That's the part where he or she collects the information before telling everyone about it. That's the hard part.

A good reporter ought to be part detective, part puzzle solver and part writer. A reporter has to find the facts, piece them together so they make sense and then put them down on paper in a manner that makes them clear to everyone else.

People often complain about inaccuracies in news stories. They talk as if reporters were deliberately inaccurate or in on some conspiracy, and this is almost never the case. No reporter sets out to write a distorted or inaccurate story. They sometimes come out that way because reporting is hard and some reporters aren't good enough. They also come out that way because a lot of people are very secretive and tell the reporter what they'd like to have printed, not what the facts are.

This all comes to me now, because this morning I got a letter from a boyhood friend I haven't seen in thirty-five years. I knew him as "Bud," but now his letterhead says his first name is "Cornelius" and he's vice-chairman of a big corporation in Oregon. He was a wonderful friend when I was young, but I don't think I know him at all now. After some personal words, he went into a tirade against the news organizations.

Being attacked by businessmen isn't a new experience for most reporters. I heard Lewis Lapham, then editor of *Harper's Magazine,* attacked one evening by a Texan with huge coal interests in Montana.

"You people know nothing about business," the businessman yelled at Lapham.

"You're right," Lapham yelled back, "and it's probably a damn good thing for business."

When businessmen say newspapers and television don't cover business very well, it makes me nervous because in many cases I think it's true. It is also true that it is business's own fault. Information about any business in town is almost impossible to get. They say they have a right to privacy, and I agree with that, but they're being stupid by not being more open, and I'll bet they *won't* agree with me.

It is possible now, because of the Freedom of Information Act, to get information out of government. It has been a great thing for the American public but, of course, there is nothing like that requiring business to reveal *its* business. Some businessmen claim they are secretive so their competition won't find out what they're doing and how, but that

Contemplating a model of New York City

seldom stands up to inspection. The competitor usually knows *all* about the business across town. As a matter of fact, the plant manager used to work for Acme and one member of the Board of Directors of Allied is a former vice president of Acme.

The average business keeps its operation a deep, dark secret mostly out of habit. If the secret is not dark, at least that's the impression they give the American public. It is Mike Wallace standing in front of the locked gates saying, "They refused to talk to us." It suggests there is something evil going on in there, and nine times out of ten there is not. The average businessman in America takes as much pleasure and pride from making a good product as he does from the money, but you'd never guess it from the public image he projects.

You could take the books and the production plans of any good company in America and print them on page one of the local newspaper, and it wouldn't alter the operation one bit. That includes printing the salary of every maintenance man and executive in the place. Business is simply too secretive about everything. They don't have anything more to hide than the rest of us.

The corporate public relations people who do the best job for their company are the ones who lay it on the line. They tell you the truth, even if it hurts a little. The ones who do their companies the most damage are those who try to hide little mistakes or keep information secret that would be better made public even when there is no law demanding it.

The American public is as suspicious of Big Business as it is of Big Government, and what I'd like to say to my old friend Bud is, business would do itself a favor and get better reporting in newspapers and on television if it opened up. If the company is making a good product for an honest profit, the truth won't hurt it.

ON WORK AND MONEY: PROCRASTINATION

It isn't working that's so hard, it's getting ready to work.

It isn't *being* up we all dislike in the morning, it's *getting* up.

Once I get started at almost any job, I'm happy. I can plug away at any dull job for hours and get some satisfaction from doing it. The trouble is that sometimes I'll put off doing that job for months because it's so tough to get started.

It doesn't seem to matter what the job is. For me it can be getting at writing, getting at mowing the lawn, getting at cleaning out the trunk of the car, making a piece of furniture or putting up a shed. It's a good thing I wasn't hired to build the Golden Gate Bridge. I'd never have figured out where to put that first piece of steel to make it possible to get across all that water.

There is some complex thing going on in our brains that keeps us from getting started on a job. No matter how often we do something, we always forget how long it took us to do it last time and how hard it was. Even though we forget in our conscious mind, there is some subconscious part of the brain that remembers. This is what keeps us from getting at things. *We* may not know but our subconscious knows that the job is going to be harder than we think. It tries to keep us from rushing into it in a hurry.

There is a war going on between different elements of our brain. If I consciously remembered how difficult something was the last time I did it, I'd never do it again. The wonderful thing about memory is that it's just great at forgetting. Every Friday afternoon in summer I drive 150 miles to our summer house in the country. I always look forward to *being* there and I always forget how much I hate *getting* there. My subconscious remembers. It keeps me fiddling around the office Friday afternoons, putting off leaving. The drive can take anywhere from three to four hours, depending on the traffic, and I hate it so much that sometimes I spend two of those four hours contemplating selling the place.

The following Friday, I can't wait to leave the office for the country again but my

With longtime editor Robert Forte

subconscious puts it off. It keeps me from getting started. *It* remembers the drive even if I don't.

One of the jobs my subconscious is best at putting me off getting at is painting. My subconscious is absolutely right. I probably shouldn't start it even though I enjoy it once I get going. Once again, my subconscious remembers what I forget.

I look at a door or a fence or a room and I say to myself, "I ought to give that a coat of paint. It'll take two quarts of paint. I'll need some turpentine and a new brush. No sense fooling with those old brushes."

My subconscious sometimes puts me off

the paint job for months but eventually, against its better judgment, I buy the paint, the turpentine and the brush. I put on my old clothes, get a screwdriver to remove the top of the paint can and then I look more carefully at the room. Now I begin to see what my subconscious saw all along.

There are many things to do before I start to paint. I have to move everything out of the room, I have to replace a piece of the baseboard that is broken and I have to scrape and sand the places where the paint is peeling. And I better go back to the hardware store to get some spackle to fill the cracks in the ceiling. While I'm there, I'll pick up some undercoater for the new piece of baseboard and the spackled cracks. I'll have to let it dry overnight so I can't start painting today.

It is quite probable that it is this wonderfully intelligent subconscious part of our brain that makes us want to stay in bed another hour every morning. *We* want to get up. *It* knows that just as soon as we get up, the trouble will start all over again.

FIRED

There's something wrong with anyone who's never been fired from a job. If I'm ever in a position to hire someone, I'm going to be very suspicious of anyone who comes in looking for work with a resume that doesn't include the information that he or she got the ax a couple of times either for incompetence or insubordination.

What's all this resignation business? Doesn't anyone get fired anymore? You read the business pages of the paper, and presidents of corporations are always resigning. From a cushy $250,000-a-year job? Come on, fellas. We're not business tycoons, but we're not that dumb. You got canned.

The whole business of resignation is false, and it's part of a new philosophy we seem to have adopted. There aren't any losers anymore.

At children's birthday parties, they play games in the cellar or the backyard, and the parents having the party give away prizes. It doesn't matter how well or poorly a child plays a game, he'll probably get a prize anyway, because the adults don't want to damage his little psyche by making him think he might not always win in life.

Most high school teams in any sport have co-captains now. Sometimes they have more than two. No one wants to hurt the feelings of a good player by choosing someone over him for the job. Sometimes the professional football teams have six or eight men trot out on the field for the coin-tossing ceremonies. They're all co-captains. Not a loser in the crowd.

I hope we never decide not to hurt the feelings of one of the presidential candidates by electing co-Presidents. One President is plenty.

Last week I read where someone won $34,000 for finishing second in a golf tournament. Second! Imagine making $34,000 for *losing* a game of golf!

The President is always saying he's "sorry" to have to accept someone's resignation. If he was really sorry he shouldn't have accepted it. All of us are using the word "sorry" too lightly. We're always saying we're sorry when we aren't really sorry at all. It's all part of the same refusal to face things as they are.

We're excusing everyone for everything. A boy of seventeen kills the man who runs the candy store for $1.35 and a Tootsie Roll.

The boy's parents find a bloody hammer under his bed and they confront him with it.

"I'm sorry," the boy says. "I killed him, but I didn't mean to do it."

The father looks at the mother with tears in his eyes and says, "At least he's honest."

The next day the neighbors are interviewed by a television reporter. They all say he was a nice quiet boy who always went to church. They don't bother to say that he was a bully, that he'd been stealing all his life and that he was rotten through and through.

We keep letting ourselves off the hook. No one wants to judge anyone else by strict standards for fear he'll be judged by them too. No one wants to say to someone on the job, "You just aren't good enough. You're fired."

BROKE

Has everyone been desperately broke?

Maybe not. I always assume that there are very few experiences or emotions that aren't universal. I've been seriously broke twice in my life.

It's a feeling you never forget and although it's been twenty-six years since I didn't know which way to turn for money, I never see anyone out of a job and without a dollar in his pocket without knowing how he feels.

There are still times when I think about being broke. At night when I empty the change out of my pocket and put it on top of my dresser, I often recall, in those terrible old days, adding up my change to see if I had two dollars.

There are chronically poor people who would laugh at what I went through because it wouldn't seem very bad to them. My wife and I were never hungry. My father was retired but he had made a comfortable living even during the Depression, and my wife's father was a doctor. They wouldn't have let us get to the point where we were out on the street and without food, but you know how that is. There's an unwritten code. There are people you don't ask for money and my father and my wife's father were two of them.

I don't know who makes those rules but we all know them. Certainly if I'd asked, either would have given me money. Maybe that was it. They'd have given it to me, not loaned it to me. They would have been disappointed that I had to ask.

My father's brother was a salt-of-the-earth lawyer in a small town in New York State, fighting petty political corruption and providing free legal services to people who couldn't afford to pay him. He and my aunt never had children and I was the closest thing to a son he had. When he came to visit us when I was a child he would often slip me a five-dollar bill as he was leaving. You don't forget an uncle like that.

In desperation one year, I went to him and asked for five hundred dollars. One of the terrible memories of my life is that I never repaid him. He died three years later without ever having been able to take pleasure from thinking that his favorite nephew was a responsible person. He didn't need the money but he must have looked for some token payment from me and I never made it. I always meant to but I never did.

About fifteen years ago we were doing better but we needed $2,500 to help pay for one of the kids' college tuition and my wife went to the bank for a loan. Banks are a better place to go for a loan than an uncle is. They aren't disappointed if you don't pay them back. They get you.

By this time I was making enough money so we weren't in desperate need of the loan, so as the joke goes, we didn't have any trouble getting it. The interest was probably 7 percent.

A year or so later I asked my wife if we were going to pay off the loan in a lump sum, or just continue paying the 7 percent interest each year. Being in no way a business tycoon, I had the feeling we should pay it off. She does all our bookkeeping and banking, and she didn't think we should.

She was right. I'm not sure to this day if we ever paid off the loan.

Now, of course, I appreciate that it's the only good joke we ever played on a bank. We won because interest rates rose. If we have the $2,500, and it's invested, maybe in the same bank's money-market fund, and we get 9 percent interest, we are beating the bank for 2 percent on $2,500. It is not at all like failing to pay back my uncle.

This all occurred to me today because yesterday an old friend asked me to loan him money. Of course I'll loan it to him but I wish he hadn't asked. It breaks the unwritten law. It changes our relationship. I don't want to think about it every time I see him and I don't want him feeling uneasy about it when he sees me but that's what will happen.

Being broke is a terrible feeling but it's probably an experience everyone ought to have once in a lifetime. If you've never been really broke, you can't possibly understand how nice it is to have a little money in the bank.

A CASH STANDARD

There's something about having a thick stack of money in your pocket that gives you a feeling of wellbeing. I smile more when I have money in my pocket. Even too much change will do it for me if the change is mostly in quarters and quite heavy.

It occurs to me to mention this today because I've noticed that the more money I make, the less I use. I'm talking about actual cash, green paper money. Earlier in the week I took an overnight trip from New York to Washington. Before I left, I cashed a check for a hundred and fifty dollars. When I got back to New York late the next afternoon, I still had more than a hundred dollars. The surprising thing was that I had that little left because I hadn't really paid for anything. The fifty dollars went out in petty cash for tips, taxis and newspapers. I charged my airfare, my hotel room and my meals.

Like most people, when I sign for something on my credit card I consider it to be free. Paying for the item is postponed to some indefinite time in the future. The bill will come in a lump sum and will bear no relationship in my mind to any service or goods that I actually got for that amount.

The trouble with doing all these things with numbers instead of with real money is that it takes the fun and the satisfaction out of the exchange process. What's rewarding is to work hard to make money and then to take that money and buy something with it that makes life pleasant or easier.

There used to be a joke about a wealthy recluse who went to his bank once a week and made them show him his money. He wanted to make sure it was still there.

We all know our money isn't really in the bank, it's in the bookkeeping machinery, but I feel the way that old guy did. I'd like to see my money in real life once in a while. Those numbers they send me aren't any fun at all.

I can't get over how little I see of my money these days. One summer when I was in college I worked at a paper mill for forty dollars a week. Every Friday afternoon they gave me my pay in an envelope and I've never made money that was as satisfying to me as that. I don't care how big my check is, it can't match that forty dollars I got in cold cash.

Today the company mails my check directly to the bank. After a while, the bank mails me a slip of paper saying the check has been deposited. When I owe someone something, I write out a check and my bank deducts that from my account. It's all terribly unsatisfactory. Collecting money or paying it out can be a rewarding experience but bookkeeping is no fun at all. If I had my way, I'd have every penny I earned turned over to me in cash and I'd pay most of the people I owe with the money in my pocket.

I understand perfectly well that it wouldn't be practical sometimes but it would be more satisfactory and, furthermore, if the federal government handled its accounts in cash, there'd be a lot less waste. It's one thing for a government official to sign his name to a piece of paper transferring a billion dollars from one place to another, but it would be quite different if he had to show up with the actual money in dollar bills and hand it over. Just counting it would make everyone think twice and there'd surely be cameras around to record the event.

Money ought to be more tangible than it is today, not less. We're treating it too lightly because we can't see it. I don't understand the ramifications of a return to the gold standard but I have a feeling pennies ought to be copper, dimes ought to be silver and it wouldn't do any harm if we had some little fifty- or hundred-dollar gold coins in circulation. We need money that's really worth something.

The money game is being played with numbers that are too big for most of us to comprehend. Only lawyers, bankers, computer experts and government officials understand money as a statistic. Most of us get no kick at all from a computer printout of a bank's idea of our net worth. What we want is that lump in our pocket.

SAVINGS

How much of your income do you spend and how much do you save for later?

Some of those people who are always announcing things in Washington announced that Americans saved less of what they made last year than they have in all history. The savings figure the Commerce Department gave was 1.9 percent of income after taxes. That means people saved just $19 out of every $1,000.

The experts have a lot of theories, naturally, on why people aren't saving. They say, for instance, that car prices were low and good deals on loans were available so people bought cars instead of saving.

To use a word that was popular among my classmates in high school, "Baloney!" People aren't saving money because when they do, they get taken and end up having less than they started with. The trouble is, there is no longer a good way to save money.

It used to be that people put it under their mattresses, in the sugar bowl or in savings banks, but none of these makes any sense now. Neither the mattress nor the sugar bowl pays interest and the banks don't pay much more. Not only that, people have learned that by the time they want to use the dollars they've saved, their money is going to be worth less than when they stashed it away.

Banks are smarter about money than people are. People have learned that and they're bank-shy. Even though people aren't saving much money, savings banks and other savings businesses are going to make $5 billion in profit this year. That's because of all that mortgage money they loaned out a few years ago at figures like 14 percent. The savings banks are paying something like 5 percent in interest to the people with savings accounts whose money the banks are loaning out now.

A lot of us have had to relearn what our fathers, mothers and Ben Franklin taught us about thrift. We all grew up on phrases like "A penny saved is a penny earned," "Waste not, want not" and "Prepare today for the wants of tomorrow." Savings these days, we've discovered, are better for the bank than they are for us.

When I made money delivering news-papers, my mother got me to open a savings account. Every once in a while I'd put an amount like $1.70 in the bank, and at Christmas I'd add the twenty-five dollars Uncle Bill gave me. My mother said I'd need it to help pay for my college education. Over a period of years I saved $189. The bank gave me $6.25 in interest. The trouble was, by the time I got ready to go to college, tuition, room and board were $2,000 and I realized I might as well have spent my newspaper money on the expensive Duncan yo-yo and the pogo stick I always wanted.

That's what people are doing now. They aren't saving money, they're buying yo-yos with it because they know it's too hard to save.

How do you save? There are thousands of savings institutions keeping a total of $826 billion of Americans' money, but you can bet not many of the executives of those banks keep their money in a low-interest savings account.

I liked the idea of a savings bank. I liked it when I put that $1.70 away with some confidence that I was doing the right and the smart thing. Fortunately for savings banks, they still have $826 billion of our dollars that they can loan out at 10 percent and pay interest on at 5 percent. This is dumb money the banks have, and they have it because it's relatively safe and because a lot of people put it there from habit or because they don't know what else to do.

Many young people today who never had a newspaper route or a piggy bank just say the hell with it. They admit they don't know how they should handle their money so they spend it.

Our whole economy is based on spending and borrowing. You just know in your bones that it's wrong. Someone has to figure a way for us to go back to the honest pleasure of saving for our own futures.

THE ART OF LIVING:
BEING WITH PEOPLE,
BEING WITHOUT

We're all torn between the desire for privacy and the fear of loneliness.

We all want to be part of the crowd one minute and by ourselves the next.

I have wended my hot, weary way back from a crowded convention to the cool, peaceful quiet of my woodworking shop set in the woods one hundred feet from our vacation home.

Today it is unlikely that I will see anyone at all between breakfast and late afternoon, when I shake the sawdust out of my hair and go down to the house for a cool drink and the evening news.

A week ago, I couldn't wait to get to where the action was. Yesterday, I went to considerable trouble and some expense to move my airline reservation up by just two hours.

A week ago, I anticipated the warmth of friendship; yesterday, I yearned for the chilly silence of solitude. At the convention, I had enjoyed a thousand handshakes, a thousand snippets of conversation on several dozen social occasions, but now I wish to be alone with myself, perhaps to finish in my mind those conversations; perhaps to put them out of my mind completely. The great virtue of being alone is that your mind can go its own way. It isn't forced to think along the lines of a conversation you didn't start and the contents of which are of no interest to you.

It is amazing how the same brain that juggles words and ideas while fencing with friends in a crowded room can turn its power to figuring the angle of a cut in a piece of cherry wood that will make the sidepiece of a drawer fit precisely into the dovetailed front.

The conversion from convention reporter and part-time well-known person didn't take long once I got into my old khaki pants. These hands with which I hit the keys already have bits of wood chips stuck to the hairs on the back of them. I shook out my shirt before I sat down at my typewriter because I didn't want to get sawdust down in the cracks between the keys. But I am alone now, and after that hectic week, I treasure these moments of blessed anonymity.

I love being alone. I don't feel the need for anyone. I know it won't last, though. Dangle an event in Los Angeles, in Florida or in Seattle in my face again next week, next month or next year and I'll endure the standing in lines, the crowded transportation, the inconvenience, noise and bustle to get there.

There doesn't seem to be any happy medium between too many people in our lives and too few. We look forward to our children coming home for a visit. They come with children of their own and it soon gets to be a crowd rubbing against itself until there's the irritation generated by friction. They're ready to go; we're ready for them to leave.

I admire people who don't feel the need to see friends on Saturday night or even to mingle with the crowd in the line at the local movie. I associate the desire for privacy with intellect. The people I know who genuinely don't want to go to a party are my smartest friends. We are naturally gregarious creatures and it's the superior people who are so self-contained over long periods as not to need the inconsequential companionship that goes with a party or a night out. We all know a few. They're either super-human beings or they're a little strange. We need each other and we need to get away from each other. We need proximity and distance, conversation and silence.

We almost always get more of each than we want at any one time.

Finding the Balance

This morning I was driving to work at about 6:45, enjoying my own thoughts and the warm red glow just below the horizon, when the weatherman on the radio said the sun would be coming up at 7:14.

"It's gradually getting lighter earlier," Herman said gleefully, as though it were good news.

There's no way to predict what's going to depress us but I suddenly found myself depressed. There were emanations of the arrival of spring in that earlier sunrise. I realized a new season was coming and I hadn't finished enjoying this one.

I savor seasons. I enjoy a good, cold winter with plenty of snow. I don't want a wimpy winter. I don't want winter to last into March but I'm disappointed when we don't get enough cold weather to freeze all the ponds solid or enough snow for skiing and sledding.

It struck me, as I drove with less enthusiasm, that Christmas and New Year's were really over. They'd joined the memories of our past.

We all spend more time preparing for pleasure than we do enjoying it, but still, it's disappointing that we cease to take pleasure from so many things before they're over. Often when I'm in the middle of doing something I've looked forward to doing for weeks, I suddenly realize the enjoyment is over before the event. I'm thinking about what's next.

At a party I'm thinking about going home to bed. In San Francisco I'm thinking about getting back to Connecticut. Monday, I think of the weekend and by Saturday night I'm looking forward to Monday.

At dinner, I often get up from the table before the meal is over to make the coffee because I've already started thinking about dessert.

This morning the first thought of the approaching spring was depressing to me because it reminded me, not of warm weather, but of the passage of time.

I like spring because, among other good things, it means I'll soon be able to get back to my summer workshop, but please, don't rush me. The idea of spring now, in the middle of winter, does nothing but make me think of how short life is. It seems as though I just left my workshop, went to a few football games, did my Christmas shopping and the New Year's party. I'm not ready for another summer so soon.

Maybe we'll get a foot of snow next week that will put these depressing how-time-flies thoughts out of my mind.

It's difficult to get time to pass at the right speed. Sometimes, in the middle of the night, I think time will never move on to morning. Some days, on the other hand, I can't hold time still long enough to do all the things I want to do.

The trick is to get a good balance of activity and inactivity in your life. You need high points to look forward to and back on but you need plenty of time in between for not doing much of anything. Not doing much of anything can be the greatest pleasure of all, if you know how to do it.

The art of living well has its geniuses just as certainly as music, painting and writing well have theirs. The greatest Old Master in the art of living that I know is Walter Cronkite. You know him as a respected newsman but believe me when I tell you his ability to live and enjoy life exceeds his greatness as a journalist. He fills all the days of his life with events, any one of which would satisfy most people for a year.

Walter works and plays at full speed all day long. He watches the whales, plays tennis, flies to Vienna for New Year's. He dances until two A.M., sails in solitude, accepts awards gracefully. He attends boards of directors' meetings, tells jokes and plays endlessly with his computers. He comes back from a trip on the *QEII* in time for the Super Bowl.

If life were fattening, Walter Cronkite would weigh five hundred pounds. He disproves the theory that you can't have your cake and eat it too.

I wish now I hadn't driven in to work this morning and gotten into this whole mess.

THE TRUTH ABOUT LYING

Lies are a part of life. In spite of the admonitions we get beginning in childhood to tell the truth, the whole truth and nothing but the truth, the most honest people among us don't live by that standard. It's too hard.

"How does this look?" a woman asks her husband as they're going out the door to a party. If he's lucky, he genuinely likes what it looks like. If he doesn't he's in trouble because either he has to lie or tell the truth and start the whole evening off on the wrong foot. He not only has to lie but has to add to the deceit by lying enthusiastically. "It's okay" is not enough.

It's at least partly the woman's fault for asking the question in the first place. Samuel Johnson put his finger on the problem when he said "Nobody has the right to put another under such a difficulty that he must either hurt the person by telling the truth or hurt himself by telling what is not true."

Truth has a much better reputation than lying. We propagandize ourselves in favor of it every chance we get. All the wise men have endorsed it:

Plato — "Truth will prevail."

H. W. Shaw — "Truth is the edict of God."

Emerson — "Every violation of truth is a stab at the health of human society."

Woodrow Wilson — "The truth always matches, piece by piece, with other parts of the truth."

Mark Twain — "When in doubt, tell the truth."

In spite of the lip service we pay truth, we spend a lot of time deciding when to lie. It's good that it doesn't come easily or naturally to most of us. We spend even more time trying to determine when we're being lied to and when we're being told the truth.

Advertising puts us to the test and gives us a lot of experience in detecting untruths. We know they lie so how good is this product they're telling us about? And what about politicians? Not many people pick up the newspaper and read a story coming out of Washington without wondering whether they're getting the truth or some altered version of it. The elected official who lies or tells less than the whole truth may, like the husband, believe that it's best for everyone if he doesn't go overboard being honest. He can get himself believing it's best for the American people if they do not know the whole truth. He is not lying for personal gain. This is called "Lying Made Easy."

It is even sadder to consider the possibility that many Americans know it and accept it. They don't want the burden of knowing the truth because they are then confronted with solving some of the problems.

Trying to discern whether we've been lied to or not is complicated when we start considering that maybe we were told part of the truth but not all the truth. Part of the truth is like a lie but worse because it's more devious and more difficult to detect.

As a guest on the Larry King show one night I said some things, in answer to his questions, that I would have been better off lying about or avoiding. My superiors at CBS were angry. It was not that the people who objected to what I said necessarily thought I was wrong. They simply thought I shouldn't have said it. It was, they thought, disloyal to be critical of CBS while I still took a salary from the company.

In my own defense, I told a boss of mine that I thought if all the truth were known by everyone about everything, it would be a better world. He scoffed. I think "scoff" is what he did. I know he rejected the idea.

I've thought about it and in retrospect decided he was right. It was a pompous statement that sounds true but probably isn't. Our lives could not survive all the truth about everything. If my boss asks me about it again though, I'm going to lie and repeat it. I like the sound of it. Maybe I can get my name in Bartlett's *Familiar Quotations* by saying, "It would be a better world if everyone in it knew all the truth about everything."

THE SWEET SPOT IN TIME

I'm lukewarm on both yesterday and tomorrow. Neither science fiction nor nostalgia interests me as much as today. I am tempted by the promise of all the great things coming up tomorrow, of course, and I do enjoy all the good memories and the graceful, simple and efficient artifacts of yesterday, the antiques, but this moment is the moment I like best.

These thoughts inevitably come at Christmas time. It's easy to get sentimental about the memories of Christmases past and years past and the people you spent them with. The advertising for gifts with which to commemorate the season, on the other hand, often emphasizes the new technology. "Buy her a computer, the tool of the future!"

So I feel a certain ambivalence toward both the past and the future. I dislike retyping a piece to correct mistakes or rearrange paragraphs. My son, Brian, said that if I got with it and bought myself a word processor, I wouldn't have to do those things. He said that if I tried one for just a few days, I'd never go back to my ancient Underwood #5.

Well, I did buy a word processor and I've tried it for a year but I still write primarily on my old machine. There are times when it's best for all of us to close our eyes to the future. There's just so much progress we have time for in our lives. Mostly we are too busy doing it the old way to take time to learn a new way. I do close my eyes to progress when it comes to typewriters. This may spring, in part, from a deep feeling I have that it's wrong to try to impose efficiency on a writer.

My antipathy for too much nostalgia can probably be traced to several hundred little antique shops where I have stopped to talk with conniving antiquaries. It seems as though every time people find out there's money in something, they ruin it. The good antique shops are outnumbered by the bad ones.

The revival of the style of the 1920s and 1930s has helped turn me off nostalgia. They call it Art Deco but to me it was the ugliest era that progress ever took us through. It's all phony frou-frou. Its ashtray art and gilded replicas of the Empire State Building put me off. The emphasis was on how it looked and not much on how it worked. Except for being old it has no virtue and it isn't even very old. Being old isn't reason enough to originate a revival of anything anyway. Age is no guarantee of quality in objects or people.

Too many of the revivals in art forms are fads based more on commercial enterprise than artistic worth. Someone stumbles across an obscure style in architecture, painting or furniture practiced by an ap-

261

propriately unknown artist and they revive that style because they know where they can lay their hands on fifty examples of it and make themselves a quick buck. Art doesn't enter into it and nostalgia works as well for the dealer as fear does for the insurance salesman.

It isn't easy to live in the present. The temptation to sit thinking about the past or dreaming of the future is always there because it's easier than getting up off your tail and doing something today.

I love the electronic gadgets that promise a magic future in which we can do the hardest jobs with the touch of a button. It's just that experience has taught me that the promise usually precedes the product by so many years that it's better to put off anticipating it until it's actually in the store window.

I like old movies, old music, old furniture and old books but if I had to choose between spending the day with dreams of the future or memories of the past or this day I have at hand, I think I'd take pot luck with today.

Life, Long and Short

I change my mind a lot about whether life is long or short. Looking back at how quickly a son or daughter grew up or at how many years I've been out of high school, life seems to be passing frighteningly fast. Then I look around me at the evidence of the day-to-day things I've done and life seems long. Just looking at the coffee cans I've saved makes life look like practically forever. We only use eight or ten tablespoons of coffee a day. Those cans sure represent a lot of days.

Used coffee cans are the kind of statistics on life that we don't keep. Maybe if we kept them, it would help give a feeling of longevity. Maybe when each of us has his own computer at home, we'll be able to save the kinds of statistics the announcers use during baseball games.

It's always fun, for instance, to try *to* remember how many cars you've owned. Think back to your first car, and it makes life seem longer. If you're fifty years old, you've probably owned so many cars you can't even remember all of them in order. I've also wondered how many miles I've driven. That's a statistic most people could probably make a fair guess at. If you've put roughly seventy-five thousand miles on twenty cars, you've driven a million and a half miles. You've probably spent something like twenty-five thousand dollars on gas.

It's more difficult to estimate the number of miles you've walked. Is there any chance you've walked as far as you've driven in a car? I'm not sure. You don't go out on a weekend and walk four hundred miles the way you'd drive a car. On the other hand, every time you cross a street or walk across the room, you're adding to the steps you've taken. All those little walks every day must add up to a lot of miles, even if you aren't a hiker.

And how much have you climbed? I must have lifted myself ten thousand miles straight up with all the stairs I've negotiated in my life. There are seventeen nine-inch steps in our front hallway and I often climb them twenty times a day, so I've lifted my two hundred pounds two hundred and fifty feet on the stairs in the house in one day alone. That doesn't include the day I climbed the Washington Monument with the kids or the time my uncle took me up the Statue of Liberty.

And how many pairs of shoes have I worn out walking and climbing all that distance? I'm always looking for the perfect pair of shoes and I've never found them yet, so I buy more shoes than I wear. There must be six old pairs of sneaks of mine in closets around the house. All in all, I'll bet I've had two hundred fifty pairs of shoes in my life. Easy, two hundred fifty.

How long would your hair be if you'd never cut it? Everyone has wondered about that at some time. What length would my beard be if I hadn't shaved every morning? And, it's a repulsive thought, but I suppose my fingernails would be several feet long if I hadn't hacked them off about every ten days. I don't know. Does hair stop growing once it gets a few feet long? I don't ever recall seeing anyone with hair ten feet long. My hair must grow at least an inch a month. That's a foot a year. I've certainly never seen anyone my age with hair sixty feet long.

This is the kind of thinking that helps make life seem longer to me. When I think of how many times I've been to the barber or even to the dentist, life seems to stretch back practically forever.

The one statistic I hate to think about is how many pounds of food I've consumed. Pounds would be an unmanageably large number. I'd have to estimate it in tons. I must have eaten ten tons of ice cream alone in my lifetime.

It makes life seem long and lovely just

thinking about every bite of it.

THE GLORIES OF MATURITY

I don't do as many things I don't like to do as I had to when I was young.

Except that you have more years ahead of you, youth isn't necessarily a better time of life than any other. When I was young, I was always having to do things I hated.

School was harder than work has ever been. I enjoy working and I never enjoyed studying. I liked learning but found the process of education tedious. There are still nights I dream I'm back in school with an exam the next morning. The scenario is always the same. I haven't read any of the books and I skipped class most of the time so I'm totally unprepared for the exam.

Staying up all night to study for an exam was a terrible experience, and I did it a lot in college. My parents and all the teachers said cramming didn't work but they were wrong. It may be the wrong way to learn but cramming is a good way to pass an exam. It just hurts a lot while you're doing it.

I no longer stay up all night for anything. If I have something I should have written and haven't, I go to bed and try to get it

A young Andy outside his home in Albany, New York

done the next morning. If I don't get it done? Sue me.

There is no single thing in my adult life so

regularly unpleasant and burdensome as homework was in my youth. If I bring work home from the office now, it's because the work interests me. It is not drudgery and if I don't feel like doing it, I put it off.

There are still things that come up in my life for which I'm unprepared but they don't bother me the way they did when I was a teenager. They no longer seem like life-or-death situations. If my income-tax stuff isn't all together when I go to my accountant, so what?

Love is more pleasant once you get out of your twenties. It doesn't hurt all the time. I no longer fall in and out of love. I have my love.

As a grown-up, I don't eat things that are good for me if I don't like them. My mother was always insisting that something was good for me and I had to eat it. Now the most I do is try to avoid things that are bad for me. I'm not doing much for the carrot farmers.

Shoveling snow is my idea of hard fun so I shovel snow in the winter, but I've always hated cutting the grass so in the summer I pay someone to do that.

On Saturdays, I always had to stop playing with the other kids and have lunch at twelve o'clock. I still play a lot on Saturdays but I quit playing and come in for lunch when I feel like it. I don't care what time it is.

They can write about the glories of youth but there are advantages to maturity, too. I don't read anything I don't want to read, I don't go places I don't want to go, I don't spend a lot of time talking to people I don't feel like talking to.

I feel no need to wear what the other fellows are wearing, listen to the music other people listen to or go to movies I don't want to see.

Every other Sunday my father and mother would put everyone in the car and drive to Troy to see some relatives. I liked the relatives but I hated ruining Sunday to go see them. I sat on the floor and looked at books while the adults talked. I'm glad I don't have to go to Troy anymore.

When I was drafted into the Army, I detested the discipline. When First Sergeant Hardy M. Harrell ordered me to get rid of the books I kept under my bunk at Fort Bragg, I made the mistake of telling him he didn't like books because he couldn't read. This turned out to be the wrong thing for a private to tell a first sergeant and I spent the next thirty days doing a great many things I didn't like doing.

Now there are books under my bed again.

I'm happy not doing all the things I had to do in the Army.

I offer all this to young people who are wondering about life. Don't think things keep getting worse. Youth can be a terrible time of life just because of all the things you hate to do, but have to do anyway.

PLAIN-SPOKEN WISDOM: TRUST

Last night I was driving from Harrisburg to Lewisburg, Pennsylvania, a distance of about eighty miles. It was late, I was late and if anyone asked me how fast I was driving, I'd have to plead the Fifth Amendment to avoid self-incrimination. Several times I got stuck behind a slow-moving truck on a narrow road with a solid white line on my left, and I was clinching my fists with impatience.

At one point along an open highway, I came to a crossroads with a traffic light. I was alone on the road by now, but as I approached the light, it turned red and I braked to a halt. I looked left, right and behind me. Nothing. Not a car, no suggestion of headlights, but there I sat, waiting for the light to change, the only human being for at least a mile in any direction.

I started wondering why I refused to run the light. I was not afraid of being arrested, because there was obviously no cop anywhere around, and there certainly would have been no danger in going through it.

Much later that night, after I'd met with a group in Lewisburg and had climbed into bed near midnight, the question of why I'd stopped for that light came back to me. I think I stopped because it's part of a contract we all have with each other. It's not only the law, but it's an agreement we have, and we trust each other to honor it: we don't go through red lights. Like most of us, I'm more apt to be restrained from doing something bad by the social convention that disapproves of it than by any law against it.

It's amazing that we ever trust each other to do the right thing, isn't it? And we do, too. Trust is our first inclination. We have to make a deliberate decision to mistrust someone or to be suspicious or skeptical. Those attitudes don't come naturally to us.

It's a damn good thing too, because the whole structure of our society depends on mutual trust, not distrust. This whole thing; we have going for us would fall apart if we didn't trust each other most of the time. In Italy, they have an awful time getting any money for the government, because many people just plain don't pay their income tax.

Here the Internal Revenue Service makes some gestures toward enforcing the law, but mostly they just have to trust that we'll pay what we owe. There has often been talk of a tax revolt in this country, most recently among unemployed auto workers in Michigan, and our government pretty much admits if there was a widespread tax revolt here, they wouldn't be able to do anything about it.

We do what we say we'll do; we show up when we say we'll show up; we deliver when we say we'll deliver; and we pay when we say we'll pay. We trust each other in these matters, and when we don't do what we've promised, it's a deviation from the normal. It happens often that we don't act in good faith and in a trustworthy manner, but we still consider it unusual, and we're angry or disappointed with the person or organization that violates the trust we have in them. (I'm looking for something good to say about mankind today.)

I hate to see a story about a bank swindler who has jiggered the books to his own advantage, because I trust banks. I don't *like* them, but I trust them. I don't go in and demand that they show me my money all the time just to make sure they still have it.

It's the same buying a can of coffee or a quart of milk. You don't take the coffee home and weigh it to make sure it's a pound. There isn't time in life to distrust every person you meet or every company you do business with. I hated the company that started selling beer in eleven-ounce bottles years ago. One of the million things we take on trust is that a beer bottle contains twelve ounces.

It's interesting to look around and at people and compare their faith or lack of faith in other people with their success or lack of success in life. The patsies, the suckers, the people who always assume everyone else is as honest as they are, make out better in the long run than the people who distrust everyone — and they're a lot happier even if they get taken once in a while.

I was so proud of myself for stopping for that red light, and inasmuch as no one would ever have known what a good person I was on the road from Harrisburg to Lewisburg, I had to tell someone.

INTELLIGENCE

If you are not the smartest person in the world, you usually find some way to be satisfied most of the time with the brain you've got. I was thinking about all this in bed last night because I made a dumb mistake yesterday and I was looking for some way to excuse myself for it so I could go to sleep.

The thing that saves most of us from feeling terrible about our limited intellect is some small part of our personality or character that makes us different. Being uniquely ourselves makes us feel better about not being smart. It's those little differences we have that keep us from committing suicide when we realize, early in life, that a lot of people have more brains than we have.

There are two kinds of intelligence, too. One can be measured in numbers from tests but the other and better kind of intelligence is something no one has ever been able to measure. The second kind is a sort of understanding of life that some of the people with the most intelligence of the first type, don't have any of. They may have scored 145 in the I.Q. tests they took in school but they're idiots out in the real world. This is also a great consolation to those of us who did *not* score 145 in our I.Q. tests.

It almost seems as though the second type of intelligence comes from somewhere other than the brain. A poet would say it comes

Enjoying a good laugh with Lesley Stahl, Art Buch-wald, and Mike Wallace (hands clasped); note reads: Andy—Straighten up, dammit! Thanks—Mike

from the heart. I'm not a poet and I wouldn't say that but it does appear as though some of the best decisions we make spring spontaneously to our minds from somewhere else in our bodies.

How do you otherwise account for love, tears or the quickened heartbeat that comes with fear? All these things strike us independently of any real thought process. We don't think things through and decide to fall in love or decide to cry or have our heart beat faster.

There is so much evidence that there's more than one kind of intelligence that we can relax, believing that we have a lot of the less obvious kind. I prefer to ignore the possibility that someone with a higher I.Q. than mine might also have more of the second kind of intelligence. One person should not be so lucky as to have intelligence of both the brain and the heart.

I wish there was some way to decide who the five smartest people are in the world because I've always wanted to ask them the five hardest questions. I haven't decided who the five smartest people are and I haven't settled on all five questions, either.

One question I've considered for my list is this:

"Are people smarter than they were a thousand years ago?"

It's a hard one. Athletes are running faster, jumping farther and lifting heavier weights. This suggests our brains must also be performing better.

On the other hand, are our eyes and ears any better than the eyes and ears of the Romans who watched the lions eat the Christians in the year 200 A.D.? Probably not. My guess would be that our eyes and our ears haven't changed for better or for worse except as we abuse them through misuse.

If our eyes and ears haven't changed in size or improved in performance, the chances are our brains haven't either. I forget when they invented the wheel but did it take any less intelligence to invent the wheel centuries ago than it took this century to invent the windshield wiper, the ballpoint pen or the toaster oven?

It must have been 2:30 before I finally fell asleep.

DIRECTIONS

Early next year I'm going to take a week off and read the directions for all the things I've bought that came with the warning READ DIRECTIONS CAREFULLY BEFORE OPERATING.

There's no sense reading directions to something before you understand a little bit about it, because they don't mean anything to you. You have to know enough about something to be confused before directions help. Once I've pressed some wrong buttons or tried to open something by pressing on it when I should have been pulling on it or sliding it sideways, then I can understand the directions.

I have a whole box of directions I've never read. Many of them are still in their plastic wrappers. When Christmas comes again, I'll probably be getting more. Last Christmas my kids gave me a new camera. I've shot ten rolls of film with it and I've made about all the mistakes there are to be made. It will be fun now to see if the directions have any good suggestions.

It is always surprising to me to see how many issues divide our population almost in half. For example, I think it's safe to say that we are about evenly divided between people who read directions before operating, as they're warned to do under threat of death, and people who don't ever read the directions. The same people who don't read the maps in the glove compartments of their cars are the ones who don't pore over the instructions for operating their new washing machine or video cassette player.

My wife drives a Saab and during the three years we've had it, I've used it a dozen times. For the life of me I can't figure out how the heater works. I almost froze last winter driving into the city one day. This summer I drove in with it on a hot day and fussed with the controls the whole hour trying to get the air conditioning to work. That night I complained to my wife about how complicated the controls were. I said I was going to read the directions about how to work the air conditioning.

"Forget it," she said. "It doesn't have air conditioning."

In spite of some bad experiences, I'm a firm believer in the trial and error method of learning. If I were asked to take the space shuttle into outer space, I'd first want to climb on board and start fooling with the controls before I read anything about it. If I do read the directions about something before I know a single thing about it, I get so discouraged I give up. If, on the other hand, I bumble along making mistakes, confident that I can always look at the directions if I have to, then I usually find out how to do it the hard way.

Direction writers have improved over the years. Even the directions that come with a piece of Japanese electronic equipment are written in better English than they used to be.

You'd think it might be dangerous to ignore written directions but usually those little red tags say something like DANGER: UNDER NO CIRCUMSTANCES SHOULD THIS BE PUT IN A BATHTUB FULL OF WATER!

They warn you against some very obvious things. Most of us know by now that you don't put a toaster in the dishwasher and that you shouldn't drop the television set when you're bringing it in the house. On the other hand, it has been my experience that FRAGILE THIS SIDE UP can usually be ignored with no ill effects. Unless you've bought a cut-glass crystal pitcher that comes filled with champagne, there aren't many things you can't carry upside down.

I'm going to look through my box of directions for the ones about my camera but usually if I really want the directions for one specific piece of equipment, those are the directions I threw out.

THE QUALITY OF MERCY

When a man came and knocked on our back door and asked for something to eat, my mother always fried him two eggs and made him toast and coffee but, no matter how cold it was, she made him eat it outside. Her quality of mercy was tempered with caution.

This was during the Depression in the late 1930s when I was growing up in Albany, New York. There was seldom any question that the man was anything but hungry. He was not looking for money with which to buy whiskey. All the man ever wanted was food. I remember asking Mother why no women ever came begging for food. She didn't know.

All this came flooding back to me last evening when I was standing in line at Grand Central Station to buy a train ticket. There were five or six people in front of me and the line was moving slowly. I contemplated switching to another line, but experience has taught me this is usually a mistake so I started reading my newspaper.

In the middle of a paragraph, I sensed someone standing next to me. I looked up and into the eyes of a small young woman wearing a belted trench coat that wasn't very clean. She had straggly, dark blond hair and, while she was not unattractive, she appeared to be no cleaner than her coat.

"Could you spare a quarter?" she asked.

She said it perfunctorily, in a manner that suggested she'd said it thousands of times before. "No," I said, without malice. I looked into her eyes but didn't get any feeling I was seeing her. There was a curtain behind the cornea so I turned back to my newspaper. I wasn't reading it anymore, though.

"No" had not been exactly the right answer, I thought to myself. Of course, I could have spared a quarter. I must have had nearly fifty dollars in my pocket, three of them in change.

Why hadn't I given this poor soul something? Or is she a poor soul?

Where did she come from? I wondered. What are her parents like? What did her classmates in school think of her? Does she have friends? When did she eat last? Where did she sleep?

If it was peace of mind I was looking for, it would have been easier to give her the quarter. I can't get her out of my mind and yet the people who drop change in cups and hats anger me. It seems like cheap gratification that does more for the psyche of the giver than the receiver. I don't like their smug assumption that they are compassionate people.

I pretended to be reading the paper for thirty seconds more and then looked up to see where the young woman had gone. She was standing a short way off, on the heartless marble floor of the station, doing nothing. I thought how close to barefoot she looked in her thin, old leather shoes.

Most beggars in New York City are either con artists or alcoholics. She didn't seem to be a con artist or an alcoholic, and I don't know what someone looks like who's on drugs or smoking marijuana. You can't make enough begging to be a drug addict, anyway. Drug addicts steal. She didn't look like a thief.

There aren't a lot of beggars in New York but there are all kinds, and every passerby has a decision to make. The black kids stand at the clogged entrance to the bridges and tunnels and slop soapy water on your windshield with a dirty sponge. If you give them a quarter, they clean it off. If you don't, they don't. I'm torn between compassion and anger at times like this. It's blackmail but it's better than stealing and I laugh and give.

The ordinary street beggar will not be helped by what anyone gives him, though. And, anyway, I have the feeling the saddest cases and the ones who need money most desperately don't beg for it.

Everyone in New York is approached at least once a month. You have to have a policy. Mine is simple! To beggars on the street, I give nothing. I wish I was certain I'm right, I keep thinking of the young woman in Grand Central and the two fried eggs.

Morning People and Night People

Are you consistently dumber during some hours of the day than others? I certainly am. I'm smartest in the morning. You might not think so if you met me in the morning, but that's the fact. After about 11:30 A.M., my brain begins getting progressively duller, until by late afternoon I can't remember my middle name. It is morning as I write. My middle name is Aitken.

Each of us has his best hours. The people who have to have a cup of coffee to activate their brain in the morning are the slow starters. I have a cup of coffee to get my body going, but my brain starts up without it.

It's always best if what we are coincides with the way we wish we were. It doesn't happen often to most of us, but both morning people and night people seem to be pleased with themselves the way they are.

I know I'm pleased to be a morning person. I think it's best. I associate it with virtue. It works out best for me, too. Not perfect, but best. I get to work very early, taper off around noon and have a very unproductive period between about 1:30 and 4:30. Unproductive periods are important too, you know.

Somewhere around 4:30, my brain begins to stage a mild comeback, but by then it's time to quit and go home.

I feel sorry for the people who think best in the evening and I'd like to tell you why. Night people awaken grudgingly. They dread getting up but eventually drag themselves out of bed, put themselves through their morning ablutions and stumble to work hating every minute of it. By noon their metabolism is finally moving at the same speed as the current of activity that surrounds them and they begin to blend in. It is now lunchtime.

In the early evening, after the sun has gone down and the rest of the world is settling in, they're ready to go. They waste some of their smartest hours, when they should be most productive, watching some of the dumbest shows on television.

Prime-time television was designed for those of us who are smartest in the morning. By 8 P.M., we've lost most of our critical faculties, and "Dallas" and "Laverne and Shirley" are just perfect for our level of intellectual activity. Even if we don't like them, they don't bother us enough to make it worth our while getting up to turn them off.

The night people sit there doing the crossword puzzle or reading the paper and grumbling because there's nothing on the tube worth watching.

It seems apparent to me that we ought to rethink the whole pattern of our daily lives. We've got to make some changes.

If each of us really does need seven hours' sleep, it would probably be better if we took it in shorter periods. I often get more sleep than I need or want all in one piece during the night. Even when I go to bed at 11:30 and get up at 5:45, which is my habit, there's something wrong with just lying there in one place for six hours and fifteen minutes.

I'll bet it would be better for both our brains and our bodies if we took our seven hours in sections instead of all at once. Say we slept for three hours between 1 A.M. and 4 A.M., two hours from noon until 2 P.M. and another two hours between 7 P.M. and 9 P.M. This would give us the same seven hours, but better distributed over the twenty-four-hour period.

There are some problems that would have to be worked out, of course. The reason all of us now try to get what is known as "a good night's rest" is not because that's the way our bodies like it, but because the whole civilized process of going to bed and getting up is such a time-consuming activity that we couldn't afford to do it three or four times a day. And, of course, if it took the night people a couple of hours to get going again after each sleep period, they'd be less help than they are now. A personal opinion, you understand.

And, of course, there are other questions that would have to be resolved. When, for instance, would we change our underwear, take a shower and make the bed?

THE SOUND OF SILENCE

There's no telling what wakes you on those nights you can't sleep. Last night, I awoke at 2:20. It was the sound of falling snow that did it. I knew it was snow because there was not a single, solitary sound. The silence of falling snow is deafening.

I lay there for several minutes, trying to breathe quietly so as not to obliterate the soundlessness. Finally, I couldn't handle my doubt any longer. I got up (I'm fighting off "arose"), pulled back the curtain and looked out on the backyard. Sure enough, there it was — gently falling snow hitting the ground silently, covering the little slate walk and clinging, half an inch thick, to tiny branches that are themselves no more than half an inch thick. It perched on top of the points of the picket fence in a beautifully symmetrical peak that no human hand could fashion. They say no two snowflakes have ever been the same but we don't know, do we? I saw two that looked very much alike.

There are all kinds of sounds in nature that are better than noise. Some sounds are good or bad depending on where you are and what you're doing when you hear them. Nothing is worse than a downpour of rain when you're caught out in it without a coat or umbrella. But inside, the sound of the same downpour is a pleasure that makes you appreciate your shelter.

Of all the sounds combining weather with nature, none is so persistently loud and impossible to turn off as the roar of the sea rolling up onto a broad, sandy beach. I envy people who live on expensive property near the ocean. There's the roar as thousands of tons of water advance on a broad front along the width of the beach, or the crash when the waves hit the immovable rocks that cup the shoreline at either end of a sandy crescent. There is the soft, seething sound as the water recedes. It pauses briefly out at sea, gathering strength for its next attack. A beach confounds angry waters by accepting them and defeating their destructive intentions, waiting patiently for the waves to go back where they came from, out to sea.

The heat of summer is as silent as snow but it's an oppressive silence. There is no pleasurable relief from heat comparable to the great feeling of pulling up the extra blanket on a cold night. Air conditioning is a modern marvel but it is loud, heartless and mechanical, with no charm. I don't like it but I don't know how we ever lived without it.

Wind is nature's most unpredictable sound. You never know for sure what it's doing, where it's coming from, or where it's going when it leaves. It's going somewhere but while it blows, it seems to stand still. The trees in front of my house are miraculously strong standing up to the wrath of a gale. The trunks creak, the branches crack, but the big maple has stood through hundreds of storms since it was a slip of a tree whipping in the wind fifty years ago. The tree will, in all probability, survive many more years.

My perfect day would be to awaken to a cool and sunny day with a sun that shone in the kitchen window while I ate breakfast. I'd take my own shower under circumstances that improve on nature's showers by allowing me to control the force and temperature of the spray with the twist of a dial.

By the time I sat down at my typewriter, which is not a typewriter at all any longer, my ideal day would be cloudy with a threat of rain that discouraged my considering even grocery store travel and encouraged this kind of overwriting.

THE SEARCH FOR QUALITY: WHERE ARE ALL THE PLUMBERS?

For the past few days I've spent most of the time in my woodworking shop making a complicated little oak stool for Emily.

I like the whole process of writing but when I get back there in my workshop, I notice that I'm quite contented. Yesterday I worked until 2:30 before I remembered I hadn't eaten lunch. It even has occurred to me that I could give up writing and spend the rest of my life making pieces of furniture that amuse me. Who knows? I might get good at it.

It's a mystery to me why more people don't derive their satisfactions from working with their hands. Somehow, a hundred or more years ago something strange happened in this country. Americans began to assume that all the people who did the good, hard work with their hands were not as smart as those who worked exclusively with their brains. The carpenters, the plumbers, the mechanics, the painters, the electricians and the farmers were put in a social category of their own below the one the bankers, the insurance salesmen, the doctors and the lawyers were in. The jobs that required people to work with their hands were generally lower-paying jobs and the people who took them had less education.

Another strange thing has happened in recent years. It's almost as though the working people who really know how to do something other than make money are striking back at the white-collar society. In all but the top executive jobs, the blue-collar workers are making as much as or more than the teachers, the accountants and the airline clerks.

The apprentice carpenters are making more than the young people starting out as bank clerks. Master craftsmen in any line are making $60,000 a year and many are making double that. In most large cities, automobile mechanics charge $45 an hour. A mechanic in Los Angeles or New York, working in the service department of an authorized car dealer, can make $60,000 a year. A sanitation worker in Chicago can make $35,000 a year. All this has happened, in part at least, because the fathers who

Hard at work in his woodworking shop in Rensselaerville, New York

Ellen Rooney

were plumbers made enough money to send
their children to college so they wouldn't
have to be plumbers.

In England, a child's future *is* determined
at an early age when he or she is assigned
either to a school that features a classical
education or one that emphasizes learning a
trade. Even though we never have had the
same kind of class system in America that
they have in England, our lines are drawn,
too. The people who work with their hands

as well as their brains still aren't apt to belong to the local country club. The mechanic at the car dealer's may make more than the car salesman, but the salesman belongs to the club and the mechanic doesn't.

It's hard to account for why we're so short of people who do things well with their hands. You can only conclude that it's because of some mixed-up sense of values we have that makes us think it is more prestigious to sell houses as a real-estate person than it is to build them as a carpenter.

To further confuse the matter, when anyone who works mostly with his brain, as I do, does something with his hands, as when I make a piece of furniture, friends are envious and effusive with praise. So, how come the people who do it professionally, and infinitely better than I, aren't in the country club?

If I've lost you in going the long way around to make my point, my point is that considering how satisfying it is to work with your hands and considering how remunerative those jobs have become, it is curious that more young people coming out of school aren't learning a trade instead of becoming salesmen.

ON CONSERVATION

My grandfather was right and wrong about a lot of things, but he was never undecided. When I was twelve, he told me we were using up all the good things on earth so fast that we'd run out of them.

I've worried about that. I guess we all have, and I wonder whether it's true or not. The real question is, will we run out of the things we need to survive before we find substitutes for them? Of course, we're going to run out of oil. Of course, we're going to run out of coal. And it seems very likely that there will be no substantial forests left in another hundred years.

Argue with me. Say I'm wrong. Give me statistics proving there's more oil left in the ground than we've already used. Tell me there's coal enough in the United States to last seventy-five or a hundred years. Make me read the advertisements saying they're planting more trees than they're cutting.

I've read all those arguments and I'll concede I may be wrong in suggesting impending doom, but if doom is not exactly impending, it's somewhere down the line of years if we don't find replacements for the basic materials we're taking from the earth. What about five hundred years from now if one hundred doesn't worry you? What about a thousand years from now? Will there be an oak tree left two feet in diameter? How much will it cost in a hundred years to buy an oak plank eight feet long, two inches thick and a foot wide? My guess is it will cost the equivalent in today's money of a thousand dollars. A piece of oak like that will be treasured as diamonds are treasured today because of its rarity.

I don't think there is a more difficult question we're faced with than that of preservation. A large number of Americans feel we should use everything we have because things will work out. They are not necessarily selfish. They just don't believe you can worry about the future much past your own grandchildren's foreseeable life expectancy. They feel someone will find the answer. Pump the oil, mine the coal, cut the trees and take from the earth anything you can find there. There may not be more where that came from, but we'll find something else, somewhere else, that will be a good substitute.

The preservationists, on the other hand, would set aside a lot of everything. They'd save the forests and reduce our dependency on coal and oil in order to conserve them as though no satisfactory substitutes would ever be found.

It's too bad the argument between these groups is as bitter as it is, because neither wants to do, intentionally, what is wrong. The preservationists think business interests who want to use what they can find are greedy and short-sighted. Businessmen think the preservationists are, in their own way, short-sighted. (One of the strange things that has happened to our language is that people like the ones who run the oil companies are called "conservatives," although they do not approve of conserving at all.)

All this comes to me now because I have just returned from Hawaii and seen what havoc unrestricted use can bring to an area. To my grandfather, Honolulu would probably look like the end of the world if he could see it now.

We have just about used up the island of Oahu. Now we're starting on Maui. Is it right or wrong? Do the hotels crowded along the beach not give great pleasure to large numbers of us? Would it be better to preserve the beauty of Hawaii by limiting the number of people allowed to be there? Would it be better if we saved the forests, the oil and the coal in the world and did without the things they provide? If there is middle ground, where is it?

The answer will have to come from someone smarter than I am. I want to save oil and drive a big car fast, I want to cut smoke pollution but burn coal to save oil, and I want to pursue my woodworking hobby without cutting down any trees.

Design

Last summer I made a chair. The wood was maple and cherry, and I invented what kind of a chair it was as I went along. When I finished, the chair looked great, but it has one shortcoming. It tips over backwards when anyone sits in it.

My design was better than my engineering.

Most of us are so engrossed in whatever it is we do with our days that we fail to consider what anyone else is doing with theirs. I attended a meeting in Washington, D.C., a short time ago and everyone there but me was a designer of things. I never knew there were so many. I came away realizing that designing what a product will look like is a substantial part of any business. There are thousands of people who spend their lives doing it.

Everything we use has been designed, well

or poorly . . . your car, your toaster, your watch. When Alexander Graham Bell finished inventing the telephone, all he had was wires. Someone had to decide on the shape of the instrument it would be housed in, and they came up with that great old standup telephone. That was industrial design.

There is usually trouble between engineers and designers. Most designers are creative artists who tend to ignore the practical aspects of a product. Most engineers, on the other hand, don't usually care much what a product looks like as long as it works.

The only time the consumer wins is when design and function blend together in one harmonious unit that looks great and works perfectly. We know it doesn't happen often.

A lot of artists who can't make a living selling their paintings or anything else that is commonly called art often turn to commerce. Sometimes they are apologetic about having to make a living, but they ought not be. If they are bad artists that's one thing, but if they are competent or even talented artists they ought to take a lot of satisfaction from being able to provide the rest of us, who don't have their talent, with some visual niceties. Making the practical, everyday world good-looking is not a job to be embarrassed about.

It may even be that industrial design and commercial art are more important than art for art's sake. Art always appeals to me most when it has had some restrictions placed on it. I like art that solves a problem or says something a new way. Uninhibited, free-form, far-out art never seems very artistic to me. Artists who can do anything in the whole world they want to do don't usually do anything. Even Michelangelo was at his best when he had a ceiling to paint.

The danger industrial designers face is that they'll be turned into salesmen. The first rule of industrial design should be that the product must look like what it is, not like something else. If something looks like what it is and works, it's beautiful and no amount of dolling it up will help it. This accounts for why bridges are so attractive to us. The best bridges are built from plans that come from some basic engineering principle that hasn't been altered by a salesman who thinks he could get more people to cross it by making it a different shape. I always liked the Shredded Wheat box for the same reason.

The best-designed packages are those whose first priority is to contain the product. The ones we are all suspicious of are the packages that are too big and too fancy for what they were built to contain. We are tired of false cardboard bottoms and boxes twice as big as they need to be to hold something.

The original green six-ounce Coca-Cola bottle was one of the great designs of all time. It was perfect in almost every way and has, naturally, been all but abandoned. The salesmen took over the bottle from the designers, and now it's too big or not a bottle at all.

I hope our industrial designers can maintain their artistic integrity, even though they have turned to commerce, because what worries me about all this is the same thing that worries me about that chair I made. Too often we're making things that look better than they are.

QUALITY?

It is unceasingly sickening to see someone make a bad product and run a good one out of business. It happens all the time, and we look around to see whose fault it is. I have a sneaking feeling we aren't looking hard enough. It's *our* fault, all of us.

If it isn't our fault — the fault of the American people — whose fault is it? Who is it that makes so many bad television shows so popular? Why were *Life, Look* and the *Saturday Evening Post* driven out of business in their original forms while our magazine stands are filled with the worst kind of junk? Why are so many good newspapers having a tough time, when the trash "newspapers" in the supermarkets are prospering? No one is forcing any of us to buy them.

Around the office I work in, they changed the paper towels in the men's room several months ago. The new ones are nowhere near as good as the brand they had for years, and it takes three to do what one of the old ones would do. Somebody in the company decided it would look good if they bought cheaper paper towels. It is just incredible that smart people decide to save money in such petty ways.

I had a friend whose father owned a drugstore in a small town in South Carolina. It was beautifully kept and well run. My friend's father was an experienced druggist who knew the whole town's medical history. During the 1950s, one of those big chain drugstores moved in selling umbrellas, plastic beach balls, tote bags and dirty books, and that was the end of the good, honest, little drugstore.

We are fond of repeating familiar old sayings like "It's quality not quantity that matters," but we don't buy as though we believe that very often. We take the jumbo size advertised at 20 percent off — no matter what the quality is. I'm glad I'm not in the business of making anything, because it must be heartbreaking for the individual making something the best way he knows how to see a competitor come in and get rich making the same thing with cheap materials and shoddy workmanship.

America's great contribution to mankind has been the invention of mass production. We showed the world how to make things quickly, inexpensively and in such great numbers that even people who didn't have a lot of money could afford them. Automobiles were our outstanding example for a long time. We made cars that weren't Rolls-Royces but they were good cars, and just about everyone could scrape together the money to buy one.

Somewhere, somehow, we went wrong. One by one, the good carmakers were driven out of business by another company making a cheaper one. I could have cried when Packard went out of business, but there were thirty other automobile makers that went the same way, until all that was left was General Motors, American Motors,

Chrysler and Ford. And in a few years we may not have all of them.

We found a way to mass-assemble homes after World War II. We started slapping them up with cinder block and plywood, and it seemed good because a lot of people who never could afford a home before were able to buy them.

They didn't need carpenters who were master craftsmen to build those homes, and young people working on them never really got to know how to do anything but hammer a nail.

We have a lot to be proud of, but there is such a proliferation of inferior products on the market now that it seems as though we have to find a way to go in another direction. The term "Made by hand" is still the classiest stamp you can put on a product and we need more of them. We need things made by people who care more about the quality of what they're making than the money they're going to get selling it.

It's our own fault and no amount of good government, bad government, more government or less government is going to turn us around. The only way we're going to get started in the right direction again is to stop buying junk.

Signed by Hand

The other night I was sitting looking at a brick wall in the living room of some friends. It has become popular to tear the plaster off old brick walls of houses in downtown areas of big cities, and leave the mellow, irregular shape of old red brick exposed. It adds warmth and charm to a room.

The house was something like 125 years old and the wall must have gone up with the house. Many of the bricks weren't perfectly oblong, being handmade, and you could see that the bricklayer had a problem getting the whole thing plumb and square.

It was a great brick wall though, and the people who owned the house had derived a great deal of pleasure from it over the years. There were pictures hung on it, a mirror, pieces of brass and some cherished old family china plates. They loved it.

Who built the wall? I wondered. Who spent months of his life putting up that wall, trying to make a perfect wall out of bricks that were not perfect? Who did this laborer's work of art? I asked my friends if they knew.

They beckoned me to come to a remote corner of the wall over by the door and near the baseboard. There, scratched in the ancient mortar that still held the bricks

A contemplative Mr. Rooney, armed with a pen, ready to strike

together, was the name "T. Morin."

Maybe signed work is the answer to getting better workmanship again. Everything that anyone makes should have his or her name on it for praise or blame and reference. Work is frequently so anonymously done that the workman has no reason to identify with it and be proud of it. If everyone is going to know who made it, the person making it will be more careful.

I can understand why people don't always put their names on their work. The workman is seldom completely satisfied with what he's done. The man who built the brick wall in my friends' house was proud enough to want his name there for the life of his wall but modest enough not to want it in a prominent place.

During World War II, I stayed in the home of a British aircraft worker in Bristol, England. The British aircraft engines had a reputation for being the best. When the man came home from work one night, we talked about what he was doing.

"Me and my buddies are making an engine," he said.

And that's what he meant. He and two other men were actually assembling from scratch an engine for a Spitfire fighter plane. They were intensely proud of their work and you can bet the RAF fighter pilot who sat in the cockpit with a Luftwaffe F-W 109 in the sights of his guns had confidence his airplane wasn't going to let him down.

Each Rolls-Royce, the best automobile in the world, is still made by hand by just a few men, not on an assembly line. The work on that airplane, or on a Rolls-Royce, is a long way from the work on the U.S. planes that are reported to have been made with bogus parts. Fake parts might get past an assembly line worker. They wouldn't get past one man making an engine.

Everything should be signed by the people who make it. We live in a house that was built about one hundred years ago. We have raised four children in it. I know every nook and cranny, every strength, every defect it has. I know the beams in the basement, the rafters in the attic. I know the crack between the foundation and where the cellar steps lead down into my workshop — but I don't know who built the house. This is wrong.

Every builder of every house should be compelled to attach his name, in some permanent but inconspicuous way, to that house . . . for better or for worse.

What we need in our country is fewer mile-long assembly lines turning out instant junk and fewer "project" builders turning out ticky-tack houses by the hundreds. We need more builders of solid brick walls willing to put "T. Morin" on their work.

LOYALTY

For years I kept my money in the same bank and filled my car at the same gas station. I liked the idea that I was loyal.

Over the years there's been a big turnover in bank personnel, and it occurred to me that when I went there, no one in the bank knew I was a loyal customer but me. It was the same with the gas station. I flattered myself into thinking they appreciated my business. When they gave me my change and said, "Thank you, have a nice day," I thought they were thankful and wanted me to have a nice day because I was such a good customer. Several years ago I realized I was kidding myself. The gas station had changed hands three times, and they didn't have the vaguest idea that I'd been buying my gas there for seventeen years.

Lately I've been banking and buying gas at my own convenience. I buy gas at the station nearest me when I need it or I drive to one I know is a penny cheaper. I've changed banks twice recently because they opened a branch a block closer to my office. Give me a toaster or move in next door and you have my allegiance. Loyalty got me nowhere.

I suppose both gas stations and banks would object to being linked together, but they serve the same purpose in my life. When I run out of gas or money, I have to go to a place where I can get more. Gas stations used to compete for my business by offering free air, free water and a battery and oil check. Now you're lucky if the attendant bothers to put the gas cap back on.

Banks used to care about my business. They knew me. I didn't have to bring my birth certificate, a copy of my listing in *Who's Who,* and four other pieces of positive identification to cash a check for twenty-five dollars. If I wrote a check for more money than I had, Mr. Gaffney used to call and sound real angry. But he *did* call. He knew where to find me. No one at the bank knows me anymore. I went in yesterday to pick up a new Master Charge card that was supposed to be there, but they wouldn't give it to me because I hadn't brought the letter with me that they sent saying the card was ready.

If the bank doesn't know me by name, the feeling's mutual, because I don't know my bank's name anymore, either. It usually changes before I've used up all the checks they've sent me with the old name on it. My bank seems to keep acquiring other banks — with my money, I suppose — and they throw the other bank a bone by putting some little part of its name in with their primary name.

My bank's name was originally the Chemical Bank, plain and simple. They changed it to Chemical National Bank, then Chemical Bank and Trust Co., then they acquired the Corn Exchange Bank and my checks said the Chemical Corn Exchange Bank. I always liked that best, but it didn't last. They bought another bank, dropped the "Corn" and called themselves Chemical Bank New York Trust Co. This was unwieldy, and I was pleased several years ago when they renamed the bank once again. The new name? The Chemical Bank.

There is a bank in New York called the Irving Trust Company, and I've always sort of hoped they'd buy my bank and call it Irving's Chemical Bank.

It's too bad everything is as big and impersonal as it is now. I'm sorry to have lost personal touch with the people running the establishments where I do business, but if they don't care, I can't afford to be sentimental. When I was a little boy, we patronized Evans Grocery Store. It had oiled wood floors, and Mr. Evans always gave me a free candy bar when I brought him the check for the month's groceries. The supermarkets were just getting started, and eventually, of course, they ran almost all the little neighborhood grocery stores out of business. My mother kept buying things from Mr. Evans, even though the same loaf of bread was two cents cheaper at the new supermarket. She wanted to help him survive, but apparently the two cents wasn't enough, because he didn't make it for long. He never got to be Evans New York Chemical Corn Grocery Store.

On Home and Family: A Nest to Come Home To

Everyone should have a nest to come home to when the public part of the day is over. Having a little room with a comfortable chair to settle into is important. You should be surrounded by familiar things. You can talk or read or watch television or doze off but you're in your basic place. You're home and you don't have to watch yourself.

I'm not sure the furniture stores and the room designers are in tune with what most Americans want. We've never had a designer design anything in our house. It's all happened by accident. I like our house a lot better than I like those rooms I see in magazines that have been put together by designers. They look more like the rooms they have just outside the men's room or the ladies' room on the ballroom floor of an expensive hotel. There isn't a decorator who ever lived who could surround me with the things I like to have around me in my living room.

Decorators go for fuzzy white rugs that show the dirt, glass-topped tables you can't put your feet on and gilt-edged mirrors that only Napoleon wearing his uniform would look good in.

I like to have the windows covered so the neighbors can't see in and I agree you shouldn't just cover them with newspaper but it's very easy to carry curtains too far. When strangers come into your living room and say right away how nice the curtains are, then you know you've gone too far with the curtains. Friends who come to your house once in a while should not be able to remember what the curtains look like.

It must be difficult to sell furniture. No one in a store would sell you a chair in which the springs were beginning to sag but most chairs aren't very comfortable until that begins to happen. No one wants to pay a lot of money for a secondhand piece of furniture and yet furniture looks better when it has a well-worn look.

My green leather chair is eighteen years old now and the rest of the family complains about what it looks like but I notice they take every chance they get to sit in it. I don't take that chair when I come into the room

315

because I'm the husband or the father. I sit in that chair because it's *my* chair. It's as much mine as my shoes. If they want one like it they can have one but I like a chair I can call my own. Familiar things are a great comfort to us all.

When the Christmas catalogs begin to come in and there's a noticeable increase in the amount of mail coming into the house, I usually make a decorating change of my own. I move another little table over by my chair so I have a table on either side of me. It's a temporary thing for one time of year. When the Christmas cards start coming, I have a better way of separating the cards from the bills and the junk mail from the personal letters. If you keep the newspaper, the mail, a letter opener, a glass, scissors, three elastic bands, some paper clips, some loose change, the television guide, two books and a magazine next to you, one table next to your chair isn't enough at Christmas.

When I sit down in my chair at night, it's the one place in the world I have no complaint with. It's just the way I like it. I'm wearing comfortable clothes, my feet are up and I'm surrounded by things that are there because I choose to have them there.

I was telling my wife how quickly and how well American soldiers make a nest for themselves, no matter what their circumstances are. They can be out in a field somewhere but first thing you know they've dug a foxhole and invented some conveniences for themselves out of empty coffee cans and cardboard containers. They've made that one little spot in the world their own. It's true but I never should have told my wife.

"That's what this place looks like," she said, "a foxhole."

REAL REAL ESTATE

When the real-estate people talk about space in houses, they put too much emphasis on the number of bedrooms and bathrooms and too little on how much stuff the kitchen counters will hold.

If we ever have to move out of our house it would be because we've run out of places in the kitchen to put all the pots, pans and electrical appliances we've bought or been given for Christmas. Things are approaching the crisis stage now on our kitchen counters. I don't buy sliced bread, and it's getting very difficult to clear enough space to operate with a bread knife.

In addition to running out of counter space, we're running out of places underneath the counter to put pots, pans and a wide variety of culinary miscellany. When we had the kitchen redone five years ago, we made sure we had plenty of storage space for pots and pans under the counter, but that was five years ago. The pots have expanded to fit the space available to them and now we have more.

It's the odd-sized, odd-shaped pots and pans that are most difficult. There are things we don't use more than twice a year taking up valuable real estate under the kitchen counters but I don't know what to do with them. Where do you keep the fluted cake pans, the cookie cutters, a pressure cooker, Pyrex dishes, big baking pans for the turkey, a fondue pot, the cast-iron popover pan and the muffin tins?

We need double the number of electrical outlets on the back wall of the counter.

Let me see if I can make a list of the major items on the counters without going upstairs to the kitchen to look. The kitchen counters now hold: a toaster-oven, a blender, a heavy-duty mixer, an electric can opener, one orange-juice squeezer, a Cuisinart, a radio, one small black-and-white TV.

Don't tell me some of these items are repetitious because I know it, but if you're given a Cuisinart you can't throw it away even if you have a Mixmaster and a Waring blender.

In addition to these electrical devices, there are, below the counter, a pancake grill, a waffle iron, an egg poacher that hasn't poached an egg in twelve years, an electric fry pan, a deep fryer we never use and a small ice-cream freezer. Pushed to the back is an electric knife that I've only used twice although it was given to us by a relative who now has been dead for nine years.

It's apparent we need either a great deal more counter space in the kitchen or we need someone to invent a compact combination radio-TV-toaster-oven that would open cans, squeeze oranges, whip egg whites and mix cake batters.

I have my house, but my advice to anyone about to buy a new one is to ask some questions beyond how many bedrooms there are. Don't think you're smart because you've asked about the type of heating and the amount of insulation. Ask the real-estate salesperson some really hard questions. Ask, for instance, how much room is left on either side after you've put two cars in the two-car garage.

Have the real-estate salesman demonstrate how to put the vacuum cleaner away in a closet that's already full of heavy winter coats and leaves for the dining-room table.

Ask the person selling you the house where you're going to put the wheelbarrow and the snow tires and try to figure out where you'd hang the leaf rakes and the shovel.

Look at the new house carefully and estimate how far you're going to have to carry the garbage can to get it to a place near the road where the garbagemen will take it . . . then figure out where the garbage can is going to go when it isn't by the edge of the road. Measure the distance between the big outside garbage can and the little inside garbage can that you have to empty into it.

Measure everything and make sure you know where you're going to be able to store the screens and the screen door when you replace them with the storm doors and the storm windows.

HOME

One Saturday night we were sitting around our somewhat shopworn living room with some old friends when one of them started trying to remember how long we'd lived there.

"Since 1952," I said. "We paid off the

mortgage eight years ago."

"If you don't have a mortgage," he said, "the house isn't worth as much as if you did have one."

Being in no way clever with money except when it comes to spending it, this irritated me.

"To whom is it not worth as much," I asked him in a voice that was louder than necessary for him to hear what I was saying. "Not to me, and I'm the one who lives here. As a matter of fact, I like it about fifty percent more than I did when the bank owned part of it."

"What did you pay for it?" he asked.

"We paid $29,500 in 1952."

My friend nodded knowingly and thought a minute.

"I'll bet you," he said, "that you could get $85,000 for it today . . . you ought to ask $95,000."

I don't know why this is such a popular topic of conversation these days, but if any real-estate dealers are reading this, I'll give them some money-saving advice. Don't waste any stamps on me with your offers to buy. You can take me off your mailing list.

Our house is not an investment. It is not a hastily erected shelter in which to spend the night before we rise in the morning to forge on farther west to locate in another campsite at dusk. Our house is our home. We live there. It is an anchor. It is the place we go to when we don't feel like going anyplace.

We do not plan to move.

The last census indicated that forty million Americans move every year. One out of every five packs up his things and goes to live somewhere else.

Where is everyone moving to? Why are they moving there? Is it really better someplace else?

If people want a better house, why don't they fix the one they have?

If the boss says they're being transferred and have to move, why don't they get another job? Jobs are easier to come by than a home. I can't imagine giving up my home because my job was moving.

I have put up twenty-nine Christmas trees in the bay window of the living room, each a little too tall. There are scars on the ceiling to prove it.

Behind the curtain of the window nearest my wife's desk, there is a vertical strip of wall four inches wide that has missed the last four coats of paint so that the little pencil marks with dates opposite them would not be obliterated. If we moved, someone would certainly paint that patch and how would we ever know again how tall the twins were when they were four?

My son Brian has finished college and is working and no longer lives at home, but his marbles are in the bottom drawer of his dresser if he ever wants them.

There's always been talk of moving. As many as ten times a year we talk about it. The talk was usually brought on by a leaky faucet, some peeling paint or a neighbor we didn't like.

When you own a house you learn to live with its imperfections. You accommodate yourself to them and, like your own short-comings, you find ways to ignore them.

Our house provides me with a simple pleasure every time I come home to it. I am welcomed by familiar things when I enter, and I'm warmed by some ambience that may merely be dust, but it is our dust and I like it. There are reverberations of the past everywhere, but it is not a sad place, because all the things left undone hold great hope for its future.

The talk of moving came up at dinner one night ten years ago. Brian was only half-listening, but at one point he looked up from his plate, gazed around the room and asked idly, "Why would we want to move away from home?"

When anyone asks me how much I think our house is worth, I just smile. They couldn't buy what that house means to me for all the money in both local banks.

The house is not for sale.

STRUCK BY THE CHRISTMAS LULL

A strange lull sets in sometime during the afternoon of Christmas Day in our house.

The early-morning excitement is over, the tension is gone and dinner isn't ready yet. One of our problems may be that we don't have Christmas dinner until about six. We plan it for four but we have it at six.

The first evidence of any non-Christmas spirit usually comes about one o'clock. We've had a big, late breakfast that didn't end until 9:30 or 10: 00 and the dishes for that aren't done until after we open our presents.

Washing the breakfast dishes runs into getting Christmas dinner. The first little flare-up comes when someone wanders into the kitchen and starts poking around looking for lunch. With dinner planned for four o'clock, there's no lunch on the schedule. Margie's busy trying to get the cranberry jelly out of the molds and she isn't interested in serving lunch or having anyone get their own. To her, at this point, food means dirty dishes.

It isn't easy to organize the meals over a Christmas weekend. Everyone is always complaining about eating too much one minute and out in the kitchen looking for food the next. We might be able to get away with just two meals if we had Christmas dinner at two. I forget why we don't but we don't.

We have thirteen people this year. The lull will strike them all but each will handle it differently.

A few will sit around the living room. Someone will decide to tidy up the place by putting all the wrapping paper and ribbons in a big, empty box that held a Christmas present a few hours earlier.

I don't do any of this because I love the mess. As soon as you clean up the living room, Christmas is over.

At one end of the couch, someone will be reading the newspaper. It's usually pretty thin. There isn't much news and very little advertising. One of the editors has had a reporter do the story about what the homeless will be having for Christmas dinner at the Salvation Army kitchen, but it's slim pickin's in the paper.

The Rooney clan with friends, circa 1983; behind Marge (seated) are daughter Martha and son Brian (with moustache); to Andy's left are daughters Ellen and Emily

My sister Nancy sits there reading out Christmas cards and looking at presents given to other people that she missed when they were being opened.

There are usually a few nappers. Someone will hog the whole couch by stretching out and falling asleep on it. The smart, serious nappers will disappear into an upstairs bedroom.

One of the kids will be working on or putting together a present he or she got. Someone will be reading a new book. (No one watches television in our house on Christmas Day.)

At some point there's a flurry of phone calls, in and out. We'll start making calls to other members of the family who can't be there or who are close but not in our inner circle. Usually one of the twins' classmates will call to see if they can get together during the few days they're both in town.

There's always someone who wants to know if the drugstore is open. They don't really want anything, they're just looking for some excuse to get out of the house.

If I've been given some new tool, I go down to the basement and try it out on a piece of wood. That's usually interrupted by a call from the head of the stairs asking if I want to go over to the indoor courts and play tennis. I'm always touched by the fact the kids want me to play tennis with them. It wouldn't be because I pay for the courts, would it?

By about four o'clock the Christmas Day lull is over. We all congregate in the living room again to have a drink. Nancy has slow-baked almonds and pecans that have been kept hidden from Brian and Ellen all day.

Everyone's relaxed again now. Dinner's

Andy and Marge Rooney, at home in Rowayton, Connecticut

ready but a Christmas dinner can be put on hold, so there's no rush. A turkey is better left at least half an hour after it comes out of the oven before it's carved. Mashed potatoes, creamed onions and squash are all easy to keep warm. The peppermint candy cane ice cream stays frozen.

I hate to have Christmas end.

AN APPRECIATIVE HUSBAND'S GRATITUDE

Wives do a thousand little things for their husbands that they don't get credit for.

Right here I want to give credit where credit is due. A few weeks ago, while I was away, Margie did something for me I'll never forget. She cleaned up my shop in the basement. She got our friend Joe to come in and help and between them they tidied up everything. It must have taken several days because it would have been impossible to put that many things in places where I can't find them in less than several days.

I confess that the shop would have looked as though it was a mess to anyone but me. To me, everything was in its place. I had little scraps of wood everywhere. If I use six feet of a seven-foot piece of maple, I don't throw away the leftover foot. I save it. I don't always put my scraps of wood away neatly in a pile of other scraps, but I know where they are. Now my scraps of wood are in neat piles. I can't find them, but they're neatly piled.

I would be the first to admit that I'm not neat. (Come to think of it, I was not the first to admit it. Other people have said it several hundred times before I ever did.)

My wood treasures, pieces of lumber, were leaning against the basement walls or were stashed up in between the beams under the dining-room floor upstairs. Because there were years of accumulated sawdust everywhere, Margie and Joe moved everything. Margie said she was afraid of fire, but if the house had burned down, it wouldn't have disrupted my shop any more than the cleaning job did.

There were dozens of different sizes of nuts, bolts, nails and screws on my workbench. When I wanted one I pawed through the pile until I found the size I wanted. No longer. Now only the three of them — Margie, Joe and God — know where anything is. Margie's out shopping, I don't know where Joe is and God has more important things to do than tell me where they put my dovetail jig.

All those nuts and bolts and screws are in dozens of little jars with tops on them now. When I want one, I dump them out of the jar onto my workbench and paw through them just like before.

Tools like chisels and screwdrivers were lying helter-skelter on my workbench. No longer. Margie put each and every item somewhere. That's the key word. Everything is "somewhere."

I go to the bottom of the cellar steps and yell up, "Hey, Margie! Where did you put the chuck key to my drill?"

"I put it right there somewhere," she yells back in obvious irritation over my lack of appreciation for the work she did.

She hung hammers, saws and extension cords. She put two tri-squares down behind some cans on a shelf. I found my level in a box over by the shelves with the paint. Margie and Joe piled my lathe chisels under my workbench and put my drill bits — well, actually I don't know where they put my drill bits, because I haven't found them yet.

Listen, it's just another reason to thank her. Most of those bits were dull anyway, so I went out and bought a set of new ones.

How can I ever express my appreciation for the job Margie did? I've been considering some ways. Margie does all our bookkeeping in what used to be the twins' room. Her papers are spread out all over several tables and desks and piled on the little couch that pulls out and turns into a bed at Christmas when everyone's home. I think that one of these days I'll repay Margie's kindness. I'll pick up her workroom the way she picked up mine. I'll pile all her papers, government forms, tax receipts and bank records, and put them in boxes. I'll tidy up. I'll try and make that room as spick-and-span and free of anything out-of-place as Margie made my shop.

There must be a rule of life here somewhere. I think the rule may be, "It may be a mess, but it is MY mess."

MY HOUSE RUNNETH OVER

Let me tell you a heartbreaking story of
people with no place to sleep at Christmas.

Once upon a long, long time ago there
was a house on a hill owned by a writer and
his wife. They had four children and five
bedrooms. Three of the children were girls
and one was a boy. Two of the three girls
were twins and sleeping accommodations in
the house were ample.

Ah, but that was long ago. The house still
has five bedrooms but since Margie took
over one of them as her workroom, the bed
that was there has been replaced by a
convertible sofa that is only made into a
double bed in an emergency and even then
the foot of it hits her file cabinets.

Two of the remaining four rooms have
single beds. The other bedroom sleeps two.
Counting the convertible couch, this makes
places for eight sleepers.

Our four children come from London,
Los Angeles, Boston and Washington for
Christmas. They are no longer little kids
and they don't come alone. The twins, with
one husband each and three children between them, come as seven. Nancy, my

The Rooney children; from left to right: Brian, Ellen, Emily, and Martha

sister, is with us.

To save counting, that's twelve in all . . . twelve people in a house with real sleeping places for eight.

The couch in the living room and the old couch that was retired to the catch-all room in the basement are pressed into service. That's ten. I've never gotten into the details of where the others go. We close our bedroom door and hope for the best. We have two television reporters in the family but we've never seen overcrowding in the shelters they do stories about at Thanksgiving that can compare with the squalid conditions in our house at Christmas. It's enough to bring tears to a grown man's eyes.

There are clothes, open suitcases everywhere. The three bathrooms are strewn with stray toothbrushes, hair dryers and an assortment of beauty products . . . although I can't tell from looking at any of the six women in the house which one uses them. The refrigerator, the washing machine and the dryer get heavy use. The iron is never cool. Someone is always washing himself, herself, hair, clothes or the car. Because of nighttime sleeping conditions, there is random couch-napping during the day and some of the beds are working more than eight-hour shifts.

One year we rented two hotel rooms and another year we used the house of friends who graciously offered it while they were away for Christmas. Neither of these alternatives is popular with the family members who have to leave the chaotic, friendly warmth in our house Christmas Eve to go to sleep in a strange place.

All things come to an end and I dread the

end of Christmas at our house. I'm not sure how or when it will come. Someone will probably decide it's too hard. The friends who loaned us their homes have made the Big Switch. They now go to the home of one of their children for Christmas. It could happen to us, I suppose. One more husband, one more wife or another grandchild might do it . . . but then where does everyone go? Do we break up the family and have separate Christmases in different parts of the country? Would this really be as merry? Am I suffering post-Christmas depression? I've thought a lot about it and I've decided what I want for Christmas next year.

I'd like Santa to bring me an addition to our house with two more bedrooms and another bathroom, even though they'd be empty 363 days a year.

MOTHER

My mother died today.

She was a great mom and I am typing with tears in my eyes. There were a lot of things she wasn't so good at, but no one was ever better at being a mother.

She never wanted to be anything *but* a good mother. It would not satisfy many women today. If I were a woman it would not satisfy me, but there was something good about her being one that exceeded any good I will ever do.

I think I know why she was a world champion mother. She had unlimited love and forgiveness in her heart for those close to her. Neither my sister nor I ever did anything so wrong in her eyes that she couldn't explain it in terms of right. She assumed our goodness, and no amount of badness in either of us could change her mind. It made us better.

Mother gave the same love to our four children and even had enough left for our family bulldog, Gifford. One summer afternoon at her cottage in a wooded area with a lot of wildlife, some food was left on the table on the front patio. When we came back later, part of it had been eaten, and everyone but Mother suspected our bulldog.

"It couldn't have been Gifford," Mother said. "It must have been some animal."

From the day she went into the hospital, there was never any question about her living. The doctor treated her as though she might recover, but he knew she would not. I hope he is treated as well on his deathbed.

Something has to be done about the way we die, though. Too often it is not good enough. Some of the people who have heard of Mother's death at age ninety-three and knew of her protracted illness said, "It's a blessing," but there was nothing blessed about it.

For seven terrible weeks after a stroke, Mother held on to life with a determination she would not have had if she hadn't wanted to live.

Visiting her, at first, I was pleased that she seemed unaware of anything and not suffering. I would bend over, stroke her hair, and whisper in her ear, "It's Andrew, Mom." It would not seem as though she heard, but her hand, which had been picking at the blanket in a manner distinctively her own, groped for mine. She did hear. She did know. She was in a terrible half-dream from which she could not arouse herself. She was suffering and in fear of death, and I could not console myself that she was not.

My wife stood on the other side of the bed. They got along during the twenty years Mother lived with us. Mother lifted her other hand vaguely toward her. Dying, she wished to include my wife, who had been so good to her, in her affection.

Something is wrong, though. She has something in her throat, or one of her legs is caught in an uncomfortable position. You don't dare touch anything for fear of disconnecting one of the tubes leading from the bottles hanging overhead into her. The nurses are busy with their bookwork, or they are down the hall working routinely toward Mother's room. Other patients there are caught or choking, too. The nurses know Mother will probably not choke before they get there. They've done it all before.

The nurses are very good, but without apparent compassion, and you realize it has to be that way. They could not possibly work as nurses without some protective coating against tragedy. We all have it. In those seven weeks Mother lay dying, I visited the hospital fifty times, but when I left, it was impossible not to lose some of the sense of her suffering. I knew she was still lying there picking vaguely at the blankets in that sad, familiar way, but it didn't hurt as much as when I was there, watching.

I wondered — if she was the President of the United States, what extraordinary measures would they be taking for her? How could I get them for her? She is not President, she is only my mother. The doctors and nurses cannot know that this frail, dying old woman did a million kindnesses for me. They wouldn't know or care that she was girls' high-jump champion of Ballston Spa in 1902 or that she often got up early

Sunday morning to make hot popovers for us or that she drove her old Packard too fast and too close to the righthand side of the road. No stranger would have guessed any of those things looking at her there and perhaps would not have cared.

There is no time for each of us to weep for the whole world. We each weep for our own.

GRANDFATHERHOOD

It seems to me that grandfathers are a lot younger than they used to be before I got to be one.

When I had a grandfather, all grandfathers and grandmothers were born at that age. It seemed as though they had always been what they were, grandmothers and grandfathers. They were kindly old folks and their grandchildren could do no wrong in their elderly eyes.

I guess I haven't taken naturally to being a grandfather. I have no interest whatsoever in being a lovable, gray-haired old codger who approves of everything his grandchild does.

Up until last week, I thought of Justin as my daughter's son. I had seen him for a day or two five or six times a year since he was born six years ago, but I'd never spent an extended length of time with him. Either his father or his mother had always been present when Justin was at our house.

Last week was different. Margie and I had this cute little blond, brown-eyed person with us all week. I seemed to have him more than Margie when I was there because he wanted to do what I was doing. I was trying to enjoy what little's left of my vacation in my workshop. If I hammered, he wanted to hammer. If I sawed, he wanted to saw. It's one-hundred-percent impossible to accomplish anything in a workshop with dangerous tools and a grandchild who insists on being there with you.

"Are we going to do our work?" he asked as soon as he got up every day. Some work.

I kept waiting to feel like a regular grandfather. I kept waiting to excuse him when he did something dumb or thoughtless. Instead, I found myself treating Justin more like a person than a grandchild. I was liking him more and more as a little friend.

The only thing this kid seemed to remember me for from last summer was that I got up early and made him pancakes for breakfast. Naturally, everyone else thought that was cute so I had to get up early this year and make him pancakes for breakfast, too.

Giving granddaughter Alexis Perkins a tow from the tractor in Rensselaerville, New York

Ellen Rooney

Elephants and grandchildren never forget.

I spent quite a bit of time with Justin, trying to break him of his eating habits. He must have gotten them from my daughter Martha, or his father, Leo. He never got them from me. I never saw a young boy so interested in fruit and vegetables and so uninterested in candy, soft drinks or junk food. I don't know what's wrong with him, anyway.

He doesn't want ice cream. The next thing he'll be telling me is he doesn't want anything for Christmas. I queried Martha about

341

his aberrant behavior in regard to food, trying to determine how in the world this kin of mine ever got off on the wrong foot by not liking ice cream. Can they get government help for a condition like this?

I remember enough old Art Linkletter shows to know that kids ask a lot of cute questions, but I was unprepared for those Justin asked.

During a long drive over country roads to the grocery store, the sun shone in his eyes. I had a baseball cap with a long peak on it in back of the car and I suggested he put it on. First, he put it on straight but the sun was still hitting his face so directly that he pulled the cap down over his eyes and was looking through the woven fibers of the dark blue material.

"Hey, Granddad!" he said suddenly. Even though there were only two of us in the car, it took me a minute to realize he meant me.

"What's all these colors?" he asked. "I see all colors. What makes all the colors, Granddad?"

I knew instantly I was about to fail my first quiz as a grandfather. I know that the light from the sun contains every color in the spectrum and I know that under certain circumstances it's possible to bend light beams so that the colors break down and separate. The process is called refraction. I know that but I can't explain it.

I can't figure out how Justin learned how to be a grandchild faster than I learned how to be a grandfather.

SIMPLE PLEASURES:
A TRIP TO THE DUMP

The President says this country is in desperate need of a moral revival. He isn't the first one to say it, either. Almost anyone who says anything has been saying it for years. The trouble is, no one knows how to revive us morally.

I have a simple idea that might just do the trick. I say we should all take our own garbage to the dump. Every able-bodied person in the country would set aside an hour twice a week to dispose of trash and garbage. There would be no exceptions. The President would pack up whatever waste was produced in the private rooms of the White House and take it to the dump just like the rest of us. A President should keep in touch with reality, too.

Going to the dump is a real and exhilarating experience. It is both satisfying and educational. It makes you acutely aware of what you have used in your home and what you have wasted. There's no faking it with garbage.

In a family, dump duty would be divided up. The kids would take their turns going to the dump with the adults. A kid can get to be voting age without knowing that the wastebasket or the garbage pail isn't the end of the line if he or she has never been to the dump. Children too young to drive would, of course, be accompanied by an adult to the dump.

The first thing you realize when you go to the dump is that we should be a lot more careful in separating what professional garbage collectors call "wet garbage" and just trash. All garbage is not the same. Trash is cans, bottles, papers, cardboard boxes and broken electrical appliances. "Wet garbage" comes from the kitchen.

Next, you have to get over that natural feeling of revulsion that garbage tends to induce. Keep in mind that coffee grounds, watermelon rinds, potato peels and corn-cobs were not revolting before we made them what they are today and mixed them together in our garbage pail. Think of them separately and in their original state and make a little game of breaking down the odor into its component parts.

It is possible to be overcome by a sense of

your place in history at the dump. You are, at that moment, a part of the future of the universe. You are helping to rearrange the planet Earth. Man has always considered himself separate from Nature but a trip to the garbage dump can make him aware that he is not. In the millions and millions of years Earth has existed, there have been constant changes taking place. You probably live in a city that was once a lake or an ocean. The mountains you see may have had their cliffs sheared clean by a glacier when it moved relentlessly through your area an eon ago, dropping rich, loamy topsoil in the valley when it melted. Now, like the glaciers, you are doing your part to rearrange the location of the elements on Earth.

Little by little, we are taking up material from the ground in large amounts in one place, making something of it, shipping it across the country to other places, using the things, turning them into trash or garbage and burying them in ten thousand separate little piles called dumps in other places. In the process, we often ruin both places, of course, but that's another story.

If being in on this cosmic kind of cosmetics doesn't interest you to think about the dump, there are other pleasures. There is a cathartic pleasure to be enjoyed from getting rid of stuff at the dump and there is a camaraderie among neighbors there that doesn't exist at the supermarket. Everyone at the dump feels he is doing a good and honest thing and it gives him a warm sense of fellow feeling to know that others, many with more expensive cars, are doing the same grubby, down-to-earth job.

Nowhere is morality higher in America than at the dump Saturday morning and I recommend a trip there as a possible cure for what so many people think ails America, morally.

VACATION

May and June are the months I enjoy my vacation the most.

My vacation doesn't begin until July but looking forward to it is the best part.

Once a vacation begins, I can't keep myself from counting the days until it ends and that diminishes the pleasure of it. It always goes so fast. I can remember thinking that when I was eight. In July the sun starts coming up later and going down earlier. There's a depressing dwindling sense about the afternoon shadows in late July. It's no longer Spring. The longest day of the year should be in August, not June.

The end of my vacation hangs over my head in July like the income tax deadline in April or a dental appointment in January. As the days dwindle down (to a precious few), it's depressing to realize that what I've been looking forward to for so long is almost over.

There are some things you can do to lengthen your vacation. Or, at least, give it a sense of length. For instance, it's best if you don't have dates when you have to do something or go somewhere. Dates that interrupt a month make a vacation shorter. If it's interrupted by someone's wedding in another city or by a dental appointment, it divides your days off into little compartments. A good vacation is one during which nothing happens so eventful that you can remember it when you get back to work and people ask, "What did you do on your vacation?"

We start going to our summer house on weekends in May and keep on going weekends right through September but for all of July and for three or four days I steal on each end of the month, we're there seven days a week. No commuting. We have an extra bedroom so we can accommodate guests but I don't like having guests during my vacation. If we have friends come to visit

With twin daughters, Emily and Martha

us, it's usually on weekends before or after my July vacation. That way, they don't interrupt my vacation. I like having them, mind you, but not during my vacation.

There's a big difference in guests. I like the ones who get up when they feel like it without worrying about "what time do you have breakfast?"

I like guests who don't want to do what I

want to do but feel free to wander off on their own. When people are visiting, I don't want to be a tour director. The best guests do what they feel like doing. After breakfast, they may volunteer to drive over and get the newspapers twelve miles away and not show up until several hours later for lunch. I am very fond of guests who enjoy a nap after lunch. If they want to play tennis towards mid-afternoon, that's fine. If it isn't too hot, I'll join them unless they're really good — in which case I'll get someone else to play with them.

Book-readers make good guests. They don't want you to bother them with suggestions like, "Would you like to walk down to the lake?" or, "There are some good antiques shops in Schuylerville." They're engrossed in their book. The man who won't move from in front of the television set while there's a ballgame on makes a satisfactory weekend visitor.

I'm hoping no one we invite to stay with us is going to read this but I don't like guests who stand around asking whether there's anything they can do. If someone asks whether there's anything he or she can do, there almost never is because the people who ask that question aren't the kind of people who know how to do anything.

There shouldn't be many decisions to make on vacation. It's best when the biggest question you have to answer during the day is "What do you want for dinner?" or "Do you need anything at the store?"

Every year I bring several boxes of letters and miscellaneous pieces of paper from my office to go through. I have never yet gone through them. That's what a vacation is for — not doing things.

NAPPING

You're certainly not interested in how I sleep, but I'm going to tell you only because you'll relate it to yourself or to the people you know well enough to know how they sleep.

There aren't many things I do really well but when it comes to sleeping, I'm one of the best. If sleeping was an Olympic event, I'd be on the U.S. team.

Coming home from a trip recently I got on the plane, strapped myself in and fell asleep before takeoff. As always, I didn't wake up until the flight attendant shook me to ask if I was comfortable. Keep in mind, the flight was at 9 A.M., and I'd just had a good night's sleep.

Nothing seems to bother some people

Enjoying one of life's greatest, simplest pleasures

when they sleep, and I'm one of them. I can eat dinner, drink two cups of strong black coffee and drop off thirty seconds after I hit the pillow. One of the few things that keeps me awake is decaffeinated coffee.

If the village fire alarm goes off in the middle of the night, I awaken easily, try to determine where the fire is and then drop back off to sleep in a matter of seconds.

Some people sleep faster than others. I'm a very fast sleeper. I can nod off for three minutes and wake up as refreshed as though I'd had eight hours. Some people can lie around in bed for nine hours and get up sleepy. I awaken instantly, going full speed.

We probably ought to sleep more often and not for so long. The trouble is, once the bed is made, we can't get back in it, and during the day most of us get so far from our beds that it wouldn't be practical, anyway. It might pay off for a company to have a room with cots where employees could take a nap. Companies have cafeterias and bathrooms, why not a dormitory bedroom? If employees got an hour for lunch, they could divide it any way they liked between eating and sleeping.

Naps are underrated. I don't know why we dismiss napping as an inconsequential little act. The word itself doesn't even sound important. I think everyone should get off his or her feet and lie down for a few minutes at some point during a long day.

Staying in bed for eight hours a night, on the other hand, seems wasteful to me. It's like overcharging a battery. At some point, it doesn't do any good. Most people who sleep eight hours stay in bed because they don't want to get up, not because they need the sleep. Taking all your sleep in one piece doesn't make any more sense than eating too much but only eating once a day.

Napping got a bad reputation somewhere along the line and I resent it. For some reason, people who don't nap feel superior to those who do. Nappers try to hide it. They don't let on that they drop off once in a while because they know what other people will say.

"Boy, you can really sleep," or, "Look at him. He sleeps like a baby." It isn't much, but there's just a touch of scorn in the voice.

People who are awake feel superior to people who are asleep because sleeping people usually don't look so good. It's a rare person who looks or acts as well asleep as he or she does awake. You don't have any control of your face muscles, your jaw is apt to drop open and your hair is a mess. You look just the opposite of the way you look standing in front of a mirror with your hair combed and your clothes all together just before you leave the house for work. You can bet the President doesn't look too good when he's asleep. Even Miss America would probably be embarrassed to have a picture of herself taken while she was unconscious.

I'd like to form an organization of good sleepers and nappers. We'd demand the respect we deserve. We are people who dare drop off for a few minutes in the middle of the day. We're an oppressed minority and we're tired of it. Nappers of the world, unite!

WASTEBASKETS

What would you say are the ten greatest inventions of all time?

The wheel would have to be high on the list and so would the engine, steam or gasoline. The printing press, radio, airplane, the plow, telephone, cement, the spinning wheel, the automobile and now I guess you'd have to include the computer. How many's that?

You can make your own list but don't count discoveries. Discoveries are different from inventions. Nuclear energy, for instance, isn't so much an invention as it is a discovery, like electricity or fire.

The propeller to drive a boat is a good invention although you wouldn't put it in the top ten. Someone just suggested the zipper. I reject the zipper. It's a handy gadget but it's a gadget.

One of the things you never see mentioned in the schoolbooks when they talk about inventions is, in my mind, one of the greatest developments of all time. It is the wastebasket. I could live without laser beams, the phonograph record or the cotton gin, but I couldn't do without a wastebasket.

If some historian wishes to make a substantial contribution to the history of mankind, he or she might find out who invented the wastebasket. It is time we had a National Wastebasket Day in that person's honor.

There are four important wastebaskets in my life although we have nine altogether in our house. The four are in the bedroom, the kitchen, the room in which I write at home and my office away from home.

Day in and day out, I can't think of anything that gives me more service and satisfaction than those wastebaskets.

I begin using a wastebasket early in the morning. When I'm getting dressed and I get ready to put the stuff on top of my dresser back in my pants pocket, I go through it and sort out the meaningless bits of paper I've written meaningless notes on. Those I throw in the wastebasket in order to give my pockets a clean start for the day. I make room for new meaningless bits of paper.

In my writing room, nothing is more important to me than my wastebasket. This essay takes only three pieces of paper, typed and double-spaced when it's completed. You might not think so from some of the things you read in it but I seldom finish an essay in fewer than ten pages. You get three and the wastebasket gets seven.

The kitchen wastebasket is the only controversial one. Margie and I don't always agree on what goes into it. There's a fine line between what goes into the garbage can and what goes into the wastebasket.

The young people of today have television but one of the things they're missing is the experience of burning the papers in the backyard. It was a very good thing to do because it was fun, and while you were doing it you got credit for working.

Most towns have ordinances prohibiting the burning of papers now. I approve of the law but I sure miss burning the papers. Taking the wastebaskets downstairs and out into the garage to dump them into the big trash container that the garbage man picks up is not nearly so satisfying a way of disposing of their contents as burning them used to be.

In recent years there's been an unfortunate tendency to make wastebaskets more complicated and fancier than is necessary. Many of the good department stores and fancy boutiques have made them into gifts. A wastebasket is not a proper gift item. Many wastebaskets in these places have been decorated with flowers or clever things painted on them. A wastebasket doesn't want to be clever and it doesn't want to be

357

so cute or gussied up that it calls attention to itself, either. Wastebaskets should be inconspicuous.

You can make your own list of the ten greatest inventions of all time but leave a place for the wastebasket.

WOOD

It was almost dark when I got to the country last weekend but I couldn't keep from going up to my woodwork shop and turning on the lights for a look around before I unpacked the car.

The sliding barn-type door rumbled on its wheels as I pushed it open wide enough to walk in. Even before I hit the light switch, I loved it. The blend of the fragrance of a dozen kinds of wood went down into my lungs with my first breath of the air inside. The smell had been intensified by the whirling saw blade as I'd shoved the wood through it the previous Saturday. The teeth had turned the kerf into tiny sawdust chips, and those thousands of exposed pores had been exuding the wood's fragrance while I'd been gone all week.

My shop is equipped with good tools but there is nothing merely good about my wood. The wood is magnificent. I've owned some of it for twenty years and will, in all probability, never have the heart to cut into a few of the best pieces.

I sat for a minute on a little stool in front of my workbench. It suddenly struck me as death-sad that in two weeks, three at the most, we'd close up the house for the winter and I'd have to lock up and leave my wood. It would lie there alone all winter, the great smell that emanates from it gradually dissipating into thin air without ever being smelled by a human being. Such a waste.

I looked at my favorite piece of walnut, the one taken from the crotch of a hundred-year-old tree.

"What are you going to make out of that?" people ask me when I show it to them.

Make out of it? They don't understand. It already has been made into one of the most beautiful things in the world, a wooden board.

Look at it! Its grain and the pattern of growth are as distinctive as a fingerprint and ten thousand times prettier. Its colors are so complex they do not even have names. Brown, you say? Are there a thousand colors named brown?

My production of tables, chests, chairs and beds has been severely limited over the years because of my reluctance to cut a piece of my wood into smaller pieces. I have nine cherry planks twenty-five inches wide, fourteen feet long and an inch thick. There are any number of things I could make out of them but I like them better as boards than I would as furniture. To me, they're already works of art that exceed anything I might make out of them.

I wish there were an American Society for the Prevention of Cruelty to Trees. Too many people are using wood to heat their homes. I hate to see an oak or maple log sawed into eighteen-inch lengths and then split for firewood.

A piece of oak or maple, walnut, cherry, even simple pine is more beautiful to me than any painting. From time to time, I've suggested we might replace some of the paintings in our living room with pieces of wood from my collection. I've had no luck with the idea.

It would be relatively easy to attach little eye screws to the backs of boards so they could be hung like pictures from the living room walls. I wouldn't trade my cherry boards for Whistler's Mother.

When I first began to like wood, I was attracted to exotic species. Wherever I could find them I bought teak, rosewood, padauk and a wide variety of mahogany. My taste in wood has become more sophisticated now, though, and I find those exotic woods to be out of place in America, so far from where they grew. Now I look for good pieces of native American hardwood.

A good piece of wood is beautiful and strong and it does what you wish to do with it. Do you wish to make a chair? A table? Perhaps you are skilled enough to make a violin. Maybe you want to build a house, a seesaw, a boat or a fence.

I turned out the light in the shop, filled the cart with the junk in the car and went down to the house. It's going to be hard to leave my wood for the winter.

An All-American Drive

In 1966 I sold a magazine article for $3,500. It was what people used to call "found money," because I was already making a living, so I splurged with it. I bought a sports car, the aging American boy's dream. The car was a Sunbeam Tiger and it cost just about the whole amount, $3500, and it was some hot little car.

Twenty-six years later, my little Tiger, painted British Racing Green, with its huge 289-cubic-inch Mustang engine, will still blow past almost anything else on the road, although I don't drive it that way. You couldn't buy it from me for $50,000, because there's nothing I could get for $50,000 that I'd enjoy so much.

I don't drive it more than ninety days out of the year because I put it up during the winter, not wanting to subject it to the deleterious effects of ice and salt on the roads.

An enterprising group at my college, Colgate University, organized a reunion last summer of everyone who had ever played football there. I can take or leave most reunions, but this one sounded like fun and Hamilton, New York, is only a few hours from our country home. I set out early one morning to drive the 120 miles in my top-down Tiger.

I haven't felt so free-as-a-breeze as I felt on that drive in a long time. I had no obligations to anyone. It didn't matter what time I got there so I couldn't be late, and I didn't have to do anything when I arrived except eat, drink, and enjoy seeing old friends.

I went with Robert Frost and chose the road less traveled. I took the small, winding, blacktop country roads for most of the trip.

There are a lot of people with things to sell on our roadsides these days. I suppose I

Andy in his prized Sunbeam Tiger with his grand-children; Alexis Perkins (front); Ben Fishel (left) and Justin Fishel (right) (back)

passed fifty garage sales, lawn sales or tag sales. We've all bought more than we need or can use over the years and we're looking for a way to unload them on unsuspecting passersby who think, as we did when we bought them, that they're treasures.

There doesn't seem to be much difference between a garage sale, a lawn sale and a tag sale. I passed one sign that said:

TODAY! LAWN SALE IN GARAGE IN BACK

A great many people must have bought new lawnmowers this year because I passed at least fifteen secondhand mowers with FOR SALE signs on them. Even though it was a summer day, there were electric and gas-driven snow-removal machines, too. We had so little snow the previous winter that a lot of people obviously decided those machines weren't worth the space they were taking up in their garage.

There were places that had signs out front saying ANTIQUES, but it didn't look to me as though they had anything very old in them. Most of what they were selling could have been in a tag sale. Half dozen of the so-called antique stores had wagon wheels out front to lend authenticity to their claim of having antiques inside. I went in a few but I didn't buy anything. Most of what they were selling for antiques would have been called junk if I'd had it in the back of my garage or in the basement.

The towns and villages I drove through were not wealthy, but every one had at least two churches and some as many as four. They had just built a new church in Winfield but I couldn't see what denomination it was. I don't think it's important. Most of the churchgoers in town probably believe pretty much the same thing no matter which church they go to. The difference between a Baptist and a Methodist or a Presbyterian and a Catholic in America's small towns is more social than philosophical.

It's too bad religions can't get together and share a building. They'd have better churches that way. That's how the great cathedrals of Europe were built. Everyone in town pitched in. Americans like their individual little churches, though, no matter how plain they are and there's a case to be made for preferring one to a Gothic cathedral.

It was Founders' Day in Sharon Springs. The fire trucks were assembling at one end of town for a parade with odds and ends of uniformed people. As I drove slowly through town, I passed perhaps thirty people seated at intervals on folding chairs, along the main street, waiting for the parade to troop by. I didn't stay to watch, but it looked to me as though there were going to be more people in the parade than on the sidelines watching it.

I passed several hospitals and entertained fleeting sad thoughts about pain, unknown to me, behind their windows. I thought how much better a time I was having than the patients inside. I thought how strange it was that we could be so close and yet so remote in spirit from one another.

Several communities had kiosks set up as

you entered town, with signs saying: TOUR-
IST INFORMATION. It has been my
experience that the booths that offer tourist
information are usually closed.

I was having a wonderful time enjoying
America from the cockpit of my Tiger. It all
looked like a cover on an old *Saturday
Evening Post.* I suppose someone else, driving in the other direction, looked at this old
guy in his green sports car and fitted me in
as part of the Norman Rockwell look, too.

I don't remember what the article was
about that earned me $3,500. But the times
I've had with the Tiger have been worth far,
far more.

CHRISTMAS TREES

The people who think Christmas is too
commercial are the people who find something wrong with everything. They say, for
instance, that store decorations and Christmas trees in shopping areas are just a trick
of business.

Well, I'm not inclined to think of them
that way, and if there are people whose first
thought of Christmas is money, that's too
bad for them, not for the rest of us.

If a store that spends money to decorate
its windows has commerce in mind, it

doesn't ruin my Christmas. If I pay nine cents more for a pair of gloves from one of the good stores that spent that much decorating its windows to attract me inside to buy them, I'm pleased with that arrangement. It was good for their gross and my Christmas spirit. I stay away from the places that pretend they're saving me money by looking drab.

I like Christmas above any time of the year. It turns gray winter into bright colors and the world with it.

I like the lights and the crowds of people who are not sad at all. They're hurrying to do something for someone because they love them and want to please them and want to be loved and pleased in return.

In New York City, the big, lighted Christmas trees put up along Park Avenue for three weeks every year produce one of the great sights on earth.

There is a kind of glory to a lighted Christmas tree. It can give you the feeling that everything is not low and rotten and dishonest, but that people are good and capable of being elated just at the thought of being alive this year.

When I'm looking at a well-decorated Christmas tree, no amount of adverse experience can convince me that people are anything but good. If people were bad, they wouldn't go to all that trouble to display that much affection for each other and the world they live in.

The Christmas tree is a symbol of love, not money. There's a kind of glory to them when they're all lit up that exceeds anything all the money in the world could buy.

The trees in our homes do not look like the ones in public places and they ought not to. They look more the way we look, and we are all different. They reflect our personalities, and if someone is able to read palms or tea leaves and know what a person is like, they ought to be able to tell a great deal about a family by studying the Christmas tree it puts up in the living room.

Christmas trees should be real trees except where fire laws prohibit them from being real. It is better if they are fir or balsam, but Scotch pines are pretty, often more symmetrical and sometimes cheaper.

Nothing that is blue, gold, silver, pink or any color other than green is a Christmas tree.

A lot of people are ignoring the Christmas tree tradition, but just to review it, it goes like this:

You put up the Christmas tree Christmas Eve. You do not put it up three weeks in advance or three days in advance.

If you have young children, you put them to bed first.

As the children get older, you let them help decorate the tree.

As they get even older, you *make* them help decorate the tree.

When the tree is decorated, you put the presents around it.

You do not open presents Christmas Eve.

The first one down in the morning turns on the Christmas tree lights.

The best Christmas trees come very close to exceeding nature. If some of our great decorated trees had grown in a remote forest area with lights that came on every evening as it grew dark, the whole world would come to look at them and marvel at the mystery of their great beauty.

So, don't tell me Christmas is too commercial.

OH, WHAT A LOVELY GAME

I was an All-America guard at Colgate University in 1940. I went on to play in the

NFL, and later was voted into the Pro Football Hall of Fame.

Well, I wasn't *actually* an All-America and I never played professional football — you know how old football players and war veterans tend to exaggerate — but I did get into a few games in college when we were ahead by four or five touchdowns and coach Andy Kerr cleared the bench to give the substitutes a break.

That was as close as I ever got to being either All-America or in the Hall of Fame, but during those years as something less than a Heisman Trophy winner, I acquired a love for football that is undiminished fifty years later. In my view, any other game is tiddlywinks.

As a freshman at Colgate, I was a 185-pound running guard. In the Single-or Double-Wing formation, devised many years before by one of the great early football coaches, Pop Warner, I pulled to run interference for a halfback or fullback on half the plays. We had Bill Geyer, one of the all-time great players in Colgate history, who had run one hundred yards in ten seconds as a sprinter. He was one of the fastest, toughest, most elusive halfbacks in the nation. Later, he played with the Chicago Bears.

There was no intermediary, no handoff, in the Single-Wing offense, as there is in today's game in which the quarterback handles the ball on every play. Everything was Shotgun. When the play was called for Geyer to sweep wide right, the center snapped the ball directly to Bill and he took off.

Everything went well in practice those first few weeks. I got by the first couple of games okay, but then we went up to Archbold Stadium to play Syracuse. They had a big, fast, rangy end who was responsible for everything that went outside.

We ran one of those sweeps during the game. From a sprinter's stance, the Syracuse end started at the same instant Geyer began his outside charge. From my crouched position, I spun to the right and headed for the gap between the end and Geyer.

The distance between the two was shorter than the distance between me and them and with my speed, which unlike Geyer's was closer to twenty seconds for a hundred yards, there was no way I could get between them for a block.

We beat Syracuse that day, as I recall, but Geyer never gave me a lot of credit for the victory.

My career as a football player in college

371

*With friend and fellow football player Obie Slinger-
land at The Albany Academy*

was one stumbling block after another. I
was determined not to let the game dominate my life and become a culturally de-
prived jock, so I decided; to take piano lessons during the football season.

The wife of a history professor undertook,
at $2 for each one-hour lesson, to teach me.
During my first lesson, I recall thinking that
it was quite probable that I had more
potential as a football player than I had as a
musician. My first day of piano lessons also
turned out to be my last. I went directly
from that lesson to football practice. It was
a game-style scrimmage between substitutes

and the first team, with officials.

During the second half of the scrimmage that day, I was playing opposite Bill Chemowkowski, one of those ape-like athletes whose weight was mostly at or above the waist. He had short, relatively small legs and a huge torso with stomach to match. At 260 pounds, "Cherno" was the heaviest man on the squad.

As things turned out, it didn't matter where he carried most of his weight or how much of it there was. When he stepped on the back of my right hand in the middle of the third quarter, that ended, for all time, any thought I might have had of being another Horowitz. My hand still is slightly deformed, and I often look at it with the same sense of pride with which I view the television Emmys in my bookcase.

One of the saddest days of my life was the day I realized I'd played my last game of football. It was as final as death. As a young boy, I'd played in vacant lots — back in the days when there were vacant lots — every Saturday during the fall. By the time I got to high school, I knew I loved the game better than any other.

I played all through high school and in college and then, one day, it was over. It was like the day my dog died.

It probably wouldn't occur to anyone who never played that even second stringers love the game. You don't have to be a star to enjoy playing football. You hear parents advise their children to learn to play a safer sport, a sport like golf or tennis that they can enjoy all their lives. I understand that argument but, as bad as I felt on that last day, I wouldn't trade my football days for golf if I could have started playing when I was eight and grown up to be Arnold Palmer.

People who have played football at any level watch a game with a different eye than someone who has never played. For one thing, they tend to watch the man playing the position they played. If you played center, you watch the center a lot. If you played end, you watch the ends.

I hear people say they can see the game better at home on television than they can see it sitting in the stadium. No one who knows much football thinks it's as good to watch at home as it is at the stadium. Watching at home is better than not watching football at all, but it isn't the same as being there.

The biggest difference in being there is that, good as the pictures, commentary, and replays are on television, the person at home is watching a small part of the total game that someone else has chosen to show him. What you watch is not your choice. At the stadium, the fans can watch what they want to watch anywhere on the field. I concede that if a person is not a knowledgeable football fan, he or she might get more out of watching it on television.

I often miss completely something that has happened to the ball carrier, because I'm watching what the guard is doing to the nose tackle or vice versa.

Every team played a seven-man defensive line when I played, with only one linebacker — always the toughest kid on the block. We all played both ways, of course, offense and defense. If they hadn't changed the rules, Joe Montana might have had to play free safety on defense. I don't know how that would have worked out for Joe, but I think New Orleans fullback Ironhead Heyward could hold his own as a middle linebacker on defense.

The great Frank Gifford, the most graceful football player I ever watched, was one of the last to play both offense and defense for the Giants.

Even relatively new football fans have seen a lot of rule changes. One of my prized possessions is a *Spalding Official Football Guide* that belonged to my uncle, who played for Williams College in 1900.

In those days they had to make only five yards for a first down (in three downs), and the literary style of the old rule book should embarrass the current rules committee.

"The game progresses," the rule book reads, "in a series of downs, the only limitation being a rule designed to prevent one side from continually keeping possession of the ball without any material advance, which would be manifestly unfair to the opponents.

"In three attempts to advance the ball, a side not having made five yards toward the opponent's goal must surrender possession of the ball.

"It is seldom that a team actually surrenders the ball in this way," the rule book continues in its elegant prose, "because, after two attempts, if the prospects of completing the five-yard gain appear small, it is so clearly politic to kick the ball as far as possible that such a method is more apt to be adopted."

Eat your heart out, John Madden!

In 1925, the NFL player limit was sixteen. As late as 1944, a team still was limited to a roster of twenty-eight players. And, of course, the uniform has changed.

One of the primary rules of life is that nothing seems to help, and that certainly is true of the protective equipment used by football players. Everything a player wears to a game today is better than the equipment of thirty-five years ago, but I don't notice that there are any fewer injuries. Of course, modern-day collisions involve bigger, stronger people. Early helmets were felt-padded leather. Today's plastic helmets are part protector, part lethal weapon.

Players used to make some individual choices about their uniforms. What a player wore frequently was not very uniform at all. There were players who liked stockings and players who didn't. In the NFL today, stockings are mandatory. I played next to a center who had an interesting theory. He refused to wear an athletic supporter because he felt he was safer from injury in this sensitive area if his private parts weren't confined like sitting ducks.

There was no rule against grabbing the facemask until 1956, for a simple reason — there were no facemasks. A lot of teeth were lost. I remember Bill Farley coming back to the huddle, leaning over, and spitting his front teeth on the ground as he listened to the signal for the next play. Broken noses were common — but not considered serious. Stanley Steinberg wore a huge rubber protector over his nose that looked like part of a clown's costume. He held it in place by clenching a mouthpiece attached to it between his teeth.

The one rule I would most like to see put into effect — and never will as long as coaches dominate the rules committee — is one that would require a man on the field to call plays. If football is a game of mind and body and there are only eleven men from each team on the field, one of those players should be responsible for making the decision about which play to run. It should be illegal for a coach or anyone on the sidelines or in a booth up in the stadium to send in or signal a play.

If that seems like a rule that would be too difficult to enforce, make it the honor system. It's an honorable game.

Position names have changed over the years. We played with a quarterback, two halfbacks, a fullback, two ends, two guards, two tackles, and a center. In today's Super Bowl, each team will have forty-five players available and the position names are different. There won't be anyone called a center on defense. He's a nose tackle now, assuming the team lines up an odd number of defensive linemen. On offense, the big, slower ends are tight ends and the smaller, fast ones are wide receivers. The tight ends block a lot, and, while they also catch (or drop) passes, they aren't called tight receivers.

Originally the quarterback was so called because he didn't stand back as far as the tailback and fullback in the Single-Wing. His position name has remained the same even though he usually no longer stands even a quarter of the way back.

Even the language of the game has evolved. Most of the football words used by fans have been popularized by radio and television commentators. Some assistant coach starts using a word in practice as a code for some action. The word is picked up by players and, eventually, by commentators and newspaper reporters hungry for authentic-sounding color.

Most of the words stick for a few years and then disappear in the lexicon of long ago. A few seem to have long lives. During the 1960s, the popular word for what a linebacker did when he abandoned his responsibility for a short pass and tried to break through the offensive line to get the quarterback was "red dog." I haven't heard "red dog" in years. Now, what they do is "blitz" and the word seems to be having a longer life than "red dog."

One phrase that's just come into its own this year is "red zone." Until a few years ago, the area inside the twenty-yard line was simply that, "the area inside the twenty-yard line." Now it's regularly being referred to as "the red zone."

"Run-and-Shoot" and the "hurry-up offense" are big these days, just the way the "flea flicker" pass and "the Statue of Liberty" used to be, but you can bet those phrases will be put out of their misery just the way "red dog" was. It's the kind thing to do to an old dog.

In spite of my failure to be chosen as an All-America during my playing days, I have great memories of it. Football locker rooms are good places. The talk is good, the feeling is good. Even the smell gets to you if you love the game.

When I go to the stadium, I bring either a small black-and-white television set or a radio. I don't watch the television set but sometimes, depending on who's doing the broadcasting, I prefer it to listening to the radio. Other times I stick with radio exclusively. All of the announcers broaden my knowledge of the game I'm watching by pointing out things I didn't see. Of course, I often feel like pointing out to them things

I saw that they didn't. "Hey, Pat!" I yell to Summerall in my mind. "You missed the block Elliott put on so and so."

In addition to the radio and television sets with earplugs, I bring a small pair of good binoculars, a tuna fish sandwich on rye, and a thermos of chicken soup when it's cold. I am indifferent to the weather. I come prepared, and, except for a few early games when it can be too hot, I don't care what the temperature is.

When Sunday dawns cold, gray, and rainy, I invariably am asked whether I'm going to the game anyway. For forty-five years I've had the same answer to that question. "Why *wouldn't* I go?"

Rain or snow are of no concern to me at a game. I actually enjoy sitting there, properly dressed and shielded, in a cold rain. The only minor problem I have with rain is that water tends to run up my sleeves when I hold the binoculars to my eyes for long periods.

Having sat with 70,000-odd strangers every Sunday for all these years, I think I understand fans better than the players do. Players seem to take fans more seriously than fans take themselves.

While it has become popular to suggest that anyone who spends time watching someone else play a game is an idiot, I happily profess to being one of those idiots. The Super Bowl is one of the highlights of my year.

If anyone here at the game is one of a small but inevitable number of people who come to every Super Bowl game, not because he or she wishes to but because a husband or friend had an extra ticket, you may wonder why some of us derive so much pleasure from a mere game. I ask you to look for a minute at the headlines in your newspaper any day of the week.

"RAGING FIRE KILLS 16!"

"AIRLINER DOWN IN MOUNTAINOUS AREA. ALL 237 ABOARD BELIEVED LOST."

"BANKRUPTCIES RISE AS ECONOMY FAILS TO RESPOND."

"PARENTS ARRESTED FOR CHILD ABUSE FOR THIRD TIME."

"AIDS EPIDEMIC ON INCREASE."

Do these tragic events make your day? Does the recent local murder make you happy all over for the rest of the week? Is reading about a raging flood or of corruption in government your idea of a good time?

It's for relief from such depressing world events and from the daily pressure of living our own lives that we turn to sports for entertainment. For many of us, there is nothing in all of sports quite as diverting as football . . . and no sporting event as much fun to watch as the Super Bowl.

The Urge to Eat:
Ice Cream

Because of the seriousness of our national and international situations, I'd like to say some things about ice cream.

The three things I have spent the most time thinking about and working with are words, wood and ice cream. Of those three things, it is possible that I'm best with the last.

Several times a year I fly into a rage as I'm reading a newspaper or magazine article on how to make ice cream. You may notice my hands are shaking this minute. The August issue of a good magazine about food called *Bon Appétit* arrived in the mail, and I've been reading a long feature story in it.

On the cover the story is called "The Best Homemade Ice Cream." Inside, the story is called "Ice Cream Greats." Magazines have gotten in the habit of calling their articles by one name on the cover and by a different name in the table of contents so they're hard to find. But this is not my complaint. My complaint is about their advice on how to make ice cream.

Under the heading "Easy Basic Vanilla Ice Cream," the writer gives this recipe: "2 cups half and half, 2 cups whipping cream, 1 vanilla bean, 8 egg yolks, 2/3 cup sugar, 4 tablespoons unsalted butter."

This recipe is not easy, it's not basic and it is not ice cream, it's frozen custard. The writer gets off to a bad start with me right away when she recommends "half and half." The assumption everyone makes is that it's half milk and half cream, but no one really knows what either half is.

I will tell you right now what easy, basic vanilla ice cream is. It is as much heavy cream as you can afford, enough sugar to make it sweet and enough pure vanilla extract to make it taste like vanilla. That is absolutely all you need to make great vanilla ice cream, and anyone who tells you something different hasn't made as much ice cream at home as I have.

I don't know why advice on how to make ice cream has been so bad over the years. The freezers they're selling have gotten a lot better just recently, but articles on how to make it are as bad as ever. When I was young, there were five kids in my summer group. We often made ice cream on hot evenings and it was no big deal. We'd decide to make it at 8:00, have it made by 8:30 and have the whole freezerful eaten by 8:40. The five of us ate it right out of the can with long spoons. It cut down on the dishwashing.

In the days before homogenized milk, about four inches of cream came to the top of each bottle. The five of us came from three families. We'd go to each icebox and take the top off whatever milk bottles were there, being careful to refill each skimmed bottle to the top with milk from another skimmed bottle. We thought this gave our parents the illusion that we hadn't taken the cream.

We used about a quart and a half of liquid, and if we didn't have enough cream, we filled in with milk or a can of evaporated milk. So, don't tell me about easy, basic vanilla ice cream that has eight egg yolks, half a stick of butter and a vanilla bean in it.

Bad or difficult ice cream recipes anger me for an obvious reason, I guess. We all like other people to enjoy what we enjoy, and these recipes are scaring people off homemade ice cream. I'd like everyone to enjoy making it and eating it as much as I do.

The first recipe in this magazine article after basic vanilla is one for "Prune and Armagnac Ice Cream." What would you serve with that, white clam sauce or ketchup? The magazine doesn't even give a recipe for the best ice cream to make in August, peach. To make peach ice cream, add mashed peaches to cream and sugar. Please don't put a lot of other stuff in it.

Part of the fascination of making ice cream is the physical principle involved. I know so few physical principles I get great satisfaction in knowing this one. The outside container of an ice cream freezer is wood or plastic. The container that holds the mixture is metal. You pack ice mixed with salt around the metal container. Salt converts ice to water without lowering its temperature. Any action like this consumes energy (heat). Neither wood nor plastic conducts heat the way metal does, so the energy to accomplish the conversion of the ice to water is drawn from the mixture inside the metal can, and when its heat is gone, it's frozen.

I'm not as sure about that, of course, as I am about how to make ice cream.

THE ANDY ROONEY UPSIDE-DOWN DIET

The two biggest sellers in any bookstore are the cookbooks and the diet books. The cookbooks tell you how to prepare the food and the diet books tell you how not to eat any of it.

The quickest way for a writer to get rich is to write a diet book. A cookbook is more difficult. With a diet book all you need is one bad idea and a lot of statistics on what has how many calories. If you want to make the book thicker, you put in a whole series of typical meals that adhere to your idea.

As someone who's been eating too much all his life, I think I'm as qualified to write a diet book as anyone, and as a writer I'm twice as ready to get rich. Not only that, I have an idea. My book would be called *The Andy Rooney Upside-Down Diet Book.*

My theory is based on the idea that the average overweight person has to change his eating habits drastically. The overweight man or woman has fallen into a pattern of eating that is making him or her fat, and the only way that person is going to lose weight is for him to turn his eating habits upside down.

The appetite itself (I'll say in the Foreword to my book) is a strange mechanism. Our stomach often signals our brain that it's ready to have something sent down when our body doesn't really need anything yet.

As I understand it — and you don't have to understand things very well to write a diet book — the appetite is depressed as the blood sugar level rises. The trouble is that the blood sugar level rises slowly as your digestive processes start taking apart the food you've consumed, so that you can still feel hungry for quite a while after you've had enough because your blood sugar level hasn't caught up to your stomach.

So much for theory. Here, in brief, is my diet. You'll want to buy the book later, I imagine.

Basically, what I'm suggesting you do is reverse the order in which you eat things at a meal, and change the habits you have in regard to what you eat for what meal.

Forget cereal, pancakes or bacon and eggs for breakfast. We're going to start the morning with a bowl of chicken soup. Chicken soup will serve a dual purpose. It's nourishing, not fattening, and because it's a hot drink you won't need coffee. If you don't have coffee, you won't need sugar. No one is going to be tempted to put sugar in chicken soup.

The beauty of my diet — and I want them to make this clear on the jacket of my book — is that you don't have to deny yourself anything. Eat absolutely anything you feel like eating. The magic of my diet is in making sure you don't feel like eating much.

Before dinner many of us consume what we call appetizers. Don't take appetizers off your diet if you like them, just don't eat them first. In our *Upside-Down Diet Book* we'll be laying out more than one hundred weight losing model meals. A typical breakfast might consist of half a grape, a bowl of chicken soup and plain butter, no toast.

Lunch might consist of ketchup, a Fig Newton, two Oreo Creme Sandwiches and lukewarm Ovaltine. In other words, Eat All You Want, but Change What You Want.

Your main meal will be dinner. Classic cuisine has called for an appetizer first, soup, a fish dish, meat, vegetables and potatoes, followed by cheese and then dessert. We're going to ask you to shake that up if you want to lose weight.

Each of our Upside-Down Diet meals will start with a bowl of ice cream or a chocolate eclair. Follow this with a small fish dish or oysters, clams or shrimp with a chocolate sauce. This will have the effect of raising your blood sugar level abruptly, and by the time the main course of oatmeal, corn flakes or Fruit Loops with buttermilk comes, you may not want any at all.

I don't want to be greedy, but after the book is published I have high hopes that it will be made into a movie.

THIN FOR CHRISTMAS

I'd buy a new suit if I wasn't about to lose weight. There's no sense buying a new suit and then having it hang on me after I've lost twenty pounds. That's about what I'll probably lose, twenty pounds.

Unlike some people, I know how to lose weight. I'm not going in for any crazy diets. I weigh too much because I eat too much. It's that simple. I'm not going to count calories or watch carbohydrates, fats and proteins. I'm just going to cut down on food.

It's time I did something. All my shoes seem a little short and not as wide as they were when I bought them and I think it's because I have more weight on my feet. The extra weight makes my feet longer and wider.

The only thing I'm going to cut out completely is ice cream. I may have a dish

In his Hacker boat, on Lake George
Ellen Rooney

of ice cream after dinner tonight but after that, that's it. No more ice cream until I drop twenty pounds. Or bread. I know who makes the best loaf of bread in America and I eat too much of it. No more bread, either.

Another thing I'll do is cut out second helpings. When I'm asked if I want more, I'll be strong. "Couldn't eat another bite," I'll say.

It's the middle of December. The average person would probably wait until after Christmas to start losing weight but not me. Those people don't have any strength of character. I'm going to start right now . . . tomorrow, probably.

I read that it's a good idea to drink a glass of water before a meal, so I'll start doing that. Maybe I'll drink several glasses because I want to drop off some weight in a hurry. The kids will all be home for Christmas and I don't want to hear them saying, "Boy, Dad, you've really put on some weight since summer."

What made me decide to lose all this weight I'm going to take off, beginning tomorrow, is that for the second day in a row I popped the top button on my pants, the one right above the zipper. It might be that I just happened to get two bad buttons but I don't think so. Anyway, I'm not taking any chances. I'm going to make it easier on the pants.

For the past few months I've been wearing wider ties because my suit jackets don't come together and button the way they used to. The wide tie helps fill the gap so that people don't see a big expanse of shirt in front. Thank goodness I'll be able to go back to wearing thin ties again pretty soon.

It's going to seem funny being as thin as I plan to get. Some people probably won't even recognize me, I'll be so thin.

"You look great, Andy," everyone will be saying.

The least I ever weighed after I got out of

college was 183 pounds. The most I ever weighed was yesterday when I hit 221 without even my socks on. I don't develop a great paunch that sticks out, I gain weight all over. Even my ears are heavier.

It's easy to see why a lot of people aren't as successful at losing weight as I'm going to be. They go for some crazy scheme that doesn't work. Not me. I'm going to do it the old-fashioned way and simply cut down on everything. After I've lost twenty pounds, I may write a book about it.

Come to think of it, later today I may call my publisher and ask if they'd be interested in a book about my weight loss. *How I Lost 20 Pounds in 20 Days,* I may call it. That would be a good title, give or take a few days.

It might even be a good idea if I started a diary the same day I start losing weight. Maybe I'll start the diary tomorrow, too, then I'll have the book done at the same time I'm twenty pounds lighter.

Of course, I don't want to get too thin. I don't want to look drawn. Doctors advise against going up and down too fast, so I don't want to overdo it. Maybe I'll have an occasional dish of ice cream. It might be better if I didn't try to get too thin too soon. If I lose weight gradually, it might be a good idea if I didn't start the book right away, either. I wouldn't want to finish the book before I'm finished losing weight.

THE URGE TO EAT

No number of books or magazine articles detailing the kind or amount of food I should eat to lose weight will ever convince me that I'm not a person who is just naturally overweight.

I don't have a potbelly or great globs of fat hanging from me anywhere in particular. I'm just overweight. There's too much of me everywhere. Right now I'm up around 210. That may not sound bad but I'm not six foot three.

No one has ever been able to prove the extent to which we can alter the course of our lives by resolve. Nine times a year I promise myself to lose weight, but at the end of the year the chances are I'm going to weigh more or less what I weighed when the year started. That's if I'm lucky.

Years ago I remember thinking I had found the answer. I had read a good book by a doctor who taught at Harvard and he convinced me that the problem of weight was a simple one. You are fat for just one reason. You take in more calories than you burn. The doctor conceded that some people burn calories faster than others and that differences in our rates of metabolism make it harder for some to lose weight than others. The fact remains, though, he wrote, that if you weigh too much, it's because you eat too much. There are a few medical exceptions to the rule but they don't involve enough people to be worth talking about.

What the doctor didn't talk about, because he was a nutritionist and not a psychiatrist, was some faulty wiring in my brain and the brains of a lot of overweight people that affects the appetite. My appetite keeps me going back for more long after I've had all the food I ought to consume. Food keeps tasting good so I want more and am unable to control my urge to take it.

I hate to be in a room with cigarette smokers but I'm sympathetic to them. I've never smoked cigarettes but I understand how difficult it must be to give them up. If I can't give up ice cream, I've got no business feeling superior to someone who can't stop smoking.

There have been periods in my life when I've lost weight. I can overcome my urge to eat for short, intense periods when I devote practically my whole life to trying not to, but it doesn't last. Overeating is as much a part of my personality as blue eyes and wide feet. I can no more keep from eating too much over a period of years than I can change the Irish look of my face.

When I look at those weight charts in a doctor's office, I laugh. According to them I ought to weigh 145 pounds. They'd have me lose a third of what I am. I'll get down to 145 pounds the day the doctor starts making house calls for ten dollars a visit.

Many things about overeating are too depressing to contemplate. Butter is certainly one of the purest, most delicious foods ever made. It's made with such a wholesome and natural collaboration between man and cow, too. It seems unfair to farmers who have so much of it, and to good cooks who love to use so much of it, that butter should be high on the list of things we shouldn't eat.

Years ago I learned that bourbon was fattening. All alcoholic beverages are high in calories. It seemed incredible to me that two things as different as butter and bourbon could produce the same deleterious effect on the system. I recall wondering whether the fat produced on my frame by bourbon would look any better or worse than that produced by butter.

Everything about being fat seems so un-fair.

SODIUM-RESTRICTED DIET

Last week I went to my doctor for my annual physical.

Things are looking up for me. My weight is up, my cholesterol is up and my blood pressure is up.

My doctor is also my friend and he was fairly insistent that I lose weight.

As I was leaving, he handed me these two brochures. This one, from the American Heart Association, is called *SODIUM-RESTRICTED DIET* and the other was put out by the Morton Salt Company.

With due respect to my doctor, let me say in the nicest way I know how — these pamphlets are ridiculous. If you're going to help someone with a diet, you don't tell them how much salt there is in one ounce of Animal Crackers, 5/6th of an ounce of Shredded Wheat or in half a bouillon cube. Its been years since I had half a bouillon cube for dinner.

If you followed the advice in this booklet, you'd be eating off a scale.

I'm suspicious of the Morton Salt pamphlet too. If their business is selling salt, are they really going to help someone use less of it?

And they keep calling salt "sodium." Salt and sodium are the same thing . . . why do they try to make it sound more important by calling it sodium? You don't notice them calling it the Morton Sodium Company.

They list the sodium content of strawberries. Half a cup of strawberries has one milligram. The average person doesn't have any idea what a milligram is and I am an average person.

And how do you measure half a cup of strawberries? Here's the half cup mark . . . do I mash them down, Morton?

I like salt. I'm the kind of person who puts salt on his sodium. If I followed the advice of Morton and the American Heart Association, there wouldn't be much I could eat. And if I do take their advice, don't expect to be seeing as much of me in the future because there won't be as much of me to see.

The American Heart Association keeps telling me to see my doctor before I do anything.

"Do not use any salt substitute that your doctor has not recommended. The important thing is to keep in touch with your physician . . ."

Why is the American Heart Association trying to get in good with doctors? Or are they doctors?

My doctor is busy. He doesn't want me hanging around asking if its all right to eat 200 milligrams of low-sodium dietetic peanut butter. He's so busy I'll bet he never even read the pamphlet before he gave it to me to read or he'd never have given it to me.

Caviar is on their list of things that are bad for you. Eleven hundred dollars a pound would make anyone sick.

I must admit, there are a couple of surprises in here.

Listen to this: "You may use carrots and celery sparingly to season a dish — one stalk of celery to a pot of stew."

The other day at a party I ate two stalks of celery so, if I'm not on next week because I dropped dead, you'll know it was that second stalk of celery that did me in.

On People and Places:
Thanks, Pal

Ernie Pyle, who wrote the book *Brave Men,* was the best kind of brave man I ever knew. He didn't have the thoughtless, macho kind of bravado that is sometimes mistaken for bravery. He was a war correspondent who was afraid of being killed but did what he had to do in spite of it.

Mostly, Ernie stayed right with the infantrymen who were doing the fighting and the dying. On the scrubby little island of Ie Shima, Ernie was moving up with the infantry when he was shot dead by a Japanese machine gunner forty years ago.

Almost everyone has heard of Ernie Pyle but in case you don't know why he was so widely read and so much loved, I thought I'd offer a little toast to the memory of this gentle, talented little man by telling you.

Unlike most correspondents, Ernie never offered any opinion about who was winning or losing the war. He just told little stories about the men fighting it. He drew vignettes with two fingers on his typewriter keys that told more about the victories and defeats of World War II than all the official communiques ever issued.

I have an Ernie Pyle kind of story about Ernie Pyle. One day sometime in July of 1944, I was sharing a tent with Ernie and two other reporters in Normandy. Ernie had decided not to go to the front that day, and he was lying on his cot when I came in and sat down on mine. I took off my boots, preparing to lie down for a while when I was dive-bombed by an angry bee.

My cot was almost directly over a hole in the ground that the bees were using as a nest. There must have been hundreds of them down there and, because it was impractical to move either my cot or the tent, I scuffed dirt over the hole so they couldn't get in or out.

The two of us lay on our cots, watching an occasional bee come into the tent looking for home. I started thinking about the bees trapped underneath the dirt.

We watched, silently, for perhaps two minutes. Ernie broke the silence.

"Aw, Andy," he said, "why don't you let 'em out?"

Ernie never seemed to be in much of a

Ernie Pyle
AP photo/Acme Pool/BertBrandt

hurry. He didn't rush to the scene of some particular bit of action with the other reporters. He made his own stories with little things others of us hardly noticed. His stories about soldiers were as apt to be about loneliness or boredom as about blood and danger.

Ernie never seemed to be interviewing anyone, either. It was more as though he were talking to the soldiers as a friend. You only realized he was working when he took out his notebook and meticulously wrote down the name and full address of every soldier near him. An infantryman could be telling Ernie a story about how his squad of eight guys wiped out a German machine-gun nest but Ernie would be as interested in getting all the names and addresses of the eight men as he was in the details of the action.

"Whereabouts in Wheeling, West Virginia?" he'd ask.

Ernie started covering the war in North Africa, and even though he didn't deal in The Big Picture, he knew North Africa was only the beginning.

"This is our war," he wrote, "and we will carry it with us as we go from one battleground to another until it is all over, leaving some of us behind on every beach, in every field. We are just beginning with the ones who lie back of us here in Tunisia. I don't know whether it was their good fortune or their misfortune to get out of it so early in the game. I guess it doesn't make any difference once a man is gone. Medals and speeches and victories are nothing anymore. They died and the others lived and no one knows why it is so. When we leave here for the next shore, there is nothing we can do for the ones underneath the wooden crosses here, except perhaps pause and murmur, 'Thanks, pal.' "

Ernie Pyle gave war correspondents a reputation not all of them deserved. All that those of us who shared that reputation can do for Ernie now is to say, "Thanks, pal."

FRANK SINATRA, BOY AND MAN

There was a small Italian bakery on Mott Street in New York City called Parisi's. Joe Parisi made his bread in two ovens on the back wall of his basement and I liked it so much that I'd often drive downtown to buy three or four loaves even though it meant an extra half hour getting home. I didn't know whether anyone else liked Joe Parisi's bread or not but I found out in a most interesting way.

Twenty-five years ago, I flew to Palm Springs with Walter Cronkite and Don Hewitt, the producer, to write an hour special about Frank Sinatra on the occasion of his fiftieth birthday. I got thinking about the experience on his seventy-fifth.

We made a mess of Frank's house by re-arranging the furniture and laying wires for lights all over the place, but he opened the house to us and was a gracious host.

The second day we were there he invited several of us to sit down and have lunch with him. The meal was prepared by an employee of Frank's who seemed to do everything for him — keep the house, take care of his clothes, and cook his meals.

We were having a good time talking and Frank passed a basket of crusty bread my way. I took a piece, looked at it suspiciously, took a bite and sat back, astonished.

"You okay?" he said.

"Where did you get this?" I asked. "I know this. This is Joe Parisi bread. He makes it in his basement on Mott Street two thousand miles from here."

"We have it flown in every week," Frank said. "Great bread."

I've been soft on Frank ever since that day I discovered he had such good taste in bread. Now, twenty-five years later, there's no one I like to hear sing a song as much as I like to hear Sinatra.

When I was young, I was cool toward him and his music and much put off by the crowds of young girls who made fools of themselves in his audience. To me, Sinatra was an awkward, gawky-looking jerk without much of a voice and no charm at all. Those fans my age were indistinguishable from the young people who, generations later, fawned over Elvis Presley.

Sinatra has made about thirty-five movies and even won an Oscar for his performance in *From Here to Eternity,* but everything he does besides singing is a sideline. He's great to see in person but it isn't necessary and that accounts for the phenomenal success of his records.

We went to a recording session of his while we were doing that show and I was surprised at how serious a musician he is. During the session, Sinatra got dickering with the orchestra leader about whether the note should be an F-sharp or an F-natural. I had always assumed the words just fell from his mouth in a random assortment of notes.

It's not just his voice or his knowledge of music that makes Sinatra sound so good, either. People who understand music hear sounds from Sinatra that no one else makes. And it all happened to him, you know it did, as he sings.

It's apparent to anyone listening to Sinatra that he enjoys his work. A performer's pleasure in his own performance is communicated to his audience and no one enjoys himself when he's singing more than Frank Sinatra.

The rap on Sinatra has always been his personal life. You can complain about the life he's lived, but he has an appealing enthusiasm for it that's part of his charm.

There are strange things going on in our brains that cannot be measured by numbers or described in words. It's impossible to say why a poem is good, or why a piece of music, a novel, or a movie is great. You can't apply reason in judging a picture painted by Picasso and come up with an answer that explains its greatness.

No amount of thinking about it can produce an answer to why so many people enjoy listening to Frank Sinatra. Genius is unfathomable . . . but whatever it is, Frank has it.

E. B. WHITE
(On the occasion of the death of E. B. White)

E. B. White may have written the English language more gracefully than any American who ever lived.

Each of us wants everyone else to know what we know, to like what we like. E. B. White was my literary hero, so give me this. Andy — he was known as Andy to his friends — was not as widely known as those movie stars, or even as well-known as a lot of writers who aren't as good as he was. Seems terribly wrong, but I'm probably better known than he was. As the phrase goes in the newspaper business, I couldn't carry his typewriter.

It was partly Andy White's own fault, although "fault" isn't the right word. He wanted no part of celebrity. All the people he cared about already knew how good he was, and that's all that mattered to him. He didn't care whether his picture was ever taken, and he refused to be interviewed for television.

Several times over the past twenty years, I told him he owed it to the world to submit to an interview on camera so everyone would know what he looked like and how he was. He just laughed. He said that people would be disappointed because he didn't talk as well as he wrote, and they'd think he was a fake.

For the past few years Andy has been ill with all the things that can go wrong with an eighty-six-year-old body, and he'd lost interest, too, after his wife died eight years ago. "Life without Katharine," he said, "is no good for me."

I talked to a mutual friend who had seen him only last week. He said Andy's eyesight was failing and the thing he most liked was to be read to from one of his own books. Strange, in a way, but I suppose for a writer it was like looking at old photographs of yourself when things were good.

I got to know Andy White when I adapted this little masterpiece of his called *Here is New York* for television, years ago. When we were finished, we were nervous about showing it to him, but he liked it. He had only one complaint: the director filmed the actor, playing the part of E. B. White as a young writer, lying on a bed in the Algonquin Hotel with his shoes on. Andy told us he'd never lie on a bed with his shoes on. His prose is like that, too.

Heroes are hard to find. He's been my hero for fifty years. Life without E. B. White is not as good as it was for me.

LONNIE

Lonnie is an institution in the building where I do a lot of my work. He shines shoes but that's only a small part of what he does. The best thing Lonnie does is keep everyone's spirits up.

The other day I had a good talk with Lonnie while he fussed over making my shoes look better. We settled some world problems and straightened out our own company. As I climbed down off the chair Lonnie has mounted on a platform so he doesn't have to bend over much, I said, as you'd say lightly to a friend, "Thanks, Lonnie, you're a good man."

"Well," Lonnie said philosophically, "we're all supposed to try and make things better, aren't we?"

That's what Lonnie does in the small piece of the world he has carved out for himself. He makes things better. He makes everyone he meets feel better and he makes their shoes look better. If all of us did as much, it would be a better world. He not only does his job but he throws in a little extra.

Lonnie is black, gray-haired and lame. I've been guessing that he's about seventy years old. His left foot is in a shoe with a four-inch lift on it and he doesn't use his left leg much. When he walks, he lifts it off the floor from the hip and swings it forward. It doesn't seem to be able to move by itself. He parks his car, a car with special controls for the handicapped, in front of the building and it's a tough job for him to make his way inside. Still, Lonnie is strong, with muscular arms and shoulders.

He has a good-looking face with prominent bones. He gets to work about 7:30 A.M. and leaves, to avoid the traffic, about 4:00 P.M. In between, he shines as many as thirty pairs of shoes. Lonnie gives every customer the feeling it's his privilege to be working for him.

A shine is apt to be interrupted half a dozen times by people passing the open door behind him who yell, "Hi, Lonnie."

"Hey, there, Mr. Edwards," Lonnie will yell back, often without looking up. He knows almost every voice in the building.

Yesterday Lonnie shined my shoes again.

"I'll be packing it in in April," he told me.

"Leaving here?" I asked, shocked at the thought of the place without him. "Why would you do that?" I asked.

"I'll be seventy-five in April," Lonnie said.

"But you're strong and healthy," I said. "Why would you quit work?"

"I want to do some things," Lonnie said. "Fix up my house. Do some things."

"Can't you fix up your house and still work here?" I asked.

There seemed to be something he wasn't telling me.

"Oh, I could," Lonnie said, "but I want to go back to school."

"That would be great," I said. "I've always wanted to do that too." I wondered what courses Lonnie was thinking of taking but decided not to ask.

"Yeah," Lonnie said, "I been working for

412

sixty-two years now. Want to go back to school. Never did get enough school. Never really learned how to read. I was a little lame boy, you know. Embarrassed to go to school. All the big kids. What I want to do is learn to read, good enough to satisfy myself."

I've known Lonnie for thirty years and never knew how handicapped he was.

THE GODFREY YOU DON'T KNOW

Arthur Godfrey has spoken more words to more people than any man since the beginning of time. Historians may someday search those words to find out what kind of man commanded so much attention. And if historians can decide exactly what kind of a man he was, they will have achieved something Godfrey's contemporaries never could.

Between 1949 and 1955, I wrote for Godfrey. Since then, I have resisted the temptation to write about him because if I did, I thought, I'd want to catch the truth, and, as any writer discovers, truth is not solely a matter of intent. Many important things about Godfrey have never been said, and many untrue and unimportant things have been repeated for years. Now perhaps it's time to fill in a few gaps.

One winter evening in 1955, Arthur taxied his DC-3 down the runway at Teterboro Airport in New Jersey, roared into the sky and turned the plane toward the Hudson for a look at New York, before heading south for Virginia. That night, I was standing between Arthur and his copilot, Frank La Vigna.

"Look," Arthur said, gazing down entranced at the sight of New York from the air. "It makes me so damn mad," he said thoughtfully. "Someday I'll be dead, and all this will still be here but I won't be able to see it."

Godfrey's zest for living takes precedence over everything else, even his career. His own programs have never been of paramount importance to him, except when they coincided with whatever else he was doing.

Godfrey has always known what many entertainers never find out. He knows people are lonely. He knows that they listen to and respond to the entertainer who reduces their loneliness, who appeals to their sense of fellow feeling. Godfrey, in his seemingly aimless talks, touches on basic elements of likeness in superficially unlike individuals, and every listener recognizes something of himself and feels he "belongs." This makes people feel good, and most of all, that is what people want.

Godfrey's instincts about what to say on air are great. "I don't like to think too much about something," Arthur often says. "If I say what comes to my mind first, that's usually the best thing. Just as soon as I start figuring it out, I get loused up."

Years ago, some of Godfrey's associates suggested that he avoid mentioning the luxurious swimming pool on his Virginia estate or his $200,000 airplane equipped with a cocktail lounge, television, beds, lounge chairs, and wing-to-wing carpeting. On instinct, he ignored the advice and spoke of both constantly, with the pride of a boy with a new bike. He was right, as usual. While the swimming pool or the private airplane might be luxuries beyond the reach of his viewers, the feeling he conveyed of unembarrassed delight in his possessions was understandable.

Within the highly regimented broadcasting industry, Godfrey is famous for his independence. Most television shows are prepared by network officials, producers, writers, directors, independent packagers, advertising agencies or various combinations of these. They are prepared *for* a performer. The performer is told how things are going to be. No one tells Godfrey anything, and if anyone does, he doesn't listen. For example, every network has a censor who checks scripts for policy, taste, and conflicts of interest. In thirty years of broadcasting, Godfrey has yet to give network officials any indication of what he is going to do or say on air. No censor passes on anything of his.

Broadcasting is a business dedicated to attracting and selling to the largest possible audience. Godfrey's answer to any complaint broadcasting executives have ever made is: "Am I selling the stuff?"

In the very beginning of his career as a broadcaster in Washington, D.C., Godfrey took a daring chance. He started treating the commercial copy of several sponsors in a lighthearted way. The story he tells most often is the one about Zlotnick, the furrier: He read some of Zlotnick's commercials with the heavy Russian-Jewish accent of the store owner. The next day, several friends asked Zlotnick why he let Godfrey make fun of his accent on the air.

As Godfrey tells it, Zlotnick looked at his

friends and said, "Heccent? Vot heccent?"

The next day, Godfrey not only made fun of Zlotnick's accent again, but told that story. Who could be mad? Not Zlotnick. His fur store, along with his accent, was becoming the best known in Washington. And Arthur Godfrey was on his way to becoming the biggest name in broadcasting.

Godfrey has a way of touching sore spots, and his relations with both CBS and several of his sponsors have often been less than friendly. If they put up with his "go to hell" attitude, it is only because he makes money for anyone connected with him.

To these two industries — television and advertising — Godfrey is a pain in the neck, to put it the nicest way I know how. He takes no nonsense from either one of them.

In ten years, more than one hundred sponsors have paid something like $125 million for Godfrey to sell their products, and he has done it with unparalleled success. He learns something about a product, convinces himself that is a good one, and sets out to convince others. His proud boast is that he has never sold a product he did not personally have faith in. Although this is literally true, it must be said in honesty that he also has an unequaled ability to convince himself of almost anything he wants to believe. So when he goes on the air and says he thinks a product is good, he isn't doing it with tongue in cheek. He *believes* what he says.

This part of Arthur's commercial approach delights his sponsors; it is the second part of his pitch that angers them. The second step is to make his audience believe as he believes. To accomplish this, he allies himself with the listeners against the sponsor. He gains their confidence by pointing out some obvious absurdity or exaggeration in advertising claims. He may complain for instance about the package the product comes in. Or he will needle the advertising men handling the product. If the sponsor has several products, he will single out one and admit he doesn't care much for that particular product. ("What a time to be selling peanut butter! I hate the stuff anyway. But, brother, if you want to try something good, taste this sponsor's peaches.")

At his best, when Godfrey has finished a commercial, he has: 1) pointed up his own honesty; 2) made certain that everyone knows the name of the product; and 3) made clear that he, an honest man, thinks the product is the best there is.

Godfrey is as independent of CBS as he is

of sponsors. At fifty-six, he is not completely tactless, but the network does not push him anywhere he doesn't want to go. There have been times when his relations with the network have been close to the breaking point. Frank Stanton, CBS president, would gladly have made an usher out of Godfrey in 1952 when Godfrey advised his *Talent Scouts* audience not to buy a television set until color sets were on the market in quantity. Color was years off, and CBS's own television manufacturing subsidiary, DBS-Hytron, was up to its ears in black-and-white sets on which the network was spending an advertising fortune.

Anyone who has ever worked for Godfrey is asked, with monotonous regularity, "Is he hard to work for?"

The answer is that Godfrey is hard, but good, to work for. Because he does not like to think that anyone can really help him, he often belittles people's efforts on his behalf.

He demands constant confirmation from the people around him that he is everything he wishes he was. He suspects himself of being a fraud — which he is not — and insists in a hundred little ways that his staff convince him that he is not. The Godfrey capacity for adulation is a bottomless pit.

"How was it?" he will ask after a show,

419

and for an hour, people will sit around thinking of new ways to say that a real stinker was great. He leaves knowing in his heart that it was a stinker.

Godfrey is thoughtful, concerned about his employees' personal problems, tight with a buck but free with a bankroll. He demands loyalty, but he returns it. Any employee of reasonably long standing who finds himself in trouble can get sympathy and real help from Arthur.

The greatest satisfaction in working for Godfrey is that he affords a refuge from all the petty pushers in the business. He takes no nonsense and protects those working for him from it. Within the limits of his absolute dictatorship, there is complete freedom, and next to getting to be the dictator, that is about all an employee can hope for.

At this point in his career, he has a nagging sense of unimportance. He underrates what he has accomplished. For instance, in 1951 Godfrey was brought into the Republican movement. He and automobile executive Charles E. Wilson had breakfast with Eisenhower in December while the general was still president of Columbia University, and Godfrey and Wilson also met with the late Sen. Robert A. Taft. "We're looking for the right guy," Arthur said one day, a little grandly but in the confines of his office.

When the Republicans decided on Eisenhower, Godfrey started on a "get out and vote" campaign that rivaled any selling job he ever did for a sponsor's product. He never said who to get out and vote for, but his sentiments were clear. Anyway, he was speaking to women on his morning shows, and in 1952, it was easy to forecast that if women got out and voted, it would be for Eisenhower. They did just that, of course, in record numbers, and Godfrey's campaign was at least partly responsible.

He has been important in another area too. He is the most genuinely open-minded man I have ever known when it comes to another's race or religion. His attitude must have had a healthy influence on his audience. As a matter of fact, one of the words Godfrey dislikes is "tolerance." To be "tolerant," he feels, suggests a superior attitude on the part of the tolerator.

I don't know what historians may say about Godfrey at some future time, but I hope they understand that he was, despite everything, a giant of a man.

Harry Reasoner

Harry Reasoner was one of the original correspondents on 60 Minutes *when it first aired in 1968. He retired in 1991.*

In 1961 CBS asked me to write a show for Harry. We'd never met so I called him and suggested we talk first. He put me off. He wasn't unfriendly, he just wasn't interested in talking about it. Harry's like that.

Writing for other people on television, I learned something. I learned that its hard to write for someone who couldn't do it without you and easy to write for someone who doesn't need you. Harry was always easy to write for.

And you could ask Harry. There are people who know things and people who don't know anything. Harry knows things. He's an omnivorous reader with a great memory. He's got a lot in his head . . . some of which he'd be better off without, of course.

Once I saw someone come to him with a blank map of Africa . . . just the outline of the countries. Harry sat down, looked at it and filled in the names of all fifty-two African countries.

Harry Reasoner's my best friend. Of the ten people I say that about, Harry's the

With Harry Reasoner, on location in California shooting the ABC documentary "A Bird's Eye View of California"

most complicated and the hardest to be best friends with. He's worth the trouble.

People wonder why he's leaving. Harry's leaving CBS because he never really liked to work. It made him mad when anyone suggested he was lazy. He's not lazy but, of all the people doing this kind of work, Harry enjoyed actually doing it the least. Mike Wallace loves to work. Harry hates it.

In 1979 I questioned the overuse of the word "superstar." I tried to say who was and who was not a real superstar.

With Walter Cronkite on his boat in Martha's Vineyard

A superstar is always a person who has something more than skill and talent that attracts the rest of us to him. In this business, Walter Cronkite's a superstar. Ten years ago, I said that of the four correspondents on *60 Minutes,* two of them were and two of them were not.

For months after that people asked me who I thought the two superstars were. I never said, of course, but I can tell you now. Harry Reasoner was one.

A Best Friend

How many really good friends do you have? If you're lucky, you have two or maybe three.

Walter Cronkite was a really good friend of mine — a best friend. I didn't just know Walter well, I didn't respect him, I didn't revere him — I just liked him a lot. We were often together and it was easy. We didn't have to think of things to talk about — things to talk about just came to us naturally.

I was with Walter recently and we didn't talk much because neither of us had much to say. You can do that with good friends too.

Walter and I met in London in 1942.

And I suppose we've been together a thousand times from then until now. It's one of those numbers in your life that you can't count.

I've been proud over the years to see Walter become not just one of the best-known people on television but one of the best-known people in the whole world of people. He was proud of me, too, and there's no better feeling in life than that. I wouldn't trade Walter Cronkite liking me for just about anything I've ever had.

THE FLAT EARTH IN KANSAS

In 1999 the Kansas Board of Education assured itself a place in the annals of ignorance by decreeing that Darwin's theory of evolution be removed from the state's school curriculum. It seems likely that board members, looking out their windows at their state's broad plains, might also conclude that the Earth is flat.

It helps restore my faith in the intelligence and good sense of the people of Kansas to know that their decision was reversed two years later.

One of the pleasures of our country house is the recurring memory it evokes of Margie's father, a doctor whose home it was. He was a self-educated intellectual who went from high school to medical college and never lost his fascination with knowledge. On either side of the fireplace in the living room, the bookcases are filled with literary masterpieces more admired than read by most Americans, including this one. Among the treasures is a twenty-volume set of red leather-bound books comprising the complete works of Charles Darwin. Over the years I have spent many hours reading them and have a ways to go to finish.

There have been no more than a handful

of people who have contributed as much to mankind's knowledge of itself as Darwin did. No one who has read any of what he wrote could question his brilliance or his dedication to searching for the truth. His two-volume book *The Origin of Species* would surprise any member of the Kansas Board of Education who undertook reading it. It seems likely none of them ever has.

"Natural selection is continually trying to economize every part of the organization," Darwin wrote. "If, under changed conditions of life, a structure, before useful, becomes less useful, its diminution will be favored, for it will profit the individual not to have its nutrient wasted in building up a useless structure."

This is merely one paragraph on page 183 of Volume I, but it summarizes Darwin's theory of natural selection and his belief that all living things change as they adapt themselves to flourish or decline under the conditions they encounter. He points out that the tallest giraffes survive the droughts because, even if they are only two inches taller than others, they can reach higher branches for food.

Darwin himself was more aware of the possibility he could be wrong than anyone on the Kansas Board of Education. He laid out some ways he might be wrong in Chapter VII of *The Origin of Species.* It runs for fifty-six pages and is called "MISCELLANEOUS OBJECTIONS TO THE THEORY OF NATURAL SELECTION."

There are scientists who doubt the broad implications of his conclusions about the origin of mankind but no scientist of any stature doubts the authenticity of his work. For "educators" in Kansas to eliminate study of it from their school curriculum is stupidity. Teach kids to doubt it if they wish, but teach it and let them decide.

Darwin always inspected his own motives and the possibility that he was wrong.

"From my early youth," he says, "I have had the strongest desire to understand or explain whatever I observed — that is to group all facts under some general laws. These causes combined have given me the patience to reflect or ponder for any number of years over any unexplained problem.

"I have steadily endeavored to keep my mind free so as to give up any hypothesis, however much beloved by me, as soon as facts are shown to be opposed to it."

The single biggest difference between those who believe that God created everything at one specific time in history and those who believe everything evolved from one simple cell over millions of years is that scientists like Darwin are willing, even anxious, to find evidence that will prove them to be wrong. Creationists are looking only for the elusive evidence that God did it.

I have mixed feelings about Kansas. The most time I ever spent there was at a political convention and Kansas City was wonderful on that occasion. On one other occasion I was filming a story in Manhattan, Kansas, and was invited to dinner at someone's home. It was the single most inedible meal I have ever faced and I learned, toward the end of it that our host, the woman who prepared it, taught a class in cooking at Kansas State University. I tell you this so you'll know I had negative feeling about education in Kansas even before the Board of Education banned Darwin.

SURRENDERING TO PARIS

Paris is a special city in my life, considering I'm not much of an international traveler. I first saw Paris on August 25, 1944, the day the city was liberated from the Germans by a combination of French and U.S. troops. I entered it across the bridge at St. Cloud. We had reached St. Cloud the night before, and the tank commanders decided to wait until morning to make their final drive into the city.

Two German Army trucks, loaded with soldiers, tried to cross the bridge in our direction in the middle of the night, not knowing we were there in such force. They ran into the barrage of fire from the 75mm guns mounted on the tanks of our armored division sitting there on the other side of the river.

The bodies of the Wehrmacht soldiers, riddled by machine-gun bullets, lay askew in the trucks and on the grated bridge roadway where some of them had fallen, their blood dripping into the Seine below. That was my gruesome introduction to what has been, ever since, an almost idyllic relationship to one of the world's great cities. (I suspect that if there were a poll taken among all the people who have been everywhere to determine their favorite city, Paris would win.)

Paris is too expensive for an American to visit now, of course, but a lot of Americans go there anyway. We try to save some money and take the trip once every few years. I'd rather go to a foreign city I'm sure I like than take a gamble on a place I don't know.

Two of us went to one of the good restaurants in Paris for a birthday celebration in 1991 and dinner cost almost two hundred dollars apiece. That included one of the least-expensive bottles of wine. French wine is as expensive in France as it is in the United States. You could say that about California wine and California, too.

When you enter a restaurant in France, an American is struck by how many people are puffing cigarettes. The French don't have no-smoking sections. Morley Safer attributes the relatively good health of the French to the amount of red wine they drink. Some people are always looking for reasons why a vice of theirs is actually good for them. I accept Morley's word on this myself.

All French restaurants add 15 percent to the bill for the waiters. Service is as good or better than in the United States, where we assume waiters try harder to get a better tip. They don't, and we should abandon tipping and add a service charge. There's a restaurant I go to in New York that gets a lot of French tourists and one waitress told me they often don't get tipped by their French customers because the French assume it's included on their bill.

The French always seem to be having a good time when they eat. When a man and a woman sit together in a cozy restaurant, it's as if they were dancing. I don't understand what French women see in French men, though. I do see what French men see in French women. Even the women who are nowhere near beautiful have an attractive, sexy way about them. French men, on the other hand, are as a whole and by my own standards not as good-looking as the average American man.

Before I left home for Paris, I bought a new pair of white pajamas, because I didn't want to be in my old, tattered ones when the maid came in every morning with the traditional French hotel breakfast of coffee, hot milk, a crusty loaf of their great bread and several croissants and jam.

I think, by the way, that the French ought to sue some of the bakeries making what they call "croissants" in our country. A soft, soggy roll is not automatically a croissant just because it's made in the shape of a crescent.

The third night I was there, I was getting ready for bed but I couldn't find my pajama bottoms. I know I'd hung them on the back of the bathroom door and it was apparent that the maid had picked them up with the white towels and bedsheets and put them in the laundry.

I didn't know whether to spend the money on a new pair, which probably would have cost as much as the expensive dinner, or sleep in just the tops for the rest of the trip. It occurred to me that it seemed almost impossible to surprise or shock the maids who brought breakfast, no matter what you were wearing, if anything at all. You can guess what I did.

I drove eighty miles from Paris to Reims, the heart of champagne country, and stopped for gas just outside the city. The superhighway gas station had everything one in the United States would have, except unleaded gas. The French don't have much unleaded gas yet. The gas station sold candy, junk food, Eiffel Tower ashtrays for tourists and trashy magazines, but, unlike any gas station I'd ever seen, it had a huge selection of expensive champagne for sale. I was tempted to buy a quart of oil, a bag of potato chips, and a magnum of Moët and Chandon.

We went to Reims, or "Rheims," as it's spelled in English, because I wanted to see where the Germans surrendered on May 7, 1945. They've made the building into a museum, but it's not very good. The French are not much interested in making a big thing of a German surrender to U.S., British and Russian troops. They seem to be vaguely embarrassed about their role in World War II.

On the way back to Paris, we came over the same bridge I had crossed forty-eight years ago when Allied forces entered the city. It's one thing I know more about than the Parisians know about their city. It gives me a kind of smug satisfaction when they're impatient, because I don't speak French very well.

I just smile quietly and think to myself, "I know something about this city you'll never know."

No, Thank You:
Waiting

Today I stood in line for seventeen minutes to cash a check for seventy-five dollars. I'd given this company, a bank, all my money to hold onto for me until I needed it, and today, when I needed some of it, it took me that long to get it back.

This is a good example of the kind of things that makes so many of us smile when we read that banks are having a hard time. We're glad. It fills us with pleasure to read about their troubles. They've made us wait so often over the years that nothing bad that happens to a bank makes us do anything but laugh. "You had it coming, bank." That's what we think.

Waiting is one of the least amusing things there is to do. Short waits are worse than long waits. If you know you're going to have to wait for four hours or six months, you can plan your time and use it and still have the pleasure of anticipating what you're waiting for. If it's a short wait of undetermined length, it's a terrible waste of time.

I've read all the proverbs about waiting and patience:

"All things come to him who waits."

"They also serve who only stand and wait."

"Patience is a virtue."

I don't happen to believe any of those old saws. *Impatience* is a virtue, that's what I think. Shifting from one foot to the other and tapping your fingers on something and getting damn mad while you stand there is the only way to behave while you're waiting. There's no sense being patient with people who make you wait, because they'll only make you wait longer the next time. The thing to do is blow up . . . hit the roof when they finally show up.

Some people seem to think they were born to get there when they're ready, while you wait. Banks are not the only big offenders in the waiting game, so are doctors. Some doctors assume their time is so much more important than anyone else's that all the rest of us ought to wait for them, "patiently," of course. What other profession or line of business routinely includes in its office setup something called "the waiting room"?

In New York City many of the parking

garages have signs over their cashier windows saying, "No charge for waiting time." What a preposterous sign! What it means is that they can take their time getting your car, but you don't have to pay them anything while you wait for it. I always tell them that I have a charge for waiting, and I think doctors ought to start knocking ten dollars off their bill for every half hour we spend in their waiting rooms. The doctor who tells all his patients to come at nine o'clock ought to be sent back to the hospital to spend another year as a resident.

All of us admire in other people the characteristics we think we have ourselves. I don't have any patience, so it's natural, I guess, that I don't admire it in other people. Sometimes I reluctantly concede it works for them, but I still don't think of it as a virtue. I secretly think that people who wait well are too lazy to go do something. Just an opinion, mind you. I don't want a lot of patient waiters mad at me.

The funny thing about that word "waiter" is that those who make a living as waiters are about the most impatient people on earth. You can't get a waiter to wait ten seconds. You go in a restaurant, he hands you a menu eighteen inches long with fifty dishes to choose from, and in three seconds he starts tapping his pencil on his order pad to let you know how impatient he is.

I'd make a great waiter. I can't wait at all.

Hot Weather

I detest hot weather. That's easy enough for me to say in the middle of a heat wave, but I'll say the same thing on the coldest day of the year.

Somehow we don't worry quite so much about the people subjected to relentless heat as we would if they had been through a flood or a hurricane. There are no pictures of it for television, and millions suffer silently.

Even though there are no pictures of heat and no one dies instantly as they might in a storm, in some ways heat may be worse than other natural disasters. In terms of physical damage to material things like houses and cars, the hurricane and the flood are worse, but when you're talking about the human spirit, a heat wave is worse. People join together and work shoulder to shoulder with a great sense of camaraderie to fight the effects of a flood or a snowstorm, but in oppressive heat all effort is impossible.

Half a dozen memories of the worst heat I've ever experienced come to my mind when it gets hot.

My first month in the Army was spent at Fort Bragg, North Carolina, in August. I will never forget having to stand at attention for hours on the red clay drill field on that one-hundred-degree day. The commanding colonel of our artillery battalion made a maddeningly slow inspection tour of the full field packs we had laid out on the ground, and our company was the one he came to last. Nine men fainted or decided to drop to the ground so they'd be carried off.

Later in World War II, I flew with the Eighth Air Force on bombing raids over Germany and I traveled across Europe with the First Army, but I never had that bad a day again.

When I go to bed at night, I often toss and turn without being able to go to sleep for as long as fifteen or twenty seconds. Insomnia has never been one of my problems. I can go to sleep when I'm worried, I can go to sleep with a headache and I can even go to sleep when I have one too few blankets over me on a cold night. There's just one thing that keeps me awake, and that's heat.

Late at night in those early Army days at Fort Bragg, I lay awake in the barracks thinking about ice water. One night I couldn't stand it any longer. I got up, waited for the guard on duty in the company street to pass, then I slipped out the door and crawled under the barracks. The barracks were built on stilts, and there was plenty of room to walk in a low crouch. Underneath, I made my way the length of the barracks to the next company street and waited silently again for the guard to pass. It was as though I was a German infiltrator about to blow up the base, but all I wanted was ice water.

I made my way under three barracks until I came to the post exchange. It was 2 A.M. by then and the PX had closed at nine. But there was something I knew. Every night as they cleaned up, they dumped all their ice on the ground outside the back door. I finally arrived, undetected, and there it was, just as I had hoped. Cakes of ice that had originally been so big that even in the heat they were still huge chunks glistened. I took two cakes so big I had to hold them braced on either hip. It was cold and wet but wonderful, as the icy water soaked through my pajamas.

It took me ten minutes to get back to the barracks and my friends were glad to see me. As a matter of fact, I do not recall a time in all my life when I was so great a hero to so many people.

We broke the ice into pieces, filled our canteen cups with them and then added water. For more than an hour, ten of us sat silently on our bunks in the sweltering heat, drinking that beautiful ice water.

I'm one of the privileged class who lives and works mostly in air-conditioned buildings. For us, hot weather is like a heavy rainstorm. We get out of our air-conditioned car and rush a short distance to an air-conditioned house. During the workday we move quickly from air-conditioned building to air-conditioned building, as if to keep from getting wet in the rainstorm.

I feel terrible for the people I read about being subjected to awful heat, and I always wish I could bring them ice water.

NEAT PEOPLE

Neat people are small, petty, nit-picking individuals who keep accurate checkbooks, get ahead in life and keep their cellars, their attics and their garages free of treasured possessions. They just don't seem to treasure anything, those neat people. If they can't use it or freeze it, they throw it away. I detest neat people. I was in a neat person's home several weeks ago and he took me down into his cellar. He must be making a dishonest living, because there was nothing down there but a few neatly stored screens and the oil burner.

I feel toward neat people the same way I used to feel toward the brightest kid in our class, who was also a good athlete and handsome.

My dislike for the tidies of the world is particularly strong this week because I realized Sunday that my desk is such a mess I can't find anything, my workshop looks like a triple-decker club sandwich with tools on top of wood on top of plans on top of sandpaper on top of tools on top of wood. If I need a Phillips screwdriver, it's easier to go out and buy a new one than to find any of the three I already own.

How do neat people do it? I hate them so much I don't want any help from them, but I would like to follow one around someday and see how they live. I bet they don't do anything, that's how they keep everything so neat. They probably do all sorts of dumb stuff like putting things back where they belong. They probably know which shelf everything is on in the refrigerator; they could probably put their finger on the nozzle to the garden hose.

What do you do with all that stuff I have cluttering my cellar, Neat People? Did you throw away the hammer with the broken handle? Mine is still down there.

What about the twenty feet of leftover aerial wire and the small empty wooden nail keg? Don't tell me you were so heartless that you tossed that out. You don't even appreciate the fact that you never know when you're going to have a good use for an empty wooden nail keg. That's how dumb you Neat People are. I, on the other hand, have been ready with an empty nail keg for the past twenty years. That's about how long it's been in the cellar, right there in the way if I ever need it.

You probably throw out broken plates and glass pitchers that can't be repaired, don't you? Tell the truth. I don't. I keep broken plates because I can't stand to throw them out. I'm waiting for them to make glue that will really mend china and glass, the way the ads say the glue will now.

Many years ago a man who owned a hairbrush factory gave me a bushel basket of odds and ends of rosewood. They're beautiful little pieces and I've never figured out what to do with them, but I wouldn't neaten up my cellar by throwing them out for anything.

My wife says the old bookcase I took out of the twins' room in 1973 should be thrown out. She gets a little neat every once in a while herself. Thank goodness that never happens to me. That's why I still have that bookcase.

We have four children and I'm not saving much money, but should I ever die, I'd like to leave the kids something. I have nineteen cans of partly used paint, some dating from the late fifties, in the cellar. I don't want them fighting over my estate when I go, so I think I'll make a will and divide the paint among them, I want it to have a good home.

DRIVING

June is the beginning of the time of year when Americans do the most driving. I often spend 20 hours a week in my car during the summer months. It seems like an awful lot of time now that I've written it down. If I sleep for 42 hours a week and drive for 20, that means I'm not doing much of anything for 62 of the 168 hours in a week. Maybe we better get a weekend place nearer home.

The trouble with driving is that you often do it in a state of agitation. I'm not usually very relaxed when I drive because I'm mad at the guy behind me or the woman in front of me or the truck that just cut me off. As soon as I do relax, I get sleepy. I'd rather be angry than sleepy when I'm driving. I'm not a very safe driver when I'm driving slowly to be safe. When I'm mad, I drive faster but at least I'm alert to everything that's going on. I'm trying to get that dirty so-and-so who cut in front of me.

It is my opinion that the slow drivers are a greater menace on the road than the ones driving at, or slightly above, the speed limit. The slow drivers sit there, slumped way down behind the wheel, smug in the knowledge that they are safe drivers but they're wrong. They're the ones who don't know how to move. They're the ones who can't get out of their own way. They cause the rest of us to pile into something to avoid them.

You can tell I'm just off the road because I'm writing in an agitated state. I just drove 150 miles from upstate New York to New York City and it was the kind of drive that makes you wonder whether the weekend was worth it.

I confess to being a competitive driver. I'm vaguely irritated when someone passes me, even when the other driver has a perfect right to do it. The chances are, though, that

With Spencer the bulldog
Ellen Rooney

he doesn't have a legal right because I'm probably driving as fast as the law allows, or faster. What irritates me on a major highway is that there are some nuts who won't let you maintain a reasonable distance between your car and the car in front of you. If you do leave a sensible opening, someone comes along and cuts into it and then you have to drop four or five car lengths behind him. You're losing ground and it makes you mad. I think this is the cause of a lot of accidents. People tailgate because they don't want anyone getting in between them and the car ahead. When there's a sudden stop or slowdown, it can be too late to brake to a

446

stop before hitting the car you're following.

The single most annoying driving habit Americans have on and off the major highways is their practice of hitting the right turn signal just after they've started to turn right. By then, you *know* they're turning right. What you would have liked is some indication of their intentions a few hundred yards back. It would have helped you make plans. Why do so many drivers think it does any good to hit the turn signal after they've started their turn?

In city driving, the principal menace for the average driver is the panel truck. I don't know where they get the people who drive panel trucks. Every year there are a lot of race drivers who fail to qualify for the Indianapolis 500. Maybe they all take jobs driving panel trucks in cities. They're trying to make enough money to enter the Indy 500 again next year.

The average driver puts 10,000 miles on his car every year, according to Federal Highway Administration statistics. One statistic I'd like to see that no one has kept is, how much I've paid out in automobile insurance in the past twenty-five years and how much I've collected. We've owned two cars for most of that time and I guess we've paid out a total of more than $20,000. The insurance company didn't get the perfect driver when they got me but they haven't done badly. During that time I doubt if they've paid out $2,000, mostly in dents.

I had all my accidents when I was driving carefully.

THE WHITE HOUSE? NO, THANK YOU

I'm always pleased but surprised that anyone will take the job of being President of the United States. Of all the jobs in the world, it's the one I'd least like to have. I know you get a big house to live in for free, a salary of $200,000, a helicopter, an airplane, your own doctor and a big staff but I still don't want the job. Don't even ask me because I won't take it.

The President doesn't even have a White House psychiatrist, which is probably the doctor he needs most.

It's always been a mystery to me why anyone would want to be President. Anyone who'd want to be President has to be some kind of nut who loves misery and criticism. If I were President, I'd call my personal physician and say, "What's wrong with me, anyhow?"

As President, any decision you make affects millions of people. You put thousands of people out of work every time you say, "Cut that." How do you sleep nights or in a Cabinet meeting knowing someone couldn't feed his family tonight because of some policy of yours that cost someone a job?

A President can't go down to the basement of the White House on a Saturday morning and putter around. He can't decide to climb up on the roof and straighten the television antenna. He never gets the satisfaction of taking a load of trash to the dump. Considering he's probably the most powerful man in the world, he's almost powerless to do anything he wants to do. If he does do something he wants to do, some newspaper or television reporter will see him doing it and claim he's wasting the taxpayers' money.

It's nice to have someone concerned about your welfare if it's a friend but I certainly wouldn't want a lot of guys running alongside my car every time I started down the street to make sure I didn't get shot. Furthermore, I'd want to drive my own car. I don't like to be driven anywhere by anyone. I like to go where I want to go the way I want to get there. The President can't do that.

You can bet there have been nights when

the President sat down after a hard day's work dealing with world affairs and wanted nothing more than to go to a good movie. Presidents of the United States can see any movie they want right in the White House but that isn't what "going to the movies" means. "Going to the movies" is getting dressed to go out, driving to the theater, finding a parking place, standing in line to buy the tickets, buying the popcorn and then groping your way down the aisle to find a seat. A President can't go to the movies. Can you imagine the complaints he'd get if he took the First Lady to one of those dirty, R-rated movies?

There are a thousand things I can do the President can't. I can go to any restaurant I want to eat dinner or I can stay home and eat leftovers. He can't do either of those things.

I can wander down a street and window-shop, eat an ice-cream cone or lie down and take a nap and not do anything at all if I feel like it. Why would I want to be President?

For all the power he has to change the world with a snap of his fingers, the President can't decide to turn over and go to sleep in the morning. He can't even make a plan for a week from Saturday. His calendar is full for the next four years . . . not just the days, but the hours.

I hope you have a happy and successful time in office, Mr. President, but frankly, you can have it.

THE AGONY OF FLIGHT

I have just taken a memorable trip I'd like to forget.

Because I was going to be in Los Angeles for only two days, I drove from my office in New York to Kennedy Airport so I'd have my car when I returned and could drive home to Connecticut. The parking area is just a minute's walk across the road from American Airlines.

When I arrived at the airport for a 9 A.M. flight at 7:30, I thought I had plenty of time. Sure. The short-term parking lot was closed for repair. I was directed to a lot two miles from the terminal. By the time I found it, parked and waited for the bus to take me to the terminal, it was 8:17. The baggage attendants outside told me my flight was "closed" and I could no longer check bags. Inside, I waited in line to check my bag anyway. By the time I got to the gate (all flights leave from the most remote gate), it was 8:40 and they were closing the door.

First class for the round trip flight cost $2,762.90. Business class cost $1,858.90. A coach seat was $517.90. I flew coach. Airlines make coach so uncomfortable that even people who can't afford it pay the "business" rate.

In flight, the pilot kept announcing that we were ahead of schedule. We landed nine minutes early, and after being told to keep our seats, we waited . . . and waited . . . and waited. Then came the inevitable: "There is a plane parked at our gate that should be moving out shortly. Please remain in your seats. Thank you for your patience." Which we were not.

Flight times should be recorded from the time they close the door for takeoff to the time they open the door to let passengers off. The advertised time of my flight was five hours and fifty-seven minutes. From the time we had to be on board to the time we were allowed off, it was seven hours and twelve minutes.

At baggage claim, the carousel went round and round. My bag never came 'round. At the lost baggage office, I waited in line. They were doing a booming business. I finally got to talk to a woman behind the desk, who said my bag would be arriving on the next flight. I opted to have the bag sent to my hotel.

In Beverly Hills, I went to the hotel I've stayed in a hundred times. It's also expensive but I could stay there for weeks for what first class costs on American.

In my room, I called American baggage service at 12:30 and was told my bag had been found and would be delivered "within six hours." I once worked at MGM, so I drove around some old familiar places, including Malibu Beach, wasting time waiting for my bag. I needed things in it to dress for dinner with friends. When I got back to the hotel, I called American again and got the "six hour" announcement again. It had now been five.

There was a huge window over the bathtub in the hotel room and by pressing a button next to the light switch, you could open a curtain that allowed you to look out on a palm frond garden.

I took a shower more to waste time than from necessity — I wasn't that dirty — and dried off with a thick towel that was six feet long. It made the bath towels at home seem puny.

After the shower, I read the paper and waited for my bag, which didn't come. It was delivered sometime after midnight, so I went out to dinner in khaki pants and slept in a terrycloth robe.

Sunday night, I ate dinner in my room because I wanted to watch *60 Minutes*. Mike Wallace interviewed Putin. Morley Safer's report on West Point was good. I could have done without Steve Kroft's chat with Ray Romano, but I watched it almost to the end. Almost. Next thing I knew, I woke up and they were showing the *60 Minutes* credits. I had missed the best part of the show.

I'll tell you about my trip home another time. It wasn't as good as the trip out.

APPENDIX:
THE FOLLOWING THINGS ARE TRUE

NINETY-NINE OPINIONS I'M STUCK WITH

A writer doesn't often tell a reader anything the reader doesn't already know or suspect. The best the writer can do is put the idea in words and by doing that make the reader aware that he or she isn't the only one who knows it. This produces the warm bond between reader and writer that they're both after because it feels so good.

The fact is, there really isn't anything new in the world and what I've always hoped to do with my writing is to say, in so many words, some of the ideas that lurk, word-lessly, in the minds of a great many people.

There's no way of knowing how we get to believe what we believe. We're all trapped within ourselves. We have this much and no more. We have our genes and our youth, during which our opinions are formed.

Most of us don't change those opinions once we get them. Instead, we spend a lot of time looking for further proof that we're right.

If we formed our opinions the way we should, we'd get all the facts together and then compare them, using logic and good sense to arrive at the right places. We don't do it that way very often, though, and as a result we acquire a lot of wrong answers that we're stuck with for life. I haven't changed my mind about anything since I was twenty-three. In my head I know I must be wrong about some things but in my heart I don't think so.

As an indication of what you'll find in the body of this book, what follows is a hundred opinions I'm stuck with. There ought to be something here to anger almost everyone:

1. I do not accept the inevitability of my own death. I secretly think there may be some other way out.

2. It's good to be loyal even when what you're loyal to doesn't deserve it.

3. We are selling things better than we're making them in the United States.

4. Capitalism and the free-enterprise system are not working very well. There are too many very rich and too many very poor

in the United States. Fortunately, the economic system that doesn't work as well as capitalism is communism. Communists are almost all poor.

5. When I was young I always assumed I'd get to like carrots when I got older but I never did.

6. In spite of all the kind things people are always saying about the poor and homeless, people with jobs and houses are usually more interesting and capable and I prefer to be with them.

7. I am often embarrassed by the people I find agreeing with me.

8. Big Business talks as if it doesn't like Big Government but the fact of the matter is, Big Business is in business with Big Government. Big Business is closer to Big Government than Big Government is to the people, but neither wants anyone to know it.

9. Most poetry is pretentious nonsense.

10. The people of the United States never worked so well or so hard or accomplished so much as they did during the four years of World War II. We need to find some substitute for war as a means of motivating ourselves to do our best. Money isn't the answer, either.

11. I don't favor abortion although I like

the people who are for it better than the people who are against it.

12. Good old friends are worth keeping whether you like them or not.

13. Although I went to Sunday school for several years at the Madison Avenue Presbyterian Church, I was not persuaded that Mary never slept with anyone before Jesus was born.

14. I'm suspicious of the academic standards of a college that always has a good basketball team. When a college loses a lot of games, I figure they're letting the students play.

15. A person is more apt to get to be the boss by making decisions quickly than by making them correctly.

16. Until we can all have the medical attention a President gets, there will not be too many doctors.

17. A great many people do not have a right to their own opinion because they don't know what they're talking about.

18. The least able among us are having the most children. Among women, college graduates are having the fewest babies, high-school graduates are having the next fewest and the people who don't get to high school or drop out once they do are having the most babies.

The most capable women are getting the best jobs and are least apt to have big families . . . or sometimes, any family at all.

19. If I were black, I would be a militant, angry black man, railing against the injustices that have been done me. Being white, I think blacks should forget it and go to work.

20. If I were a woman, I would be an angry woman. Men are satisfied having women be something women are not satisfied being. We have a problem here.

21. There are facts too painful to face. I cannot watch a documentary about the slow death facing all elephants and whales.

22. The people who speak up in public for or against something almost always lose my support by being too loud about it.

23. It doesn't interest me to watch a movie or read a novel in which the characters are put in difficult situations by a writer. I'm not interested in being reminded of difficulties. It's already on my mind.

24. It's hard for me to believe that, in the next 150 years, we'll have as many important inventions and discoveries as we've had in the last 150. What is there left comparable in importance to the electric light, the telephone, the gas engine, radio, flight, television, nuclear energy, space explora-

tion, computers and Coca-Cola?

(If anyone were to read that paragraph 150 years from now, I'm sure they'd laugh at my ignorance.)

25. People like to say, "You're only as old as you feel," but it isn't true. It's just something old people say to make themselves feel good about their age. You're as old as you are.

26. I spent fifty years of my life working to become well-known as a writer and I've spent the last ten hiding from strangers who recognize me.

27. I dislike loud-mouthed patriots who suggest they like our country more than I do. Some people's idea of patriotism is hating other countries.

28. Politicians deserve better treatment than they've been getting and we should stop using the word "politician" as an epithet. Most of them are honestly trying to accomplish something good for all of us.

29. I spent four years in the army but do not belong to any veterans' organization. As a way of getting together socially with people your own age and background, veterans' groups are fine but I disapprove of them as a pressure group. I'm suspicious of professional veterans who wear overseas caps at conventions. Except for the men

who were disabled, to whom it owes everything it can give, our country owes veterans nothing. We got what was coming to us, a free country.

30. I wish people spent less time praying and more time trying to solve the problems religion was created to help us endure.

31. It seems wrong for the United States to try to protect democracy by undemocratic means like overthrowing the government of a foreign country by undercover action.

32. A lot of people assume that we live in an orderly world where every event has a meaning and every problem has a solution. I suspect, however, that some events are meaningless and some problems insoluble.

33. I believe a lot of things I can't prove.

34. Women have better natural instincts than men and are more apt to do the right thing.

35. I'd make a bad nun. Material possessions give me great pleasure even though all the best advice we're given for happiness advises us to ignore them.

36. When someone says, "You know what I mean?" I don't usually know what they mean and I know they don't know. If someone knows what they mean, they ought to be able to tell you. I mean, you know what

I mean?

37. My only war wound is an aversion to German accents.

38. We need chefs more than headwaiters and mechanics more than car salesmen. We need good doctors more than health plans.

39. The evolution of every business enterprise is away from quality. Products always get smaller, worse and more expensive.

40. If someone chooses to live in the United States, they should learn to speak English. I recognize that this is a small, meanspirited, right-wing opinion but I hold it.

41. People will generally accept facts as truth only if the facts agree with what they already believe.

42. The accuracy of political polls is sad evidence of our predictability.

43. Most religions are designed to trick us into doing the things we'd do anyway if we used our heads.

44. It's a lot easier to object to the way things are being done than it is to do them better yourself. Being a revolutionary, even in a modest way, is a lot more fun than having to take over and do it. Castro was a great revolutionary. It wasn't until he won and started running things himself that he went wrong.

45. A lot of companies spend more to package, advertise and sell their product than they spend on making it. The toothpaste in a tube that costs $1.79 probably doesn't cost ten cents to manufacture. Something's wrong here.

46. I think women should be paid as much for doing the same job as men . . . although I don't think they can lift as much.

47. I don't believe in flying saucers or the Loch Ness monster and I'm not on drugs or religion. I don't know my astrological sign.

48. If all the truth were known by everyone about everything, it would be a better world.

49. If all the truth were known by everyone about everything, most people wouldn't like it, though. If their future depends on logical decisions based on all the evidence, they're nervous. They don't think they're smart enough to make the right decision. If, on the other hand, success and happiness depends on their astrological sign or on hoping and praying or on winning the lottery, then they feel better. They think their destiny is in better hands than their own.

50. In view of how many of them are regularly found out to be scoundrels, I have an unreasonable faith in and affection for doctors. In this regard, I am very suspicious

of anyone who uses the title "doctor" who is not an M.D. There are some very good optometrists but I do not call them "doctors."

51. People are too careful with books. If you like a book, you ought to mark it up with a pencil. Publishers put too much money in the flimsy paper dust jacket on books. The first thing I do with any book that doesn't have my picture on the jacket is throw the jacket away.

52. I don't like to lock anything or take precautions against having it stolen because every time I do, I get the feeling the bastards have beat me a little by making me do it.

53. It doesn't make sense to be against abortion and for the death penalty.

54. It's too bad we seem to need six or seven hours' sleep. Someone's going to invent a way for us to sleep faster.

55. It seems wrong for a state to take money from the poor and ignorant by selling them lottery tickets to collect money to help the state provide welfare and education to the poor and ignorant.

56. People talk as though they like the country better than the city but they move to the city.

57. Farmers have been quitting the farm and moving to the city for years but you

never see any of them there.

58. There's an acute shortage of well-known people in America. The same ones keep appearing on television talk shows. Of course, maybe what we need is not more well-known people but fewer talk shows.

59. Ronald Reagan wasn't as successful reducing the size of government as Franklin Roosevelt was in increasing it.

60. No one wants to read a lot of good writing. There's just so much good writing a reader can take.

61. If the reviews talk about how good the acting is in the movie, I don't go see it. Like writing, there's just so much good acting I can take. Acting and writing shouldn't call attention to themselves.

62. It no longer makes any sense to bother to use an apostrophe between the *n* and *t* in words like *dont* and *isnt.*

63. Most evenings I have two drinks of bourbon before dinner even though I am uneasily aware that the practice is difficult to defend against the charge that drinking is no different from using drugs. Drinking also isn't compatible with my belief that our best hope for happiness is clear thinking, but I try to have my thinking out of the way for the day by the time I have my first drink.

64. Journalists are more honest than other

businesspeople because honesty is a hobby with them. They're amused by it. They talk about honesty at lunch. They aren't naturally any more honest, but it's on their minds.

65. There are more beauty parlors than there are beauties.

65. It's harder to avoid listening to something you don't want to hear than it is to avoid seeing something you'd rather not see.

67. We're all proud of admitting little mistakes. It gives us the feeling we don't make any big ones.

68. I'm always surprised when a light bulb burns out.

69. It's amazing that bees keep making honey, cows keep giving milk and hens keep laying eggs all their lives. There certainly isn't much in it for them.

70. It's too bad Jesus didn't have a family.

71. Getting up early in the morning is a good way to gain respect without ever actually having to do anything.

72. It sounds funny in the house without the television set on.

73. I'd get a lot more reading done in bed if I read when I woke up in the morning instead of when I crawled in at night.

74. People who are wrong seem to talk louder than anyone else.

75. I don't like any music I can't hum.

76. Ice cream was just as good when they only had three flavors, vanilla, chocolate and strawberry.

77. The middle of the night seems longer than it used to.

78. I'm satisfied with the money I make until I read how much baseball players are making.

79. No matter how big the umbrella you carry or how good your raincoat is, if it rains you get wet.

80. When the telephone rings in a store, the person behind the counter will spend five minutes explaining something to the caller while all the customers who have bothered to come to the store stand there waiting.

81. They keep talking about how low the rate of inflation is but I notice that when I buy something that cost me only $1.98 last year, it costs $2.42 now.

82. If I'd known how many problems I was going to run into before I finished, I can't remember a single project I would have started.

83. Computers may save time but they sure waste a lot of paper. About 98 percent of everything printed out by a computer is garbage that no one ever reads.

84. Lawyers are more interested in winning than in justice.

85. There aren't many times in your life when your body has absolutely nothing wrong with it.

86. Vacations aren't necessarily better than other times, they're just different.

87. When someone tells you, "It was my fault," they don't expect you to agree with them. When they say, "You're the boss," they don't mean it.

88. No one who goes to prison ever admits he did it.

89. It gives you confidence in America to hear so many people talk who know how to run the country better than the President.

90. Doctors ought to think of some name for their outer office other than "waiting room."

91. It's lucky glass makes a loud noise when it breaks.

92. If dogs could talk, it would take a lot of the fun out of owning one.

93. People aren't called "the working class" much anymore unless they're unemployed.

94. Most people don't care where they're going as long as they're in something that gets them there in a hurry.

95. Blue jeans cost less when they were

called dungarees.

96. When I get sleepy driving, the only thing that really wakes me up is starting to fall asleep.

97. People in Florida talk more about the weather than people anywhere else in the world. I think it's because weather is what they're paying for and if it's good they feel it justifies the expense. If it's bad they like to think it isn't as bad as it is some places.

98. Never trust the food in a restaurant on top of the tallest building in town that spends a lot of time folding the napkins.

99. After thinking something through as well and as completely as I am able, to be sure I'm right, it often turns out that I'm wrong.

DISLIKES

Life is pleasant most of the time but there are some things it would be better without. I've made a partial list of things I dislike:

— Special or clever license plates with the owner's nickname on them.

— Magazines that hide their index where you can't find it. The index to magazine belongs inside the first page after the cover.

— Television commercials for hemorrhoid cures, toilet paper, sanitary pads or dental adhesives. Newspaper ads for these same products don't bother me.

— Flip-top beer and soft drink cans.

— People who take up two parking spaces with one car.

— Anything stapled together.

— Announcements in the mail that I'm the potential winner of a million-dollar sweepstakes.

— A space that's too small on a form where I'm supposed to put my signature. I scrawl when I write and if I have to put it in a little space, it isn't really my signature.

— Having to open a new can of coffee when I only need two tablespoons more.

— Telephone answering machines with messages at the beginning that are too long or too cute.

— Newspapers with sections that have different numbering systems from the main news sections. There may be no good way to handle this problem but that doesn't stop me from disliking it.

— The middle seat in a crowded airplane.

— Trunks of cars that have to be opened with a key. Why can't I leave the trunk of my car unlocked if I want to?

— Religious quacks on radio and television thinking up new ways to take money from ignorant listeners and incidentally from legitimate churches.

— Dirty magazines prominently displayed at a newsstand.

— A cart in the supermarket with a wobbly wheel.

—Waiting in line to pay for anything.

— Secretaries who say, "May I ask what this is in reference to?" when you call their boss.

— Admonitions from weathermen to "drive safely." All I want to know from them is whether it's going to rain or not. I'll decide how to drive.

— Recipes in a bag of flour that you can't remove without spilling flour all over.

— Hot-air hand dryers in public washrooms. I'd rather use my shirttail.

— People who play radios in public places.

— Baseball or basketball scores on the radio for teams I don't care anything about.

— People who stand too close to my face when they're talking to me. I think they're cousins of the people who move you gradually over toward the buildings when you walk down the street with them.

— Screws with slots that aren't deep enough so that they tear when you twist with the screwdriver.

— Having to check a shopping bag when I go into a store. I know shoplifting is a problem but I don't like the idea of being a suspect.

— Cars with too many red taillights.

RULES OF LIFE

What follows are some rules of life:

— Don't pin much hope on the mail, and when the phone rings, don't expect anything wonderful from that, either.

— If everyone knew the whole truth about everything, it would be a better world.

— Any line you choose to stand in during your life will usually turn out to be the one that moves the slowest.

— The best things in life are not free, they're expensive. Good health is an example.

— If you wonder what anyone thinks of you, consider what you think of them.

— Don't take a butcher's advice on how to cook meat. If he knew, he'd be a chef.

— Anything you look for in the Yellow Pages will not be listed in the category you first try to find it under. Start with the second. Keep in mind cars are under A for "automobiles."

— Not everyone has a right to his own opinion. If he doesn't know the facts, his opinion doesn't count.

— If you think you may possibly have forgotten something, there is no doubt about it. You've forgotten something.

— Happiness depends more on how life strikes you than on what happens.

— The model you own is the only one they ever had that trouble with.

— Hoping and praying are easier but do not produce as good results as hard work.

— Wherever you go for whatever reason, it will turn out you should have been there last week.

— When you buy something, it's always a seller's market. When you sell something, it's always a buyer's market.

— The same things keep happening to the same people.

— Enthusiasm on the job gets you further than education or brains.

— Money is not the root of all evil.

— Every so often you ought to do something dangerous. It doesn't have to be physical.

— Patience is a virtue. Impatience is a virtue, too.

— All men are not created equal but should be treated as though they were under the law.

— The people who write poetry are no smarter than the rest of us, and don't let them make you think they are.

— Patriotism is only an admirable trait

when the person who has a lot of it lives in the same country you do.

— Apologizing for doing something wrong is nowhere near as good as doing it right in the first place.

— If you want something you can't have, it is usually best to change what you want.

— The only way to live is as though there were an answer to every problem — although there isn't.

— New developments in science and new inventions in industry don't usually improve our lives much; the most we can hope is that they'll help us stay even.

— You may be wrong.

— You should be careful about when to go to all the trouble it takes to be different.

— It is impossible to feel sorry for everyone who deserves being felt sorry for.

— One of the best things about life is that we are happy more than we are unhappy.

— Not many of us are able to change our lives on purpose; we are all permanent victims of the way we are, but we should proceed as though this were not true.

The Following Things Are True

A great number of people are unsure of what's true and what isn't. From time to time, in an effort to help those who are confused, I present lists of things that are true. Herewith:

— More movies are too long than too short.

— In spite of any recession, prices always go up. They may not be going up as fast in hard times, but they still go up.

— If Beethoven was played as loud as rock music, I wouldn't like that, either.

— People don't think they really look like pictures of themselves.

— You don't see as many parakeets or canaries in cages as you used to.

— Chinese food isn't as popular as it was twenty years ago. Here, I mean. It's just as popular as ever in China.

— Self-service hasn't made gas any cheaper.

— A gas station attendant always screws the cap back on the tank tighter than I do.

— If there was no crime, local television news broadcasts would have to go out of business.

— Considering how poor they say they are in Russia these days, it's surprising how many of them wear those mink hats.

— Imelda Marcos' popularity in the Philippines is enough to shake your faith in democracy.

— Cough drops aren't much help when

you want to stop coughing.

— We're all a little prejudiced about something.

— We make more friends than we have time to keep, but we make more enemies than we have time to fight, so it evens out.

— Believing there are differences in races doesn't make anyone a racist.

— It's surprising how convincingly someone who's guilty can say he didn't do it.

— There's a delicate balance between the pleasure of being with people and the pleasure of being alone.

— Things are at their worst when you can't sleep in the middle of the night.

— A lot of people spend too much time being careful.

— People who say that breakfast is their favorite meal don't enjoy food much.

— Getting up and down off the floor is easier when you're young.

— It doesn't snow as much as it used to and, furthermore, it never did.

— If you have a vague feeling you may have forgotten something, it's absolutely certain that you've forgotten something.

— The handicapped don't use many of the parking spaces set aside for them.

— We all assume we're smarter than when we were younger — but probably not.

— Licking a stamp or an envelope is a disgusting thing to do.

— No matter where you stood, the war in Vietnam was one of the worst episodes in American history.

—You get so used to what everyone looks like in their clothes that you don't think about what anyone looks like naked — and it's a good thing.

— When checking a cookbook, look for the noun, not the adjective. For molasses cookies, don't look for "molasses." Look under "Cookies, molasses."

— We're lucky the Japanese don't speak English.

— Generally speaking, shoes don't fit very well. We just get used to where they hurt.

— Cheerleaders with short skirts and megaphones are out-of-date and have no effect whatsoever on the performance of the team they are exhorting.

— People use coffee tables a lot more to put junk and magazines on than they use them to put coffee on, but the name sticks anyway.

— A dining room table twenty-nine inches high is too tall to eat from comfortably, but that's what most tables are. In some restaurants, the table is too high and the chair is too low.

— All television programs should be broadcast simultaneously on radio.

— Three-quarters of the homeowners in America never use their front door.

— Men's undershirts aren't long enough when you're working around the house Saturday because they pull out at the waist when you bend over.

— I don't drink beer from a bottle and I don't see why anyone ever drinks it from a can. I don't drink a beer very often and cannot imagine drinking two. When I drink a beer, it tastes best if I wet the glass and chill it in the freezer for a few minutes first. Two make me bilious.

— No one in prison for murder is guilty when they tell their story on television. I've never seen a guilty murderer.

— Two-door cars are a pain in the neck and I'm never buying another.

— They ought to play the second half of the Monday Night Football game first so we'd all know how it came out without staying up past midnight.

— It's apparent to me how old I am when I read in the paper that they're handing out condoms to kids in the New York City schools. I didn't know what one was in high school and wouldn't mention the word in mixed company to this day.

— The shades are always down in my office. If it's a beautiful day outside, I don't want to know.

— People who don't remember when you had to choke a car to get it started are lucky.

— When you come up to the checkout counter in the supermarket with a shopping cart full of groceries, the cashier always says, "Will that be all?" or "Is that it?" Does she think you're just leaving the stuff with her while you go get more?

— There is a definite difference between Coca-Cola and Pepsi Cola and one is clearly better than the other. I can't even drink the other.

— They say squid and octopus are catching on in American kitchens but not in ours.

— Most kids in school like their teachers.

— Not many Americans could fill in a blank map with names of the United States even if it had the outline of the states on it.

— Stores with the cheapest merchandise use cheap bags that often break through at the bottom before you get to the car.

— If it wasn't so annoying, it would be amusing to hear politicians speak less than the truth most of the time.

— I'm fed up with stories every year about whether this is going to be a good or a bad Christmas for stores. There's just so much economic news I want at Christmas. What I want to know is, is it going to be a good year for *us?*

— It's hard to get used to your age no matter what age you are. The trouble is, you're that age for such a short time. Just when you begin to get used to it, you get older.

— When I hear a promotional ad on television for news shows and they tell me about a story they're going to have on tomorrow, I don't watch it. If they knew what the story was yesterday, it's not news, it's history.

— It's easy to start hating someone on a television news broadcast. If the newscaster's mannerisms annoy you, man or woman, you start paying more attention to them than to the news and it ruins the show for you. It accounts for why you hear people say, "I can't stand Peter Jennings. I hate Dan Rather. Tom Brokaw is terrible." Not to mention Andy Rooney, of course.

— Less than half the fresh fruit you buy is any good, but you keep buying it anyway. You're always hoping for that perfect tangerine, that perfect melon, that perfect peach or pear. Most fruit-store fruit rots before it ripens. Melons are the most expensive disappointment. Only one out of ten is any good. Unfortunately, that can be great.

— On vacation I sleep less. I hate to waste it.

—When you pump your own gas at a self-service place, it's hard not to end up with a little gas on your hands. There might be a market for a machine that dispenses little packets containing a piece of wet cloth or paper that you could clean your hands with. I'd pay a nickel but not a quarter. Maybe that's the business we'll go into.

— It's difficult to stop the gas pump on an even amount of money.

—You still see someone paddling a canoe on a lake or river once in a while, but I haven't seen anyone rowing a boat in years. The basic flaw in a rowboat has always been that you can't see where you're getting to.

— There's too much glass in a car on a hot, sunny day. We don't need all that windshield to see out.

— There are a lot of things around the house that aren't any good that I don't throw out.

— I've passed a lot of Christian Science reading rooms in cities around the country, but I've never seen anyone reading in one. I'm not sure whether they're for Christian Scientists or whether they're to attract people from other religions to Christian Science.

— People don't know much about any religion but their own — and a lot of times, they don't know much about that one, either.

— It's hard not to drop at least one sock or a piece of underwear when you're emptying the clothes dryer.

— The weather is almost always something other than normal.

— Hollywood movies are the best art America produces.

— I can't help wondering where all the Russians are today who bugged the hotel rooms of American visitors and spied on everyone who came there just a few years ago.

— The pencil that comes with an expensive pen and pencil set is never satisfactory. You have to be able to sharpen a pencil.

— If the mailman knew what I was going to throw out without opening, he could save both of us a lot of trouble by throwing it away before he delivered it. I'd like to give our mailman power of attorney over the mail.

— The best thing that's bad for you is butter.

— I can name everyone who lived on our

block on Partridge Street fifty years ago. Most people don't know the names of all their neighbors today.

— Tying a shoelace is a small but satisfying thing to do.

— The lives of people who plan carefully don't go according to plan any more often than the lives of people who don't plan them at all.

— There are a lot of magazines with one or two articles in them that I want to read but the magazines are too expensive to buy for one or two articles. The time should come when we can each make up our own magazine from a computer index in our home and have every article we want to read from a lot of different magazines.

— Automobile tires are better than they used to be. Paper handkerchiefs like Kleenex are not.

— If a bottle of wine is really good, you can't afford it.

— There aren't nearly as many shoe repair shops as there used to be because people don't wear out the soles and heels of shoes by walking on them much anymore.

— Learning how to type should be mandatory in grade school.

— When I was in high school, the final score of a basketball game was 38 to 29 or, at the very most, 47 to 36.

— There are some good things on television except when you want to watch. If there are two good things on the same night, they're opposite each other. There are usually some good things on the night you have to go out, too.

— It is comforting for people with illegible handwriting to know that a lot of brilliant people have terrible handwriting.

On the other hand, of course, a lot of dumb people don't write so you can read it, either.

— New clothes always look good in the mirror at the store, but I end up not wearing about half of all the clothes I buy.

— Stores have got to make a greater effort to have prices come out even so we don't get left with so many useless pennies.

— It would be good if there were some way to feed information to the brain intravenously.

— If I could start over, I'd be a much better person.

THE FOLLOWING THINGS ARE TRUE ABOUT SPORTS

— There's more talk about money on the sports pages than in the business pages of the newspaper.

— Of all the balls we use to play games, the football is the most interesting. It was a crazy idea to play a game with a ball that isn't round, but it's worked out fine. As a matter of fact, the football is a work of genius. You can kick it or throw it as well or maybe even better than a round ball, and its bounce is just unpredictable enough to add an interesting element to the game.

— When I hear about a golf tournament, I still expect Arnold Palmer to win it.

— I saw Muhammad Ali referred to as "the best-known fistic gladiator the world has ever known."

Not by me, he isn't. I'd put two boxers ahead of Ali, both for well-knownness and fighting ability. They are Joe Louis and Jack Dempsey.

Sports heroes from one generation who never compete against each other are hard to compare. Some athletes remain well-known long after their playing days are over and sometimes after anyone is left alive who saw them play. The name Babe Ruth has probably survived the years better than any other sports figure. It's amazing, when you consider that he played before television, that Babe Ruth is still the best-known American sports figure of all time.

— What talent major league baseball

managers have escapes me. Football coaches sound like Phi Beta Kappas by comparison. Baseball managers may have some brains, but I've never heard one with an education.

— I'm not clear why the man running a baseball team is called a manager while the one running a football team is called a coach.

— Another difference is in the way they dress. A baseball manager wears a baseball uniform to work. A football coach doesn't wear a football uniform on the sidelines, even though it wouldn't look any sillier.

— The game of baseball may be in trouble in the near future and it won't be simply because of the multimillion-dollar salaries of so many of its players. The biggest problem for baseball's future is kids aren't playing it as much as they once did. In big cities, they're playing basketball instead.

There aren't any empty lots left, so the city kids are all over at the blacktop behind the school shooting baskets.

A sign of the problem shows in the makeup of major league baseball teams. Fewer than 18 percent of major league baseball players are black. In pro basketball, 72 percent of the players are black.

— When we were kids, we used to cut the cover off old golf balls and unwind the rubber string underneath. Someone spoiled our fun by saying a golf ball might explode if you cut into it, so we stopped playing with them.

— I don't resent the players' salaries being so high. What I resent is the price of a hot dog or a beer at the stadium.

— I'd rather play tennis indoors on a rainy day than outdoors on a sunny day.

— It's a mystery to me why there are no black jockeys.

— I love to watch a football game on television, but it's nowhere near as good as being there. If you're at the game, you watch what you want to watch. At home in front of the TV screen, you watch what someone else chooses to show you.

— Players for the home team ought not be allowed to encourage the crowd to drown out the opposing quarterback's voice when he's trying to call signals.

— It's surprising that so many cities and towns have enough open land left for golf courses. I should think members of most golf clubs would have voted to sell the land to developers. That's what I think of golf club members.

— I was thinking of taking steroids but I wouldn't know what to do with a lot of muscles if I had them.

In full Giants regalia, after a 60 Minutes *spot on his favorite team*

— Sometimes when I'm watching a game, I hope a team wins so much that you'd think it really mattered.

— Sports announcers usually work in pairs and none of them seem to be clear in their own minds about whether they're talking to each other or to us.

— Some games are better on television than others. It makes a big difference how interesting the waiting time is between the action. There's a lot of time when nothing's going on in both football and baseball, but serious fans enjoy anticipating what their team's going to do next. The waiting time isn't dull.

Hockey is the worst sport on television and there's no waiting time.

That's partly true of basketball too, but there's so much scoring you can enjoy thinking about whether your team can catch up.

If you think hockey is a bad sport for television, try listening to it on radio sometime.

— A lot of men turn to the sports pages of their paper first, but that doesn't mean they think sports are the most important thing in the paper.

"HAPPY HOLIDAY" DOESN'T DO IT

The following things are true about Christmas:

— Sometimes it's joyous and merry but it's never easy.

— Old weather records do not substantiate the suggestion, given by today's Christmas cards, showing scenes from old-fashioned Christmases, that it used to snow more than it does now. Horses did not dash through the snow pulling sleighs on the way to grandmother's house any more a hundred years ago than cars do now. It almost never snows on Christmas even in northern parts of the country and if it does, the snow is wet and slushy and not conducive to horses pulling sleighs through it.

— It's a sign of the new sensitivity to political correctness that, more and more, the greeting "Happy Holidays" is replacing "Merry Christmas." Most Jews I know accept "Merry Christmas" in the spirit in which it was intended without adding any heavy religious baggage to it. Most atheists or agnostics I know use "Merry Christmas."

— I never get over feeling bad about tearing open a beautifully wrapped present. It takes ten seconds to destroy a work of art that took someone ten minutes to accomplish.

— Someone in the family is always better at wrapping than anyone else. My sister stays up in the back bedroom in our house and we all deliver presents to her to be wrapped as if she was the package room behind the scenes in a department store.

— Of course it's true that some presents are better to get than others but some are better to give, too.

— Some people are easy to give to, others are hard and there's always one who's impossible. Usually it isn't that the person has everything, it's that he or she is not enthusiastic about gifts.

— The knowledge that the sales will start the day after Christmas doesn't deter many people from buying presents before Christmas.

— When you buy a piece of clothing for someone, it's more apt to be too small than too big. Clothes look bigger on the rack than they do on someone.

— The store clerk who asks, "May I help you with something?" can hardly ever help.

—You read and hear a lot of advice about how to keep your Christmas tree to keep from getting dry so the needles don't fall off but most Christmas trees are cut in November and nothing anyone does can keep them from drying out and dropping their needles all over your living-room floor.

— It's interesting how good orange and black seem for Halloween and how wrong they'd be as Christmas colors.

— In spite of the old sayings to the contrary, the best presents come in large packages.

— A quarter of the Christmas cards we get are from some commercial establishment. There ought to be a law against a company or anyone with whom you have a business arrangement sending you a Christmas card. "Happy Holidays from all of us at the First National Bank" doesn't make me feel warm all over toward the bank. I don't want cards from any real estate brokers, dentists, insurance salesmen or car dealers, either. I don't want a Christmas card from anyone I don't know personally.

I'd include in this group the President of the United States. When Bill Clinton was President, we used to get two cards from Bill and Hillary, one at home and one at the office.

The Clintons wished us "a beautiful holiday season." I was flattered and touched until I came to the note in small print on the back of the card that read "PAID FOR BY THE DEMOCRATIC NATIONAL COMMITTEE." That's not in the Christmas spirit.

Apparently the Clintons didn't leave their Christmas card list with the Bushes. We haven't received one from them.

What follows is a list of the ten best tastes.

No. 1: SUGAR. This sweetener is at the top of the taste list even though too much of it is cloying and unpleasant. It's the most important ingredient in many things we eat — even things we don't consider sweet. When I make bread with six cups of flour I put a full tablespoon of sugar in the flour because of what sugar does for the yeast.

No. 2: SALT. Without salt, anything is tasteless. I like a little too much salt; a tablespoon in the bread.

(Too much sugar or too much salt is bad for us, but one of the things we all recognize is the direct relationship between how good something tastes and how bad it is for us. The better it tastes, the worse it is for us. There is some eternal equation.)

No. 3: BUTTER. Nothing improves the taste of anything as much as butter. Fake butter was an unfortunate invention and it isn't much cheaper or any better for you than the real thing.

No. 4: BREAD. It is with some hesitation that I put bread on the list because commercial bread in the United States is terrible. How it ever happened that the French eat such great bread every day and Americans eat such bad bread is a mystery.

A great breadmaker in the Bronx named Terranova makes a round loaf so hard you can drum on it with your fingers. When I asked him what he put in his bread to make it so good, he said, "It's what I *don't* put in it that makes it good."

In spite of the waxed-paper-wrapped mush in the supermarkets, almost every city or town has a good bakery where you can get real bread. You can tell a good restaurant before you eat your meal by the bread it serves.

No. 5: CHOCOLATE. Clearly one of the ten best tastes, chocolate is another thing Europeans make better than we do. A chocolate bar from Belgium, Germany, Switzerland or even England is better than one made here. Vanilla is a good taste but not as important as chocolate. Chocolate is important.

No. 6: CHICKEN. Chicken not only tastes good but it's also cheap and can be cooked in a thousand different ways. It can be baked, fried, deep-fried, stewed or broiled. It's the best leftover you can have in your refrigerator.

No. 7: STEAK: I'm embarrassed to have it on the list but can't leave it off.

No. 8: POTATO. The taste of potato isn't good or bad until you do something with it.

You can bake potatoes, mash them, boil them, fry or deep-fry them. You can scallop them and if you're good in the kitchen, soufflé them.

No. 9: PASTA. If you have a variety of pastas in the cupboard, you never have to worry about dinner. You can find something in the refrigerator or in the pantry to go with whatever pasta you have on hand. Just don't overcook it.

No. 10: RICE. Rice is on my personal ten best foods list. Basmati rice is best.

No. 11: ONION and GARLIC. I know I said ten, but I can't leave either of these out.

Maybe this was a bad idea. I'm up to eleven and I haven't mentioned the tastes of orange, lemon, tomato, strawberry, peanut or egg. I haven't even mentioned two of the world's great tastes: vanilla ice cream with chocolate sauce or a bacon, lettuce and tomato sandwich — without chocolate sauce.

LIFE AS I SEE IT: ROONEY'S WITTICISMS

— At about age forty, each of us should resolve to throw out or give away one book for each new book we acquire.

— It's a good thing we can take as much pleasure from oldness as newness because, for the most part, we have to live with more oldness.

— It isn't working that's so hard, it's getting ready to work.

— Being broke is a terrible feeling but it's probably an experience everyone ought to have once in a lifetime.

— There are idiots who will buy anything as long as it costs enough.

— I had all of my accidents when I was driving carefully.

— The thing that keeps most of us from feeling terrible about our limited intellect is some small part of our personality or character that makes us different.

— You don't have to say everything to a

friend for both of you to understand what you mean.

— I like animals who trust people.

— No machine can help anyone write.

— If I reach into my pocket to pay for something and pull out a handful of change that turns out to be mostly pennies, I get discouraged about life.

— Soothing music sets my nerves on edge.

— There's nothing that keeps you in touch with supply and demand and the sensitive balance of our earth better than knowing firsthand that there's a limit to how much you can take out and how much you can dump back into it.

— Travel is an escape from all your pressing problems. That's why we're so willing to give it our complete attention.

— I prefer cigarette smoke to perfume.

— My idea of heaven would be to die and awaken in a place that has all my lost things.

— Too many people get stuck doing the same dull thing all their lives without ever finding out whether they have the ability to do something else.

— One of the healthiest things for any community is a post office where everyone comes to pick up the mail.

— What I want, if any of you medical scientists are reading this, is a small pill that can be taken once a day before dinner, with a martini, that will cure anything I already have and prevent anything I might catch in the future.

— There's nothing more satisfying than getting mad.

— There's nothing much worse than lying awake in the middle of the night, staring at your life.

— I have never met a cat I liked.

— America's contribution to mankind has been the invention of mass production.

— Everyone should think twice before making a noise.

— There are some ideas I stick with even though I'm vaguely aware that I may be wrong.

— I'd like to put an end to all tipping but I don't dare start the movement myself.

— There are a few moments in our lives that should be preserved for ourselves alone, and breakfast is one of them.

— I'd prefer than no one put flowers on my grave if I have one. I don't like the idea of flowers dying on top of me.

— Trying to get an electrical appliance fixed is harder than trying to get a brick laid.

— The only time I feel in control of my life is when I am sitting at my typewriter —

computer now — typing.

— The best smiles come unbidden.

— Barns age more gracefully than most buildings and certainly more gracefully than people.

— Loyalty is an admirable trait even when a person is loyal to something that doesn't deserve it.

— Because I'm such a bad businessman, I tend to distrust good ones.

— I am unnecessarily wary of any man

Holding great-grandchildren Liza (left) and Drew Fishel, May 2009

who carries a fountain pen in his inside coat pocket.

— I like guests who don't want to do what I want to do but feel free to wander off on their own.

— Most time passes when we aren't watching.

CREDITS

Drafted and Meeting Marge were previously published in *My War* (New York: PublicAffairs, 2000).

Places of Business was previously published in *The Story of the Stars and Stripes* (with Bud Hutton; New York: Farrar & Rinehart, 1946).

Combat was previously published in *Air Gunner* (New York: Farrar & Rinehart, 1944).

Chairs, Mr. Rooney Goes to Dinner, In Praise of New York, and An Essay on War were previously published in *A Few Minutes with Andy Rooney* (New York: Atheneum, 1981).

Introducing Andy Rooney; Big Business; Fired; Life, Long and Short; Trust; Morning People and Night People; On Conservation; Design; Quality?; Loyalty; Home; Mother, Christmas Trees; Ice Cream, The Andy Rooney Upside-Down Diet; Waiting,

Hot Weather; Neat People; and Rules of Life were previously published in *And More by Andy Rooney* (New York: Atheneum, 1982).

An Interview with Andy Rooney, There is No Secret, Journalist's Code of Ethics, Procrastination, Broke, A Cash Standard, The Sweet Spot in Time, Intelligence, Directions, Struck by the Christmas Lull, A Nest to Come Home To, A Trip to the Dump, Wastebaskets, Driving, and Dislikes were previously published in *Pieces of My Mind* (New York: Atheneum, 1984).

Sartorial Shortcomings; A World-Class Saver; It's a Writer Who Makes a Fool of Himself; Savings; Being With People, Being Without; Finding the Balance; The Glories of Maturity; The Quality of Mercy; *Real* Real Estate; Grandfatherhood; Napping; Wood; Thin for Christmas; The Urge to Eat; Thanks, Pal; and The White House? No, Thank You were previously published in *Word for Word* (New York: G. P. Putnam's Sons, 1984).

Born to Lose; Signed by Hand; An Appreciative Husband's Gratitude; An All-American Drive; Frank Sinatra, Boy and Man; Surrendering to Paris; The Following Things Are True, and The Following Things Are True About Sports were previously published in *Sweet and Sour* (New York:

G. P. Putnam's Sons, 1992)

My Name's Been Stolen, A Report on Reporting, The Sound of Silence, The Agony of Flight, and The More You Eat were previously published in *Out of My Mind* (New York: PublicAffairs, 2006).

The Truth About Lying, Vacation, The Flat Earth in Kansas, and "Happy Holiday" Doesn't Do It were previously published in *Common Nonsense* (New York: PublicAffairs, 2002).

Where Are All the Plumbers?, My House Runneth Over, Lonnie, and Ninety-Nine Opinions I'm Stuck With were previously published in *Not That You Asked . . .* (New York: Random House, 1989).

Oh, What a Lovely Game was previously published in *Super Bowl* magazine (*Super Bowl XXVI,* Los Angeles: National Football League Properties, 1992).

Sodium-Restricted Diet, E. B. White, and Harry Reasoner were previously published in *Years of Minutes* (New York: PublicAffairs, 2003).

The Godfrey You Don't Know was previously published in *Look* magazine (December 22, 1959).

ABOUT THE AUTHOR

Known to millions for his regular commentary on the television news magazine *60 Minutes* and for his nationally syndicated newspaper column, **Andrew A. Rooney** is the author of numerous best-selling books. He lives in New York.